The French Communist Party
in Transition

Annette Eisenberg Stiefbold

The Praeger Special Studies program, through a selective worldwide distribution network, makes available to the academic, government, and business communities significant and timely research in U.S. and international economic, social, and political issues.

The French Communist Party in Transition

PCF-CPSU Relations and the Challenge to Soviet Authority

Praeger Publishers   New York   London

PRAEGER SPECIAL STUDIES IN INTERNATIONAL POLITICS AND GOVERNMENT

Library of Congress Cataloging in Publication Data

Stiefbold, Annette E
   The French Communist Party in transition.

   (Praeger special studies in international politics
and government)
   Includes index.
   1. Parti communiste français. 2. Kommunisticheskaĩa
partiia Sovetskogo Solitiza. I. Title.
JN3007.C6S7   1977   329.9'44   77-83477
ISBN 0-03-040946-2

PRAEGER SPECIAL STUDIES
200 Park Avenue, New York, N.Y., 10017, U.S.A.

Published in the United States of America in 1977
by Praeger Publishers,
A Division of Holt, Rinehart and Winston, CBS, Inc.

789   038   987654321

To My Family

At its 22nd party congress in February 1976, the French Communist Party (PCF) stunned much of the outside world with its announcement of what seemed to be radical departures from past policy: abandonment of the Marxist-Leninist doctrine of the dictatorship of the proletariat; endorsement of a peaceful, democratic path to socialism "in French colors," which would respect political pluralism and civil liberties; and insistence on the right to criticize existing socialism as practiced in the Soviet Union and Eastern Europe.

What appeared to be a radical break with the past, however, turned out on closer inspection to be merely the consolidation of a process of gradual assertion of autonomy from the CPSU, which had begun with the PCF's experiences in the momentous year of 1968—in the student-worker strikes and riots in May and June and the Soviet-led invasion of Czechoslovakia in August. The lesson of these searing events for the PCF was that henceforth its domestic strategy of seeking to attain power by forging alliances with like-minded parties on the basis of a Common Program of Government would have to take priority over allegiance to the Communist Party of the Soviet Union (CPSU), in the event of conflict between the two. While not signaling a complete breach with the CPSU, this stand inevitably placed the parties' relationship on a new basis, and brought the PCF into closer harmony with such Eurocommunist parties as those of Italy and Spain. Thus, the estrangement in PCF-CPSU relations has been accompanied by the forging of a community of interest among Western European Communist parties, and beyond them to such other important Communist parties as the Japanese, which threatens to undermine —in the Soviets' view—the bonds of traditional proletarian internationalism. The Soviets' efforts to reassert their primacy within the international Communist movement, particularly following the June 1976 Berlin conference of European Communist and Workers' parties, reflect their growing apprehension about the impact of these centrifugal tendencies on international Communist unity.

In the January 1977 issue of *Foreign Affairs,* the PCF's leading foreign policy expert asserted: "As far as we are concerned, the year 1968 played a decisive role . . . in what our policy line has become." For an author facing the necessity of drafting a conclusion to a study of the changing relationship between the French and Soviet Communist parties which had taken the events of the year 1968 as its point of departure, this statement by PCF Politburo member Jean Kanapa was the pièce de résistance. What could be more satisfying than having a hypothesis validated by one of the principal actors in the drama under study?

Yet such highly topical studies as the present one do not allow time for smugness. The events marking the evolution in PCF-CPSU relations, on the one hand, and Franco-Soviet relations on the other, do not cease merely because a manuscript goes to press. The French parliamentary election, scheduled for March 1978, will at the very least add new dimensions to the PCF-CPSU-French government triangle.

I would like to record here my appreciation to my former mentors at Cornell and Columbia Universities and the University of Paris, whose instruction and counsel of more than a decade ago in many ways were the progenitors of this book; and to my colleagues at the University of Miami's Center for Advanced International Studies, for providing invaluable insights into Soviet perceptions of contemporary international and interparty relations.

Finally, I would like to express my gratitude to members of my family, without whose help this undertaking would not have been possible: to Shirley and the late Herman Eisenberg, M.D., for lifelong encouragement; to Gwen and Paul Stiefbold, for countless hours of grandchild care; to Diana and Mark Stiefbold, for superb cooperation and understanding; and to Dr. Rodney P. Stiefbold, for constant support and encouragement. To them this book is dedicated in appreciation.

The French Communist Party in Transition

1

1968:
THE WATERSHED
YEAR

The year 1968 marked a watershed in relations between the French Communist party (Parti communiste français—PCF) and the Communist party of the Soviet Union (CPSU). In May and June student and worker strikes erupted in France, and in August the five Warsaw Pact countries, under Soviet leadership, invaded Czechoslovakia. In the first case, the PCF, vigorously challenged by dissidents within its ranks, generally adhered to a CPSU-style analysis of the events and followed its Soviet comrades' prescriptions. For this, it was penalized by considerable loss of domestic following and electoral disappointment. In the second case, which confronted the party when it was still reeling from the May-June events, the PCF, for the first time on a major issue, adopted an official position critical of the Soviet Union.

These two events first posed the principal issues which surfaced so dramatically in 1976 at the PCF and CPSU party congresses and the Conference of European Communist Parties: proletarian internationalism, strategy and tactics for coming to power, and conception of the Socialist state. While it is not the contention of this book that the PCF made a total and irrevocable break with the CPSU either in 1968 or 1976, it is suggested that the independent line heralded at the 22nd PCF party congress in 1976 actually was forged in the crucible of 1968.

THE MAY-JUNE CRISIS

The Setting

Soviet Assessment of the Class Struggle in 1968

In the ongoing Communist assessment of the class struggle in the international arena, the year 1968 was situated on something of a plateau. The great

thrust of the anticolonial struggle had occurred, Cuba had been added to the
chain of Communist successes, and the Western world was experiencing signs
of economic crisis. On the other hand, the rightwing coup in Greece had again
raised the specter of a resurgence of fascism in Europe; the Soviets' Middle
Eastern clients had suffered humiliating defeat the previous June; the "national
liberation" forces had not yet prevailed in Vietnam; and international Communist unity was beyond reach.

Yet, the overall trend on the Soviets' balance sheet was positive. "Historic
changes are taking place in the international arena in the correlation of forces,
to the benefit of socialism and the workers' and national liberation movements," a *Pravda* editorial asserted in February, and added: "The general
tendencies in world development favor a further upsurge of the basic forces
of the world revolutionary process."[1] A crisis in the capitalist foreign exchange
system, highlighted by the devaluation of the pound and the "precariousness
of the American dollar," the "desperate inter-imperialist struggle for the market," and the multiplication of strikes throughout the capitalist world were
said to be symptomatic of the fact that "the capitalist economy is currently
suffering grave shocks."[2] As a Soviet commentator observed, "the first weeks
of 1968 have been filled with sharp class conflicts and clashes, with a tense
struggle on the world scene."[3]

Significantly, at this stage the crisis of capitalism was portrayed as part
of a recurring cyclical pattern. (Only several years later did the Soviets begin
to speak of "qualitative changes" of a more permanent nature, or a "new
stage" in the crisis of capitalism, inaugurated, in their view, at the turn of the
1970s.) At this stage, the Soviets acknowledged that capitalism, "even though
it is a historically doomed system,"[4] still possessed the means to thwart tempo-
rarily the advance of the revolutionary movement. "Marxism-Leninism has
never presented the revolutionary movement as only a continuously accelerat-
ing process advancing in a straight line," Soviet commentators asserted. Anyone claiming that the revolution would proceed to victory without suffering
"the most heavy sacrifices" was not a true revolutionary.[5]

However, in the Soviet view, the class struggle in the capitalist countries
was becoming more acute. Rising levels of unemployment, taxation, cost of
living, inflation, and the aggravation of the international monetary crisis combined to account for the "growing contradictions within the capitalist world."[6]
The form of class struggle was also seen as changing, in response to the
increasing fusion of state and economy in capitalist countries. Thus, in the era
of state-monopoly capitalism, the working class struggle against the monopolies was increasingly becoming a struggle against the state as well. This process,
in the Soviet view, revealed the internal contradictions of state-monopoly
capitalism, which, in essence, prepares the way for its own replacement by
socialism.

In addition to the growing politicization of the strikes, the Soviets hailed the broadening of their social base. Engineers, technicians, office employees, and other members of the intelligentsia "are more and more often resorting to purely proletarian forms of organization and methods of struggle" in such capitalist countries as Italy, France, Britain, and Japan, an expert on the international workers' movement observed.[7] From their initial concentration on increased wages, the Soviets noted, the strikers' demands had expanded to include improvements in the social security, credit, and tax systems; nationalization; worker control of enterprises; and changes in foreign policy, particularly "in defense of peace and against the U.S. aggression in Vietnam."[8]

Thus, although they were not yet announcing the advent of the next great round in the class struggle, the Soviets did believe events were generally moving in their favor in the year 1968.

Soviet Prescriptions for Revolutionary Transformation in Capitalist Countries

Anticipating a "further accentuation of the class struggle" in developed capitalist countries, the CPSU had advanced general guidelines for the correct strategy and tactics Communist parties in these countries should pursue. Additional elaboration of these guidelines was to be forthcoming with the convening of the next international conference of Communist and workers' parties, then in the planning stages, at which the question of strategy and tactics was to figure prominently on the agenda.

Determining the correct strategy and tactics was accomplished by carrying out a correct Marxist-Leninist "scientific analysis of the correlation of forces inside the country and in the international arena."[9] Such an analysis was said to enable the Communists to "oppose imperialism by tactics and forms and methods of struggle which most comprehensively take concrete conditions into account."[10] With prescient candor that would seem remarkably suited to the soon-to-erupt French crisis, *Pravda* acknowledged, however, that "at times it is difficult to quickly find a correct solution to the problems at hand," and therefore called for "constant study and profound generalization, creative development of Marxist-Leninist theory, and intensification of this influence in the ranks of the revolutionary movement."[11]

Three principal tasks were said to confront the workers' movement in developed capitalist countries at this stage. The first was to achieve unity of action of the various segments of the working class. In practice, this meant trade union alliance, "to insure united actions by all political units of the working class movement," particularly the Communist, Socialist, and Social Democratic branches, which represented the majority of the organized labor movement.[12] According to the Soviets, "the 1967 class battles attest to the fact that the trend toward united actions by trade unions with different ideological directions is rising to a new level."[13] Moreover, this growing unity of trade union action was accomplished with the simultaneous increasing politicization of trade union activity on the part of those segments that had previously restricted their demands to the economic sphere. Efforts by Communist parties in France, Finland, and Japan were credited with the positive results achieved in those countries.

Thus, in defining the current stage of the class struggle as being waged essentially against the monopolies and for democracy, the CPSU designated as the second task required for success of the workers' movement the extension of united action to include "all antimonopoly forces" in the developed capitalist countries. "Antimonopoly alliance is called upon to play a leading part in solving what is the central task of the present stage of revolutionary struggle in developed countries, that of limiting and then eliminating monopoly domination," a high Soviet official responsible for relations with fraternal parties in capitalist countries wrote.[14] This meant primarily "establishing and developing the unity of action of Communist and Social Democratic parties," as exemplified by the "dialogue between the French Communists and Socialists" which had culminated in the "impressive victory" of the united front in the 1967 French legislative elections.[15]

The Soviets considered that the conditions of the present stage created "complexity and diversity" in the forms and methods of the class struggle: "the range of requirements has . . . gone far beyond the limits of the direct, everyday needs and demands of the worker. . . . The working class is now making demands which can not be solved by the traditional methods of struggle, that is, by isolated strikes."[16] Thus, in addition to strikes on an expanded scale, "the working class widely and successfully uses . . . the legislature, local authority organs, factory and plant committees, and the system of settlement through collective bargaining."[17] While they noted that "forms of revolutionary work have arisen which were not characteristic or even known in the past stage of historic development,"[18] however, the Soviets apparently did not anticipate that occupation of factories by workers could become one of the new forms of revolutionary activity, as would soon occur in France.

The Soviets acknowledged that the goal of achieving further democratization of capitalist countries as a prelude to Socialist revolution was challenged by "dogmatists and sectarians" (that is, Maoists), who "think that more radical methods of struggle are required" and that the struggle for democracy is almost a betrayal of the socialist revolution.[19] It would be a fundamental error, the Soviets insisted, to contend that the struggle for democracy would draw the proletariat away from the socialist revolution. On the contrary, as Lenin asserted, just as socialism cannot be achieved without realizing full democracy, the "proletariat can not prepare itself for victory over the bourgeoisie without waging a fully supported, consistent, and revolutionary struggle for democracy."[20]

The final task to ensure remaining "on the right revolutionary road" was "to strengthen the internationalist ties of the working class in developed capitalist countries."[21] The cohesion of all currents of the revolutionary movement was essential to maintaining a favorable position in the world power balance, the Soviets maintained. The forthcoming international conference of Communist and workers' parties was to be devoted to this end.

The May-June Crisis in the Context of the Class Struggle in France in 1968

Soviet appreciation of the historic importance of the May-June events in France apparently grew with hindsight. Writing in 1976, a Soviet expert on the strategy and tactics of revolutionary transformation in capitalist countries, A. I. Sobolev, defined the period from the late 1940s through the end of the 1960s as essentially "preparatory"—a period of "gathering strength, preparing reserves" in the class struggle. However, he asserted, a definite shift had occurred at the end of the decade, for which the French strikes in 1968 receive a large share of the credit: "The situation changes considerably at the end of the sixties and the beginning of the seventies. The mighty May demonstrations by the French working class in 1968 and the tremendous scale of the strike movement in Italy in 1969 marked a change in the correlation of forces."[22]

The Soviets describe the France of 1968 as having a "contradictory appearance," which "capriciously combined authoritarian structures and a 'liberal' facade," with the totality kept in balance by the personal prestige of de Gaulle.[23] A "virtually all-powerful bureaucracy," a powerful financial oligarchy, and "emasculated rights of the elective institutions," combined with the existence of "basic bourgeois-democratic freedoms," was how the Soviets characterized the regime of the Fifth Republic.[24] It was the accumulated resentment of the working class, laborers, intelligentsia, petit and middle bourgeoisie, they said, that gradually built up to form the combustible material that sparked the antigovernment crisis.

The Soviets attributed the crisis to the "dictatorship by the monopolies," which were endeavoring to solve the problems of French capitalism, brought on by the scientific-technological revolution and the pressures to remain economically competitive with France's Common Market partners, at the expense of the workers. By means of state regulation of the economy and economic rationalization, increases in production had been obtained, but the price was the systematic reduction of the workers' standard of living and the appearance in France, for the first time since the war, of mass unemployment.[25]

In striking, the workers demanded solution of their "most burning economic problems," the Soviets said, including increased wages, guaranteed employment, shorter working hours without diminished earnings, social security reforms, and recognition of trade union rights in enterprises. In addition, according to Soviet accounts, the French working class expressed its solidarity with the students' and professors' struggle for reforms of higher education, and with the peasants' struggle against agricultural monopolies.[26] Moreover, the Soviets asserted, the economic demands were linked with social and political demands for limiting the powers of the monopolies and democratizing the country's political life, and thus were aimed at the policies of the bourgeois state as a whole. Finally, they maintained, the strikes belied the efforts of the capitalists to buy off the workers with promises of codetermination and worker control.[27]

The Soviets clearly chose to view the events in France within the context of a struggle for democratization of the existing regime, not its violent overthrow. They termed the upheaval a "testimony to the powerful effort of the class struggle of the proletariat against capital, for social transformations and democratic rights."[28] The PCF, too, deliberately situated the strike within the context of the continuing struggle of the French workers against the power of the government and the monopolies. Thus, according to Secretary General Waldeck Rochet, "the cause of the strike of May–June 1968, unprecedented in its scope, is nothing mysterious. . . . It is the cynical indifference of the ruling circles to the most pressing needs of the workers and the confiscation of all the fruits of scientific-technological progress by the oligarchy."[29]

Stretching the student movement to fit the parameters of the class struggle required a feat of ideological gymnastics. The CPSU and the PCF rose to the occasion. As a lengthy *Pravda* article on the role of the intellectual under socialism (which appeared coincidentally with the events in France) asserted, intellectuals in bourgeois societies are, as hired workers, subject to the same exploitation as the working class: "This is the basic reason for the ever-increasing participation of the intelligentsia, like other categories of working people, in the antimonopolistic struggle."[30]

Within the PCF the task of integrating the student movement fell to party ideologue Roger Garaudy, whose efforts to embrace the student movement were, some critics contended, excessively generous. As Garaudy explained, Marx did not define class membership on the basis of "background or original environment," but on the basis of one's place in the production process. Thus, on the basis of their *future* place in society, students could be defined as members of the working class, part of the "collective worker." The May 13 general strike, the key event in the PCF analytical schema because it brought out the workers in support of the students, thereby became a "class problem." However, Garaudy admits, "this is certainly not very clear in the minds of all students [or] of a great many workers. If it were, they'd all be militant revolutionaries."[31]

While the PCF asserted that the root cause of the crisis was in the political structures of the Fifth Republic, it also perceived reluctance on the part of the mass of workers to carry the strikes beyond satisfaction of their economic demands: "although the masses of workers were united in bringing their economic and social demands to a successful conclusion, they were not united for prolonging the strike when a large part of these demands had been met, and still less united in assigning political aims to their demands."[32] Therefore the PCF, in not allowing itself to be drawn more actively into the unfolding events, avoided the isolation, its leaders maintained, of the "most aware and most combative elements . . . from the broad masses."[33]

The French Communists also determined, correctly as events bore out, that, although weakened, capitalism in France still possessed the preponderant power. Asked by the German weekly *Der Spiegel* why the Communist *confédération générale du travail* (CGT) and the Communist Party did not give the de Gaulle regime a "final push" when that appeared to be all that was needed, CGT President Benôit Frachon retorted that the reasons for the strike were primarily economic and social, and that capitalism did not die that easily: de Gaulle still "has all the power at his command."[34]

Why the PCF Failed to Act

The Ideological Explanation: Not a Revolutionary Situation

The Marxist-Leninist precept of the vanguard role of the Communist party in leading the struggle for socialism is the key to understanding the PCF analysis of and its limited role in the May-June events. Completely alien to Marxism-Leninism is the notion that any group, class, or party other than the working class, under the leadership of its vanguard, the Communist party, can be the engine of the revolutionary sociopolitical transformation. Thus, as a *Pravda* editorial affirmed shortly before the onset of the May-June crisis in France:

> Among the forces operating against imperialism, the working class of capitalist countries occupies an important place. It is steadfastly fighting against monopolistic capital, for political, social, and economic rights of workers, and for the triumph of socialist ideals. The Soviet people . . . are sure that the proletariat of the capitalist part of the world will achieve new decisive successes in the struggle . . . for the progress of mankind under the leadership of the Marxist-Leninist Communist vanguard.[35]

Again, virtually on the eve of the outbreak of the French crisis, a Soviet commentator reiterated: "The Communists are marching in the vanguard of the struggle of the working class. The world Communist movement is the most influential political force in modern times."[36] In reply to the question, "What is a revolutionary in France today?" PCF Secretary General Rochet answered that a true revolutionary must possess and correctly apply the scientific tools of Marxism-Leninism in accord with the realities of the situation in order to win over to socialism a majority of the people. The Communist vanguard party is charged with correctly determining the most appropriate strategy and tactics at all stages. Above all, this means deciding when, based on the objective social conditions and the subjective mood of the masses, a society is ripe for revolution: when a "revolutionary situation" exists. Because it is the party of the French working class and is inspired by Marxism-Leninism, Rochet declared, the French Communist Party is "the only revolutionary party in France."[37]

According to Lenin, the proletariat "knows . . . that for the success of its revolution . . . the sympathy of the majority of the working masses (and hence of the majority of the population) is *absolutely necessary.*"[38] Taking action prematurely would be gross political irresponsibility. Only through the continuous, patient effort of the party to unite the Left and gain acceptance for its ideas among a broad stratum of the population—the preparation of the "subjective conditions"—can a revolutionary situation be created. The party, with its Marxist-Leninist lights, thus becomes the vital interpreter of events for the proletariat. Only the party can evaluate the shifting correlation of class forces and prescribe correct strategy and tactics. As Rochet asserted, the only truly scientific approach "is accurately to estimate the actual situation and the balance of class forces, to discern and foresee new trends in time, and to determine the right policy line on this basis."[39] Thus, as interpreted by Alfred G. Myer, "This is precisely the meaning of the revolutionary situation: the masses have taken the initiative, or are about to take it. It is the test of an able revolutionary leader to make use of these 'elemental forces' and ride to power on the waves of spontaneity."[40]

Spontaneity, therefore, does have a place in the revolution, but only if it is "harnessed, transformed into political energy, and channeled into the most advantageous direction" by the revolutionary vanguard.[41] For this reason, the Soviets contend, " 'Left' petit bourgeois ideologists . . . are the opponents of Leninist teaching on the revolutionary situation as an essential objective prerequisite of revolution," because of their pretension that "such a situation can be created by artificial measures."[42]

The events of May-June clearly did not fit this definition of a revolutionary situation. Initially sparked by student dissatisfaction with bureaucratic university administrative procedures, the movement was only partly and tardily embraced by the organized workers; even then, organized trade union support at the national level was limited to calling a general strike for May 13, in "solidarity" with the students, who had suffered "police repression" during the preceding demonstrations. Otherwise, both the PCF and its union, the CGT, remained virtually on the sidelines, and in some instances ordered their militants not to participate in the student demonstrations, which Politburo member and Central Committee Secretary Georges Marchais, on behalf of the party, had initially condemned as the work of "pseudorevolutionaries" and as serving the interests of the government, the bourgeoisie, and monopoly capital.[43]

Both the PCF and the CPSU railed against the elements of "spontaneity" and anarchy within the student movement, and frequently pointed out that since workers' children comprised a mere 10 percent of the student body, the student movement was understandably permeated with petit bourgeois ideology. On the eve of the French crisis, the Soviets had noted that "deserters from the strata of the petit bourgeoisie" were continually "swelling the ranks of the proletariat" in the economically depressed capitalist countries.[44] They blamed the infusion of petit bourgeois elements for diverting the movement from a true revolutionary path into adventurism. True Marxist-Leninists were opposed to these "adventurist elements who are summoning and driving the masses toward ill-considered and unprepared actions, failing to take into account the real correlation of fighting forces at a given time and place."[45]

Much was made also of the influence of the "German-American philosopher" Herbert Marcuse and of his disciple, the "German anarchist" Daniel Cohn-Bendit, leader of the group known as the March 22 Movement. On May 30, *Pravda* published an article attacking Marcuse's "Revision of the Marxist Concepts of Revolution" speech delivered at a UNESCO colloquium in Paris shortly before the outbreak of the student unrest. *Pravda* criticized Marcuse for substituting intergenerational conflict for class struggle; for preaching a version of the "convergence" theory in which he asserted that it is necessary to struggle against all industrial societies, including Socialist ones; for his rejection of organized struggle in favor of "spontaneous rebellion" of the youth; and for charging that the working class in industrial countries has lost its revolutionary spirit and that only those outside the production process can be true revolutionaries. Such contentions are only devices of the bourgeois ideologists and Maoists, *Pravda* countered, designed to "confuse and divide the ardent but politically inexperienced youth. . . ." *Pravda* reported that on May 13, at the height of the general strike, when the working class was demonstrating in support of the "legal demands of the student body striving for democratic university reform," Cohn-Bendit and his followers issued the "provocative" call to "storm the Elysée Palace!"[46]

The May-June events brought to the fore the sensitive issue of the Communist parties' relations with the intellectuals. "It is precisely the working class, and primarily the Communists marching in its vanguard," *Pravda* reminded, "who defend everywhere the basic interests of the working people, including those of the intelligentsia and the student body."[47] The "student movement has prospects only if it integrates itself . . . into the general strategy of the class struggle under the hegemony of the working class," and does not consider itself a substitute for the vanguard workers' party, the PCF repeated.[48]

A group of PCF intellectuals openly charged that "by attempting at the outset to restrain this exceptional outburst, the leadership has cut off the party from a great force of Socialist renovation."[49] The intellectuals urged that the party act "at any cost to establish bonds with the new forces which have come to light in the struggle for socialism and liberty." Moreover, in a meeting with a party delegation, they called for the resignation of two party officials (including Marchais, the present secretary general), whom they held particularly responsible for the rift between the student movement and the party.[50]

In an article that dealt directly with the question of whether there was a revolutionary situation in France, a Swiss Communist asked rhetorically "whether the French Communist Party has not knowingly, deliberately, let one of those historical 'opportunities' slip by, whether it 'neglected,' purposely or not, the possibility of seizing a 'vacant' power in a revolutionary manner."[51] Answering in the negative, the author cites Lenin's dictum from "The childhood Disease of 'Leftism' in Communism."

> The fundamental law of the revolution . . . is this. In order for the revolution to take place, it is not enough for the exploited and oppressed masses to become aware of the impossibility of living as formerly and to demand changes . . . it is necessary that the exploiters not be able to live and govern as formerly. It is only when "those at the bottom" no longer want, and "those at the top" are no longer able, to continue to live in the old manner . . . that the revolution can triumph.. . . [52]

Thus, the majority of the workers (or at least the politically aware workers) must have understood the necessity for revolution and be "ready to die for it." Second, the governing classes must have experienced a "governmental crisis which draws even the most backward masses into political life . . . which weakens the government and makes its prompt overthrow possible for the revolutionaries." These conditions were not present in France, however, the author asserts: "There has been a profound discontent on the part of the working and popular masses, but not among the most backward, and these masses were not—not yet—'ready to die' for the revolution."

This line was echoed by the French Communists. As Georges Séguy, secretary general of the CGT, revealed, "To tell the truth, the question of whether this is the moment for the working class to seize power has never been raised by the CGT . . . at the present time it is a question of the struggle of the working class to gain concessions from the capitalist government and firms, a struggle that responds to deep democratic expectations."[53]

Moreover, PCF Politburo member Jacques Duclos implied, if the government and the private employers had more speedily granted the workers' demands, the strike movement would have quickly dissipated. Thus, he asserted, "our party correctly analyzed the character of these strikes. Though they expressed a general aspiration towards change, they were primarily strikes for stated demands. The situation was therefore not revolutionary, as the leftist groups and the bosses of the PSU [Parti socialiste unifié] alleged."[54]

In reply to an interviewer's acerbic question of how the French Communists ever hoped to achieve a classless society if not in such a favorable situation with ten million people on strike—"Do you wish to introduce socialism by parliamentary resolution?"—CGT President Frachon declared, "Socialism will come, it is life itself. The capitalist system, due to its internal contradictions, is condemned to death. However, it must not necessarily be defeated by violence. If we are able to implant socialism another way, it will not be a less worthy socialism."[55]

The PCF's behavior in the May-June events thus corresponded to its own self-image as well as to Marxist-Leninist ideological prescriptions. "We are not adventurers," Frachon reminded, and added, "And why do you insist that we rush headlong into irrational, partly provocative, partly unrealistic actions? We saw a major strike through victoriously and make no point of gambling away our conquests like big-mouths and brigands."[56]

The Soviet Foreign Policy Explanation: de Gaulle Preferred

It is tempting to explain the PCF's reluctance to take decisive action in the May-June events as pandering to the interests of Soviet foreign policy. The interpenetration of state-to-state and party-to-party relations is indeed a perpetual feature of the PCF-CPSU relationship. In recent years Franco-Soviet relations had grown very warm, particularly since de Gaulle's historic visit to the USSR in 1966; trade and scientific cooperation were in the process of being further strengthened, and French Armed Forces Minister Pierre Messmer had recently completed a successful visit to the USSR. Most important, the Soviets highly valued de Gaulle's policy of independence from the U.S. on Vietnam, NATO, and international monetary issues. De Gaulle was routinely exempted from Soviet press criticism, which concentrated instead on French "monopolists" and "oligarchs." A late-April *Pravda* article, for example, was highly laudatory of the French leadership: "The working people of France, headed by their vanguard, the French Communist Party, have always supported a policy of cooperation between France and the USSR. An understanding of the significance of this cooperation in the national interests of their country has been and is present in the most farsighted *state officials* of France in the recent past and at present."[57]

Soviet support for Gaullist foreign policy understandably placed the PCF in a delicate domestic position. Its solution was to differentiate the "positive"

aspects of Gaullist policy in foreign relations from its negative domestic counterpart, and, even within its treatment of foreign policy, to highlight what it
regarded as certain "contradictory aspects." An article by PCF Politburo
member Duclos admirably illustrated this combination tactic.

> The French imperialist forces . . . are doing their utmost to protect the
> interests of the French monopoly groups poised to exploit the setbacks of
> their imperialist rivals in capturing world markets and desirous of playing
> a prominent role in Europe, the domain of the most powerful trusts.
> That is what lies at the root of the contradictory aspects of Gaullist
> policy. The French government is encouraging the aggressive designs of the
> German revenge-seekers by refusing to recognize the GDR [German Demo-
> cratic Republic] and by continuing the nuclear arms race, on the one hand,
> while seeking to play a positive part in such issues as the Vietnam war and
> the development of East-West contacts, on the other.[58]

Moreover, although the PCF was one of the most obedient hewers to the
CPSU line among the Western European Communist parties, these fraternal
bonds had not prevented something of a CPSU double cross at French election
time. While the PCF supported the François Mitterand candidacy in the
presidential elections of 1965, the Soviet press did not disguise the USSR's
preference for de Gaulle, asserting that his independent foreign policy was
more favorable to the antiimperialist struggle than a Mitterand government's
foreign policy would be.[59] Following the elections of June 1968, which essentially wrote "finis" to the May-June events, Soviet commentators warmly
recalled the close working relationship that had been formed with the new
head of the French government, Maurice Couve de Murville, in his prior
capacity as foreign minister, and reiterated the harmony of Soviet and French
views on important international issues.

Apparent Soviet preference for a continuation of Gaullist power over the
installation of a noncommunist leftist government, however, did not prevent
the PCF from waging its own anti-Gaullist campaign. As Rochet wrote in
1967, "The Gaullist leaders . . . had imagined that, thanks primarily to the
policy of rapprochement between France and the Soviet Union that had been
outlined by de Gaulle, the French Communist Party was going to attenuate
. . . its fight against the system of personal power under cover of which the
Gaullist candidates might have been able to win over a sizable number of
Communist votes."[60] PCF spokesmen contended that the "progressive foreign
policy" was not the creation of one man, but was rooted "in the opposition
of French monopoly capital and American, English, and West German imperialism." Even if de Gaulle himself were defeated, France would never "go back
to being a vassal of American imperialism."[61]

Obviously, the PCF understood the Soviet accommodation with de Gaulle. But, equally clearly, it opted to maximize its own domestic alliance strategy, as exemplified by its electoral conduct, at certain times when its interests and those of the CPSU were in conflict. To attribute its unwillingness to act in 1968 to servitude to Soviet foreign policy interests is to condemn the party to permanent opposition status. Such an explanation ignores the genuine efforts of the PCF to expand and legitimize its position in the French political process, which will now be examined.

The Domestic Strategy Explanation: Need to Preserve Alliance and Enlarge Support

The decisive reason the PCF decided to pursue a policy of moderation in May and June was its determination to preserve its budding and still delicate alliance with the noncommunist parties of the Left. Since the 1965 presidential election, the PCF had moved painstakingly toward closer ties with the other leftist parties, which in September 1965 had themselves combined to form the *Fédération de la Gauche démocratique et socialiste* (FGDS). These efforts to promote broad-based unity were carried out in accordance with the party's policy of forming alliances to achieve an ever-expanding base of popular support. Any move to seize power illegally, the party feared, would rekindle the suspicions of its alliance partners, and of the population at large, about the antidemocratic nature of the party, and risked provoking a rightist backlash.

As an earnest of their commitment to unity of the Left and to the democratic process and parliamentary path to power, the Communists had supported Socialist Mitterand rather than presenting their own candidate for the presidency in 1965; in the second round of the legislative elections of 1967 the PCF and the FGDS had united behind their best-placed candidates; and in February 1968, after eight months of tough negotiation, the two parties had issued a historic joint declaration setting out their common goals and programs. While falling short of the joint legislative program the PCF advocated, and leaving unresolved differences on nationalization and foreign policy, it was a promising foundation on which the PCF believed it would be possible to build a unified program. The PCF was loathe to jeopardize these results of its efforts to achieve leftist unity, which, it believed, was crucial to its goal of escaping its political isolation and gaining respectability and acceptance as a responsible alternative to Gaullism. Thus, as one analyst of PCF behavior in May-June concluded: "The Communists stopped the revolution in May because . . . they are convinced that their persistent moderation over the past two decades and their alliance with the Socialists will bring them into a coalition government after de Gaulle leaves the scene."[62]

The PCF believed that the "peaceful transition to socialism" based on broad alliances was the soundest strategy; any other, including armed insurrection following a general strike, would only result in defeat. As Politburo member Paul Laurent asserted, the events of May and June provided "incontrovertible proof" of the correctness of the PCF strategy.

> ... today, after our recent experience, what we suggest for our country and its path to socialism takes on much greater force. We have seen the masses of the people reject certain forms ... of struggle, because they ... think that the barricades are not the right answer to France's problems in our time. This carries with it some imperative requirements for the party's political and ideological battle, to show what our strategic line is on rallying all the forces of democracy against the monopoly government.[63]

In its December 1968 manifesto, calling for a "broad alliance of all social classes victimized by the monopolies and by their government," the PCF Central Committee confidently asserted: "as the powerful popular movements of May and June 1968 forcefully proved, conditions are rapidly ripening for common action *by all classes harmed or threatened by the monopolies.*" The party's goal was thus "replacement of the Gaullist monopoly government with an advanced political and economic democracy, opening the way to socialism."[64]

The PCF opted for an electoral egress from the crisis, hoping, in its acceptance of de Gaulle's call for new legislative elections at the end of June, that it would benefit from its posture of responsibility and legality in the crisis, and would enlarge on its electoral gains of 1967. "The Communist Party will enter this consultation of the people with its candidates, explaining its program for progress and peace in national independence, and its policy of union of all the democratic forces," the PCF Politburo declared, following de Gaulle's announcement of the forthcoming elections. The decision to participate in the elections, which was consonant with its "peaceful road to power" strategy (and with the decisions of the CPSU 20th party congress), signaled the end of the "revolutionary" threat of the crisis.[65] As Ronald Tiersky has observed: "In the 'peaceful transition to socialism' doctrine, the key moment in strategy is no longer a general strike or widespread disorder, such as the events of May 1968. Rather, the 'revolutionary situation' is to be created at the time of general elections: by voting the Left into power, the people initiate a process with a potentially revolutionary conclusion."[66]

The Communists campaigned on the platform that to vote Communist was to help bring about a new democratic government with Communist representation and to consolidate the strike gains. The Communist program, Rochet assured Frenchmen, "offers the possibility of an original, French way for proceeding to socialism, in democracy."[67]

The PCF entered the electoral campaign with considerable optimism: "the June 23 elections may signify the undoing of the Gaullist regime in France, its definitive failure," Politburo member Roland Leroy prognosticated.[68] Soviet commentators felt safe in predicting that "at least one voter in four" would vote Communist.[69] The PCF apparently regarded the elections as an opportunity to receive concrete endorsement of its crisis behavior from the electorate, because it spurned the FGDS proposal of an alliance from the first ballot (June 23), and insisted on reinstituting the 1967 alliance for the runoff (June 30) only. In any event, PCF expectations (and those of the Left in general) were severely disappointed. While in 1967 PCF representation in the Assembly had increased from 41 to 73 seats (out of a total 486), in 1968 only 34 Communist candidates were elected.[70]

The Soviets were obviously surprised by the "clear slide to the Right" in France, which gave the ruling Gaullist *Union pour la Défense de la République* (UDR) and its allies, the *Républicains indépendants* (RI) a solid absolute majority. As one Soviet writer acknowledged, "The French cannot remember a time within their lifespan when the correlation of forces in the National Assembly between the ruling majority and the opposition was such as has resulted from the June elections. This correlation can be defined as three-and-one-half to one, in favor of the Gaullists and their allies—the Independent Republicans."[71]

Both Soviet and French commentators attributed the PCF's defeat to a rightist backlash brought on by fear, especially on the part of "vacillating" and "floating" bourgeois voters, and voters who had been newly won over to the party in 1967. Throughout the campaign, the Gaullists had deliberately laid the blame for the riots and strikes on the hapless PCF and its supporters, thus blunting the party's appeal as a responsible alternative to Gaullism. The Soviets reacted sharply to this "tactic of intimidation" by the French Government, which was "turning the course of events by setting as its main aim in the coming election the struggle against the Communist Party, against the country's democratic forces."[72] Thus, as Soviet expert on relations with non-ruling Communist parties Vadim Zagladin wrote in 1975, the Communists lost votes "because the mass of petit bourgeois strata, frightened by the revolutionary pressure of the proletariat, had taken a leap to the Right and voted for bourgeois, reactionary forces. Unfortunately, a certain section of the working class also acted the same way (chiefly the low-paid sections of workers who had recently come into production)."[73]

Ignoring the fact that it was the PCF that had spurned a first-ballot alliance, the Soviets also blamed the "refusal of Socialist and other leftwing elements to take joint action with the Communists and create a united front of leftwing forces which would help take complete state control by parliamentary means" for the failure of the May-June events to "lead to radical changes in the country's domestic affairs."[74] They also indicted the French majoritarian electoral system for the one-sided distribution of Assembly seats. "The correlation of seats in parliament still does not determine the true correlation of forces on the political scene," they asserted.[75]

In its election postmortems, the PCF also held the actions of "leftists," the distortion effects of the electoral system, and the government's campaign of fear responsible for its poor showing. But it also laid the blame on the absence of a specific joint legislative program for the PCF and FGDS. "The masses could hardly be expected to come out in favor of a change if they had no way of knowing exactly what would replace the government they had," they argued.[76]

Thus, although the 1968 election represented not only a repudiation of the PCF strategy in the immediate crisis situation, but a severe setback in its long-term strategy of legitimizing itself in the eyes of the French electorate, PCF analysts optimistically predicted an early resumption of the party's forward march. They insisted that the election results confirmed the party's analysis of the correct strategy—that not via barricades, but by means of intensified party work among the masses and solidifying the leftist alliance, would the PCF ultimately succeed in defeating the "monopoly government."[77]

THE CRISIS OF AUGUST

The PCF could scarcely have been in a worse position to confront another crisis that would threaten both its internal cohesion and its domestic alliances than it was when the five Warsaw Pact nations invaded Czechoslovakia on August 21, 1968. The new crisis placed before the party an awkward choice which was bound to reopen the not-yet-healed wounds from the previous months. Approval of the intervention would be, if anything, a graver blow to the PCF's alliance strategy, its effort to overcome the image of a "foreign party," and its relationship with its dissident intellectuals than were the May-June events. Condemnation, conversely, would complicate its relationship with the CPSU and the other members of the bloc, and rankle the hard-liners within the party.

The strategy the PCF elected was clearly designed to maximize its gains and minimize its losses in a difficult situation. By criticizing the Soviets' manner of handling the crisis, while acknowledging that some action had indeed been necessary, the PCF deftly kept its criticism within the narrowest possible bounds. Moreover, after apparently getting the criticism off its collective chest, the party moved quickly to resume the role of peacemaker and healer that it had (mistakenly) thought it was successfully playing prior to the invasion. The fact that the PCF did not allow a permanent breach to develop with the CPSU, however, should not detract from the historic nature of its original act. Its criticism of the Soviet invasion of Czechoslovakia constituted the first time the PCF had broken with the CPSU on a major issue,* and in this it marked a watershed in their relationship.

Let us examine briefly some of the antecedents of and fallout from this event.

Impact of the Crisis on the PCF

PCF Attitude toward the Dubcek Regime

One should perhaps begin a discussion of the PCF's attitude toward the Dubcek regime by recalling the party's traditional evocation, on the basis of the decisions of the CPSU 20th party congress and subsequent international Communist conferences, of the right of each party to determine, within Marxist-Leninist guidelines, the particulars of the path to socialism that best conformed to its nation's history and level of development. As Secretary General Rochet had affirmed in his report to the 18th PCF congress in January 1967: "The French Communist Party elaborates and conducts its policies in the light of practical conditions in France and in the international situation, with a firm reliance on the principles of Marxism-Leninism."[78]

In explaining its reaction to the invasion, the PCF recalled Maurice Thorez' November 17, 1946, statement to the *Times* on the French path to socialism. According to Thorez, it was "possible to envisage other routes for the march toward socialism than the one followed by the Russian Communists."[79] The PCF had almost made a fetish of its verbal endorsement of the principles of party autonomy and noninterference, most recently at the Budapest consultative conference preparatory to convening the long-anticipated international Communist conference. The PCF delegate to the Budapest conference, Georges Marchais, moreover, had emphatically registered his party's opposition to the notion that there is or could be any single international Communist center.

> All Communist parties are truly independent and equal in rights . . . there is not, and there cannot be today, when Communist parties have become major national political factors, and when the conditions under which they struggle have become so widely diversified, any "center" or "centers" directing the activity of all Communist parties. There is not now, nor could there ever be, any "dominant" or any "subordinate" party. Consequently, no party can claim the right to impose its point of view on others.[80]

---

*In the case of the Daniel-Sinyavsky trial, PCF Central Committee member Louis Aragon had signed his protest as a "private person," rather than in his official capacity.

Then, using the strongest language, Marchais reaffirmed the PCF's commitment to party autonomy, noninterference, and the centrality of national considerations in determining party conduct.

> Each party decides, and must decide in complete independence, upon its policy, its patterns of action, and its tactics in the struggle. We are resolutely devoted to this principle, and we take a vigorous stand in opposition to any attempt at interference in the formulation and conduct of our policy. It is as a function of the interests of the working class and of the French nation, as well as of the prevailing conditions for the mass struggle in our country, that the French party, on the basis of scientific socialism, determines its policies in all circumstances.

But then, in his well-practiced dialectical rhetoric, Marchais evoked the other side of the duality of a Communist party's existence: proletarian internationalism and its role as an international vanguard party. The PCF, Marchais intoned, "draws enduring sustenance from the common aims and interests" that unite workers in all countries. Success depends on the party's skill in "binding together" the national and the common interests, a task that "sometimes involves real difficulties. . . ."

Thus, the PCF claimed, its position on the invasion of Czechoslovakia was consistent with the party's positions enunciated in the past: "It is precisely because of its loyalty to principle, to past action, and to its historic mission that the French Communist Party had no choice but to take the position expressed by its Politburo on August 21, and unanimously by its Central Committee on the following day."[81]

Certain parallels existed between the French and prereform Czechoslovak Communist parties—in their lack of enthusiasm for de-Stalinization and distrust of Khrushchev; their worker-bureaucratic character (contrasted with the more intellectual cast of, for example, the Polish and Italian Communist parties); and their fidelity to Moscow.[82] In July 1967 a PCF delegation, headed by the doctrinaire Jeannette Vermeersch-Thorez, had conferred in Prague with a Czechoslovak delegation headed by First Secretary Antonin Novotny. The talks were said to have been held in the "spirit of traditionally friendly relations between the two parties; they reflected full identity of views on matters discussed as a whole. . . ."[83] The L'Humanité account of the meeting also contained the observation that "the French Communist Party delegation highly values the conquests of socialism in Czechoslovakia, and the creative meaning of the new methods of economic management which tend to favor economic progress and the flourishing of socialist democracy."[84]

Nor did the relevance of the subsequent Czechoslovak reforms to French Communists pass unnoticed. Garaudy, while still in fairly good standing as the party's chief ideologue, had written in April 1968 that the errors of excessive and prolonged centralization of powers had first "emerged with physical force" in "the only one of the Socialist states to begin building socialism in an already highly industrialized country: Czechoslovakia."[85] In a generally sympathetic vein, Garaudy added that the errors "are being corrected under difficult conditions . . . and under fire from implacable enemies who are trying . . . not to improve socialism, but to destroy it. But they are being corrected, and Czechoslovakia's success in correcting them will provide a fine example of the potential of socialism in a highly developed country."[86] Dissident communists, committed to democratizing the party structures, organized around the monthly journal *Unir-Débat,* also identified with the Prague Spring reformers, even linking the events of May-June to the attractiveness of the Czechoslovak reform ideas.[87]

In a major speech to a PCF Central Committee meeting in April, Secretary General Rochet sat out the official party position toward the Czechoslovak reform regime.[88] While affirming that the internal changes in Czechoslovakia were the "private business" of the Czechoslovak Communist Party (CPC), Rochet claimed that the bonds of international solidarity permitted the PCF to make its own evaluation of a fraternal party's activity. Rochet's assessment was that the actions of the CPC indicated that, in its "quest for better methods, more democratic practices," it was concerned with protecting "the very foundations of Socialist society from being in any way compromised." As evidence, Rochet noted Alexander Dubcek's commitments to "socialist democracy" and the guarantees of democratic rights and freedoms; and his affirmation of alliance with the USSR and the Socialist community. Rochet approvingly noted the CPC Presidium's expressed desire for strengthening Czechoslovak-Soviet economic cooperation, and voiced the expectation that party "application of the guideline ideas" of the CPC leadership "will demonstrate to the foes of socialism that they must abandon all hope of disputing socialism in Czechoslovakia."

What emerges is a PCF declaratory position that the Czechoslovak reforms were compatible with the Socialist system,[89] but that the leadership should more actively combat the antisocialist elements. Thus, it was an endorsement not of the particulars of the Czechoslovak reforms, but of the CPC's right to seek its own path to socialism.

PCF Mediation Efforts

The PCF had actively played the role of mediator in the CPSU-CPC dispute, a role for which it was well suited by virtue of both its historical affinity with the Czechoslovak party and its solid loyalist credentials. On July

14, precisely at the time the five Eastern European countries were meeting in Warsaw amid rumors of the presence of Soviet troops in Czechoslovakia, Rochet and Italian Communist officials conferred in Moscow with CPSU Central Committee Secretary Mikhail Suslov and the deputy head of the International Department of the CPSU Central Committee, Zagladin. The next day they also conferred with other CPSU leaders following their return from Warsaw. Rochet subsequently stated that the purpose of his talks in Moscow had been to "express the concern of the French Communist Party to see the difficulties existing between the fraternal parties solved by negotiation while respecting the national sovereignty of each country, and in a spirit of proletarian internationalism and fraternal cooperation among the socialist countries in the common struggle against imperialism and for socialism."[90]

Following Rochet's return to Paris, the PCF Politburo announced that "in view of the developing situation in Czechoslovakia and its resultant problems," it intended to propose a meeting of European Communist parties within the next few days.[91] It was simultaneously announced that Rochet would confer in Prague on July 19 with the CPC leaders. The thrust of the PCF initiative in proposing the conference and in Rochet's journey to Prague seems to have been an effort to find a nonmilitary resolution to the dispute that would have required fundamental CPC concessions on its liberalization program, and particularly a clampdown on freedom of expression. As Politburo member Etienne Fajon later stated, the PCF was determined "that everything must be done, by those fraternal parties directly concerned, to arrive at a political solution which will insure that Czechoslovakia remains in the world Socialist system."[92]

Rochet reportedly warned Dubcek that if he failed to overcome the difficulties through some kind of mutually acceptable agreement, "a breaking off of your alliances with the Soviet Union would undoubtedly expose your country to any sort of maneuver from West Germany and the U.S.A. The entire balance of power would be upset and European security threatened. It is understandable that the Soviet Union and the Socialist countries could never allow such a situation to arise."[93]

According to Marchais, the Czechoslovaks rejected the idea of a conference, and the proposal was withdrawn. The PCF, noting "the possibility of bilateral meetings" between the CPC and each of the parties that had participated in the Warsaw Meeting, asked the parties that had accepted the proposal for the conference "not to insist at the present on the convocation of such a meeting."[94]

The PCF seemed to breathe a collective sigh of relief at the outcome of the Cierna and Bratislava meetings between Czechoslovak and other Warsaw Pact leaders, which appeared to indicate that agreement had been reached on a political resolution of the crisis. The PCF expressed satisfaction that "the problems that had come up among the sister parties" had been settled along the lines advocated by the PCF in its July 27 Central Committee resolution, that is, "by negotiation that respects the free will of each party, and within the spirit of proletarian internationalism."[95]

PCF Reaction to the Soviet Invasion of Czechoslovakia

The PCF reacted immediately to the news of the Soviet invasion of Czechoslovakia. In a declaration datelined 10 A.M., August 21, the Politburo expressed its "surprise and disapproval of the military intervention in Czechoslovakia."[96] Indicating what must have been a genuine sense of betrayal, it recalled that it had "asserted its strong satisfaction after the Cierna and Bratislava meetings . . . with regard to their positive conclusions. . . ." At 11:30 A.M. the CGT released a statement in which it declared that "the French workers can only deplore the present intervention in Czechoslovakia."[97] The next day the PCF Central Committee, meeting in extraordinary session, expressed its "regret" and "disagreement" over the military intervention, and announced its support of the Politburo's August 21 declaration. It also revealed that during the course of Rochet's meetings with Soviet and Czechoslovak leaders in July, the PCF had "clearly expressed to the contending parties its opposition to any foreign military intervention."[98]

The PCF stated that its position on the invasion of Czechoslovakia derived from application of basic principles which it had adopted at party congresses, and which were "solemnly proclaimed" in the 1960 Declaration of 81 Marxist-Leninist parties. Politburo member François Billoux enumerated these principles as follows:

1. Each party must define its policies and actions "in complete independence, on the basis of Marxism-Leninism, with national conditions as a point of departure, and taking into account its international responsibilities."
2. All parties have the duty to combine proletarian internationalism with patriotism.
3. All parties have equal rights. No party can impose its views on others.
4. Although criticism of a fraternal party is normal, there must be "no interference . . . or intervention in internal affairs. . . ."
5. Disagreements among parties must be resolved by discussion at bilateral or multilateral meetings, "with respect for the free determination of each party and in the spirit of proletarian internationalism."[99]

In more specific terms, the PCF attributed opposition to the invasion to underlying differences in analysis and interpretation of the developments in Czechoslovakia since January 1968 between itself and the five Warsaw Pact invading states.[100] According to the PCF account, all parties directly or indirectly involved were in agreement over the necessity for the changes which the CPC had undertaken in December and January: bureaucratic inertia had stymied economic growth and the CPC had lost touch with the masses. The opening up of the system, elimination of censorship, and encouragement of individual responsibility and initiative, however, had "quite naturally" produced problems. Antisocialist elements, free to express their views, were sometimes countered by "inadequate answers." But, despite these attacks on socialism by elements taking advantage of the freedom of speech opened up by the reforms, the Czechoslovak working class remained loyal to the Socialist regime. Besides, the PCF pointed out, the very fact that it itself speaks of a "peaceful transition to socialism" reflects its own belief that the bourgeoisie might be too weak to resist; but did anyone think, it asked, that the Czechoslovakian working class and the CPC were too weak to resist an attempt to restore capitalism by "ideological erosion" of socialism?[101] The PCF, therefore, "never believed" that Czechoslovakia "might have been on the edge of counterrevolution. . . ."[102]

The PCF also discounted the danger posed by outside "imperialists" (the U.S. and West Germany), which had been cited by the invading states as justification for their "preventive action." Action by revolutionaries, *Cahiers du Communisme* editor Léo Figuères said, must be based on "concrete or verifiable realities and not possibilities." The bitter political struggle between Socialist and antisocialist forces in Czechoslovakia required *political support* of the CPC's struggle against the anti-Socialist elements. The PCF was "completely ready—within the limit of its means—to undertake efforts of a political nature" to help resolve the problems. The PCF considered military intervention a "serious error which has not facilitated a settlement of the problems" in Czechoslovakia.[103]

Thus, the PCF opposed the intervention on both ideological and practical grounds. First, it contravened fundamental principles of interparty relations —sovereignty and noninterference. Second, it was counterproductive, by allowing the proponents of counterrevolution to masquerade as Czechoslovak patriots. And third (reflecting PCF concern for the negative impact on its own efforts to gain acceptability), it had disturbed people all over the world, and "planted the seeds of doubt as to socialism's ability to insure the right of people to be their own masters. . . ."[104]

Although the PCF refused to go so far as to sign a joint statement supporting the Czechoslovak leaders, as proposed by Italian Communist leader Luigi Longo, it continued pressing for respect for party autonomy. In October Politburo member and Central Committee Secretary Gaston Plissonnier called on the Soviet leaders to put "special significance on the principles of independence, equality, and noninterference," and to assure "that they are not only proclaimed, but also respected by all parties without any exception."[105] The PCF recognized its own national and international responsibilities, the party press affirmed, but "the heaviest responsibility is that of the Communist Party of the Soviet Union. . . ."[106]

PCF Moves to Restore Good Relations with the CPSU

Having vented its genuine dismay over the Soviet invasion of Czechoslovakia, the PCF's principal preoccupation seemed to turn to restoring good relations between itself and the CPSU. Critics have contended that the restoration process began the very day after the invasion, pointing to the subtle gradations in phraseology between the Politburo's strong expression of "surprise and disapproval," the CGT's use of the more modulated word "deplore," and the Central Committee's still weaker expression of "regret" and "disagreement" over the invasion.[107]

Adding to this impression is the Central Committee's pledge, contained in its August 22 statement, that the PCF would redouble its efforts "for the cause of international Communist unity but, first and foremost, for the strengthening of the ties of fraternal friendship which have always bound it to the Communist party of the Soviet Union."[108] Secretary General Rochet put on notice those who might have anticipated a prolonged rupture with the USSR that "no one should depend upon us to participate in the anti-Soviet concert unleashed by the enemies of socialism all enchanted by such a propaganda windfall."[109] The CGT reacted to a planned symbolic strike called by the other labor unions in solidarity with the Czechoslovak workers by warning against "attempts to organize anti-Soviet and anticommunist demonstrations."[110] After the Moscow accords, which codified the Czechoslovak leaders' political capitulation, the PCF pledged to "contribute with all our strength to explaining and supporting the decisions jointly made by the Soviet and Czechoslovak comrades."[111] In early November, the PCF became the first of the protesting parties to send a delegation to renew relations with Moscow.

One of the immediate casualties of the invasion was the international conference of Communist and workers' parties which had been scheduled to convene at the end of November. The PCF had been an enthusiastic ally of the CPSU in pressing ahead with the conference plans, which it had originally endorsed as early as October 1963 as a vehicle for censoring the Chinese Communist Party. Following the Budapest consultative conference, the PCF Politburo had strongly reaffirmed its commitment to the conference. Then, on September 16, the PCF announced that it considered conditions no longer opportune for the convening of the conference, and called for its postponement.

Impact of the Invasion on Party Unity

The Soviet invasion of Czechoslovakia produced a confrontation not only between parties but within parties as well. Despite what *Le Monde* called the party's "incredibly skillful balancing act," the confusion and disarray within the PCF precipitated by the invasion could not be contained by the strictures of party discipline and secrecy. The party, already buffeted by the stains of May-June, was attacked by dissidents from both sides of its political spectrum. The resignation of Vermeersch from the Politburo and Central Committee, thereby unmasking the actual discord behind the "unanimously" adopted criticisms of the invasion, was the most dramatic manifestation of old-liner discontent over the PCF rejection of Moscow's infallibility. Vermeersch had voted with "hesitation" for the August 22 resolution, and her dissent was welcomed by the "revolutionary wing" of the PCF as "one voice raised within the party leadership to denounce the present anti-Soviet trend."[112] This wing of the party charged that the leadership's stand on the Czechoslovak invasion revealed how "bemired it is in pacifism, legalism, and an unprincipled policy of alliance with the pro-American bourgeois FGDS . . ." and it almost openly called for Soviet pressure to oust the offenders.[113]

The CPSU did overtly propagate its point of view within the PCF rank and file, many of whom could not accept the leadership's sudden departure from its history of near-total support for the Soviet party. Methods used by the CPSU in disseminating its views angered the PCF leadership. In particular, the PCF considered publication in *Pravda* of extracts from an article by Jacques Duclos on Czechoslovakia that had been written in June—"before the events in Czechoslovakia"—to be improper.[114] At a plenary session of the PCF Central Committee, Secretary Gaston Plissonnier complained about the almost daily barrage of propaganda, emanating from the USSR and East Germany, aimed at justifying the intervention, which was being distributed throughout France.[115]

High-level dissent from the opposite quarter came from such intellectual luminaries as Central Committee member Louis Aragon and Politburo member Garaudy, who was director of the party's Center for Marxist Research and Studies, implementer of its earlier efforts at overture to the Catholics, and chief party ideologue and philosopher. Garaudy's advocacy of a more conciliatory and open posture toward the students had already clashed with the party's official intransigent line, as expressed by Marchais. He again split with the party over Czechoslovakia, charging, in a statement to the Paris correspondent of the Czechoslovak press agency, that the invasion was a "return to Stalinism, both in theory and practice," and appealing to the Soviet leadership to withdraw the troops.[116] Garaudy's remarks were criticized in the party press as "inadmissible interference in the internal affairs of fraternal parties."[117] The storm really only broke, however, with his publication in early October of a collection of documents, with his own preface, by leaders of the Prague Spring. PCF Central Committee member Lucien Mathey severely attacked Garaudy for his violation of party discipline, his advocacy of adoption of the Czechoslovak model of socialism for France, his endorsement of worker self-management and Western management principles, and his advocacy of giving intellectuals a larger role in the revolutionary movement.[118]

The same day Mathey's criticisms were published, Garaudy elaborated in a Radio Luxembourg interview on his conception of the requirements of a French path to socialism. France's future, he asserted, lies neither in the People's Republic of China (PRC), the Soviet Union, nor Czechoslovakia. But, he added:

> it seemed to me that the Prague pattern was far closer to that of France by reason of the similarity between the internal structures of the two countries, and also by reason of the bourgeois democracy that had prevailed there. . . . We are talking about adapting socialism . . . to the new and changing demands of advancing techniques, to changing economic and political relationships, and even . . . to culture.[119]

As part of its early effort to mend relations with the Soviets, the PCF Politburo on August 27 publicly disavowed Garaudy's interview with the Czechoslovak news agency. His views were publicly censured by the PCF Central Committee at its October 20–21 plenum; Garaudy declared that he would accept the criticism "without reserve." In 1970, however, after a speech at the 19th party congress which restated these same views, and his failure to be reelected to the Politburo or Central Committee, Garaudy was finally expelled from the party.[120]

Impact of the Invasion on PCF Alliance Strategy

Officially, the PCF denied that concern over the probably shattering impact of the invasion on its own domestic alliance strategy had been a factor in its decision to condemn the Soviet-led move. Unofficially, however, it was acknowledged that just such a fear had motivated at least some of the most outspoken critics. Survival of the PCF-FGDS alliance in the immediate present, and PCF hopes for the ultimate institution of a popular-front government, required that the PCF disassociate itself from the invasion by the five Warsaw Pact countries. The response of the PCF's allies such as Guy Mollet and Mitterand to the party's initial criticism of the invasion was expectably favorable. Mollet specifically contrasted the party's response to its servile reaction in the face of the Soviet invasion of Hungary in 1956, and said it eliminated the issue as an obstacle to future rapprochement with the PCF. As the PCF backed away from its initial strong criticism, however, indicated its acceptance of the "normalization," and increasingly placed a premium on restoration of close relations with the CPSU, its domestic allies' support considerably cooled. After its electoral losses in June, the invasion of Czechoslovakia produced further strain within the FGDS, whose members argued over breaking off all ties with the PCF (favored by the Radicals, while the *Section Française de l'Internationale Ouvrière* [SFIO] adopted a "wait and see" position). The SFIO publicly defended Garaudy's views when he was attacked by Mathey. In December SFIO leader Mollet announced: "It is not at present possible to exercise joint power with the Communists."[121]

Thus, the Czechoslovak crisis had a serious chilling effect on the PCF's alliance strategy. Polemics between the party and various of its erstwhile allies lasted for more than a year. The party was once again on the defensive, having to prove itself, demonstrate anew its commitment to a French way to socialism, and reestablish credibility and respectability within the French political system. As the party acknowledged, the rapid evolution of the domestic and international situation made it imperative for French Communists to define in greater depth their own path to socialism.

The PCF set about reassuring its domestic allies and the French public about the kind of political system it envisaged for France. "The democracy we want," the PCF proclaimed in one of its earliest statements explaining its position on the invasion, "will be no restriction, but an expansion and extension of the individual liberties enjoyed under bourgeois democracy."[122] Dictatorship of the proletariat—"the dictatorship of a majority over a minority recently stripped of its exploiting privileges"—would be exercised "in alliance with the non-exploiting classes ... through democratic processes."[123] The party rejected, however, what it referred to as "humanistic" socialism, which would entail only some economic reorganization, but would leave the class nature of the state basically unchanged. But it admitted the need to "begin working out new patterns for relations between a Socialist state and a group of parties, among which the Communist party would seek no influence other than that which the probity of its actions, its scientific theory, and its disciplined organization would naturally warrant."[124] The Champigny Manifesto, issued on December 7, 1968, which reaffirmed the party's commitment to respect for civil rights and liberties, its openness to cooperation with all "anti-imperialist" parties, and a peaceful path to socialism, was a major first step in this effort.

NOTES

1. Editorial, "On the Eve of the Consultative Meeting," *Pravda,* February 22, 1968.
2. Editorial, "Capitalism in the Grip of Contradictions," *Pravda,* February 7, 1968.
3. L. Vinogradov, "Proletarian Banners," *Izvestiya,* February 15, 1968.
4. Ibid.

5. Roundtable discussion, Moscow Radio, April 28, 1968.
6. *Pravda* editorial, February 22, 1968.
7. Vinogradov, op. cit.
8. Ibid.; passage in boldface in original.
9. *Pravda* editorial, February 22, 1968.
10. Ibid.
11. Ibid.
12. Vadim Zagladin, "On the Right Revolutionary Road," *Pravda,* April 28, 1968.
13. Vinogradov, op. cit.
14. Zagladin, op. cit.
15. Vinogradov, op. cit.
16. Roundtable discussion, Moscow Radio, April 28, 1968.
17. Vinogradov, op. cit.
18. Nikolay Vladimirov commentary, Moscow Radio, February 12, 1968.
19. Vinogradov, op. cit.
20. Ibid.
21. Zagladin, op. cit.
22. A. I. Sobolev, "The Revolutionary-Transforming Activity of the Working Class," *Rabochiy Klass i Sovremennyy Mir,* 1976, no. 2 (March-April).
23. Yu. I. Rubinskiy, ed., *Frantsiya* (Moscow: Misl Publisher, 1973), p. 294.
24. Ibid.
25. N. Prozhogin, "Working France Submits its Account to the Monopolies," *Pravda,* June 10, 1968.
26. T. Yevleva, "Polozhenniye Trudyashchisya Frantsii," *Mezhdunarodnaya Zhizn,* September 1968, no. 9. A detailed account of the events is provided by Richard Johnson, *The French Communist Party Versus the Students: Revolutionary Politics in May–June 1968* (New Haven: Yale University Press, 1972).
27. Boris Kotov, "Labor and Capital are not to be Reconciled," *Pravda,* as reported by TASS, June 20, 1968.
28. Moscow broadcast in French to Europe, May 27, 1968.
29. Waldeck Rochet, *L'Avenir du PCF* (Paris: Grasset, 1969), cited by Philippe Bénéton and Jean Touchard in "Les Intérprétations de la Crise de mai–juin 1968," *Revue française de Science politique* (June 1970):532–33.
30. R. Kosolapov and P. Simush, "The Intelligentsia in a Socialist Society," *Pravda,* May 25, 1968.
31. Roger Garaudy, in *Démocratie nouvelle* 21 (April–May 1968): 4–9.
32. Editorial, *Cahiers du Communisme* (theoretical journal of the PCF), June–July 1968.
33. Ibid.
34. *Der Spiegel,* June 24, 1968, p. 62.
35. Editorial, "The Path of Peace and Progress," *Pravda,* April 20, 1968.
36. Roundtable discussion, Moscow Radio, April 28, 1968; cf. Zagladin, op. cit.
37. Waldeck Rochet, "What Being a Revolutionary Means in France Today," paper delivered at Maurice Thorez Institute, October 1967 (abridged), in Richard V. Allen, ed., *1968 Yearbook on International Communist Affairs* (Palo Alto: Stanford University Press, 1968), pp. 880–84.
38. "Greetings to the Italian, French, and German Communists," *Sobraniye Sochinenni,* vol. 24, pp. 480–81, cited by Alfred G. Meyer, *Leninism* (Cambridge: Harvard University Press, 1957), p. 40.
39. Rochet in Allen, op. cit., p. 880.
40. Meyer, op. cit., p. 42.
41. Ibid., p. 43.

42. S. Kovalev, "Marxism and the Contemporary Ideological Struggle," *Pravda,* April 25, 1968.

43. *L'Humanité,* May 3, 1968.

44. Zagladin, op. cit.; cf. F. Konstantinov, "Marxism-Leninism, a Single International Teaching," *Pravda,* June 14, 1968.

45. Yu. Zhukov, "The Werewolves," *Pravda,* May 30, 1968.

46. Even the New York *Times* had adopted the "terminology of the *People's Daily,*" the *Pravda* article charged, in "accusing" the French Communists of "wanting to avoid violence" and of striving to create a popular government of democratic union; Zhukov, op. cit. See also V. Petrusenko, "The Idol Comes from the Left, or Some Thoughts on Where Herbert Marcuse Summons Youth,"*Komsomolskaya Pravda,* September 19, 1969; and refutation of Marcuse by French Communist ideologue Garaudy, op. cit.

47. Zhukov, op. cit.

48.Georges Cogniot, speech, "Students, Intellectuals Face Revolution," in the weekly organ of the PCF, *France nouvelle,* October 30, 1968.

49. Letter of May 26 from 36 PCF intellectuals to the party leadership, *Le Monde,* June 6, 1968.

50. Katia D. Kaupp, "Intellectual Criticism," *Le Nouvel Observateur,* June 12–18, 1968, pp. 13–14.

51. J. Vincent, "The Revolution . . .," *Voix ouvrière,* Geneva, June 18, 1968.

52. Ibid.

53. E. Shulyukin interview with Georges Séguy, "An Important Victory Has Been Gained: The Struggle Continues," *Trud,* June 21, 1968; cf. statement by a PCF parliamentary candidate that "the situation was not revolutionary. The ten thousand strikers were not all at the same level of political consciousness. . . ." in *Le Monde,* June 15, 1968.

54. "Anarchists of Today," *Cahiers du Communism*, August-September 1968.

55. *Der Spiegel,* June 24, 1968; Frachon was awarded the Order of Lenin in Moscow on May 17, 1968, for his "services in connection with strengthening friendship between the Soviet and French people."

56. Ibid.

57. Academician S. D. Skazkin, "What Does Historical Experience Teach?" *Pravda,* April 24, 1968; emphasis added.

58. Jacques Duclos, "Imperialism and the Forces Opposing It," *World Marxist Review* 11, no. 9 (September 1968):12.

59. See Ronald Tiersky, "The French Communist Party and Détente," *Journal of International Affairs* 28, no. 2 (1974):202. François Fejtö reports that the reaction among PCF militants to the TASS communiqué in question was so strong that, according to statements made by PCF leaders to activists in the party cells, an official protest was lodged with Moscow. See Fejtö, *The French Communist Party and the Crisis of International Communism* (Cambridge, Mass.: M.I.T. Press, 1967), p. 200.

60. *L'Humanité,* December 11, 1967.

61. PCF Politburo member and Central Committee secretary André Vieuguet, interview in *Land og Folk* (Copenhagen), June 24, 1968.

62. Arthur P. Mendel, "Why the French Communists Stopped the Revolution," *The Review of Politics* 31, no. 1 (January 1969):25.

63. Paul Laurent, "Two Thoughts on the Events of May," *France nouvelle,* July 31, 1968, pp. 7–8.

64. "For an Advanced Democracy, for a Socialist France:" *L'Humanité,* December 7, 1968.

65. Georges Albertini, "The French Communist Party in the May 1968 Revolutionary Crisis," *Est et Ouest,* June 1–15, 1968, pp. 1–5.

66. Tiersky, op. cit., p. 202.

67. Waldeck Rochet television address, June 12, 1968.

68. Interview with *L'Unità* (Rome), June 5, 1968.

69. *Pravda,* June 20, 1968.

70. Frank L. Wilson, "The French Left and the Elections of 1968," *World Politics* 21, no. 4 (July 1969):539ff. The PCF share of the popular vote represented a drop from 22.46 to 20.03 percent.

71. Yu. Bochkarev, "An Unparalleled Chamber," *Komsomolskaya Pravda,* July 4, 1968.

72. Roundtable discussion, Moscow Radio, June 9, 1968.

73. Vadim Zagladin, "Preconditions of Socialism and the Struggle for Socialism," *Voprosy Filosofii,* 1975, no. 11.

74. A. Zozulya, "The Great Force of Today," *Sovetskaya Rossiya,* September 30, 1969.

75. L. Volodin, "The Results of the Second Round," *Izvestiya,* July 2, 1968.

76. Léo Figuères in *Cahiers du Communisme,* November-December 1968.

77. Laurent, op. cit.

78. Reprinted in the PCF monthly review, *La Nouvelle Critique* no. 17, October 1968.

79. Francis Cohen, "Relations among Communist Parties," *La Nouvelle Critique,* no. 17, October 1968, pp. 27–40; Thorez' entire statement published in the *Times* (London), November 17, 1946, was reprinted in François Billoux, *Quand nous étions ministres* (Paris: Éditions sociales, 1972), pp. 184–88.

80. Georges Marchais, speech at the Budapest consultative meeting, February 28, 1968, in *Cahiers du Communism,* no. 4 (1968), pp. 93–102. Some of the PCF's domestic critics charged that it was Marchais' assignment in the international Communist movement to take this position, which fully accorded with that of the CPSU.

81. *La Nouvelle Critique,* no. 17, October 1968.

82. Fejtö, op. cit., pp. 86–93.

83. *L'Humanité,* July 12, 1967.

84. Ibid.

85. *Démocratie nouvelle* no. 21 (April-May 1968).

86. Ibid.

87. *Unir-Débat,* no. 18 (June 10, 1968).

88. Waldeck Rochet, speech at PCF Central Committee meeting at Courneuve, *L'Humanité,* April 20, 1968.

89. The PCF contrasted the situation in Czechoslovakia with that of Hungary in 1956 when there was a real danger of Hungary's elimination from the Socialist camp.

90. Waldeck Rochet interview on Radio Luxembourg, *L'Humanité,* July 24, 1968.

91. *L'Humanité,* July 18, 1968. According to Heinz Timmerman, Suslov was initially receptive to Rochet's European conference idea; see "National Strategy and International Autonomy," *Studies in Comparative Communism,* Summer/Autumn, 1972, p. 270.

92. Étienne Fajon, "Rapport sur la Discussion et l'Adoption des Thèses," *Cahiers du Communisme,* no. 2 (February 1970), p. 207; cited by Annie Kriegel, "The International Role of the French Communist Party since World War II," in Donald L. M. Blackmar and Annie Kriegel, *The International Role of the Communist Parties of Italy and France* (Cambridge: Center for International Affairs, Harvard University, 1975), p. 49.

93. *L'Humanité,* May 15, 1970; cited by Kriegel, op. cit., pp. 49–50.

94. *L'Humanité,* July 22, 1968; in ibid., p. 32.

95. *L'Humanité Dimanche,* August 11, 1968.

96. *L'Humanité,* August 22, 1968.

97. Ibid.

98. *L'Humanité,* August 23, 1968.

99. François Billoux, editorial, *Cahiers du Communisme,* August-September 1968.

100. Editorial, "Why the Invasion of Czechoslovakia?" *La Nouvelle Critique,* no. 17, October 1968; Figuères, op. cit.

101. Billoux, editorial.

102. Figuères, op. cit.

103. Ibid.

104. Billoux, editorial.

105. *L'Humanité,* October 23, 1968.

106. Editorial, *La Nouvelle Critique,* no. 17, October 1968.

107. Claude Harmel, "The French Communists and the Czechoslovak Affair," *Est et Ouest,* September 1–15, 1968; and Kriegel, op. cit., p. 49.

108. *L'Humanité,* August 23, 1968.

109. Quoted by Billoux, editorial.

110. *L'Humanité,* August 24, 1968.

111. Billoux, editorial.

112. *Le Communiste* (organ of the "revolutionary wing" of the PCF), November 1968.

113. Ibid., September-October 1968. Kriegel calls Rochet the "indirect victim" of the Czechoslovak invasion; illness, not direct Soviet pressure, sapped his authority. In 1970, Georges Marchais, who had been groomed by the Soviets, was elected deputy secretary general, and served as leader of the PCF in all but name. For Kriegel's analysis of Rochet's moves toward heterodoxy, see "The French Communist Party and the Fifth Republic," *Communism in Italy and France,* Donald L. M. Blackmer and Sidney Tarrow, eds. (Princeton, N.J.: Princeton University Press, 1975), pp. 76–77.

114. *L'Humanité,* September 20, 1968.

115. *L'Humanité,* October 23, 1968.

116. *Le Monde,* August 28, 1969.

117. Ibid.

118. "Concerning a Preface by Roger Garaudy," *L'Humanité,* October 5, 1968; see also "French Communist Party Crisis Takes a New Turn: Garaudy Branded Deviationist," *Le Figaro,* October 7, 1968; and R. B., "Garaudy Stand Storm Center of French Communist Party," *Le Monde,* October 6–7, 1968.

119. *Le Figaro,* October 7, 1968.

120. Johnson attributes the expulsion of Garaudy in large part to Soviet organization and financial pressure on the PCF, as part of a coordinated international purge of the French, Italian (the "Manifesto Group"), and Austrian (Franz Marek) parties. He erroneously states, however, that Garaudy was purged in 1968; Johnson, op. cit., p. 199, fn. 12.

121. *Le Monde,* December 22–23, 1968; the PCF labeled the SFIO's position "A Step Backwards": *L'Humanité,* December 23, 1968. By year's end, the FGDS had ceased to exist.

122. Editorial, *La Nouvelle Critique,* no. 17, October 1968.

123. Ibid.

124. Ibid.

2

STRATEGY AND
TACTICS FOR
COMING TO POWER

Soviet analysts assess the current situation in the major capitalist countries as having a "vast revolutionary potential,"[1] with the situation in Western Europe appearing particularly promising. "All over the capitalist-dominated part of Europe the movement of the working people and progressive forces seeking to bring about democratic changes in all fields of economic, social, and political life has increased in scope," the assemblage of leaders of 29 European Communist parties proclaimed in East Berlin in June 1976.[2]

The opportunities and risks created by the European nations' economic and political crises have confronted the CPSU and the nonruling Western European Communist parties with new dilemmas concerning strategy and tactics for coming to power and the amount of influence and control the CPSU will exercise before, during, and after attaining it. Statements by Soviet officials suggest that the unfolding of the crisis in Europe may have occurred more rapidly than the Soviets anticipated, with the creation of opportunities for Communist advantage in some cases outstripping the concretizing of a strategy for exploiting them. The public airing of policy differences between the CPSU and some of the major Western European parties is no longer rare; less publicized is the evidence that advocates of varying degrees of militancy continue to advance contending views within the CPSU itself.

French Communists share their Soviet comrades' analysis of the pervasive nature of the crisis of capitalism as it applies to France. "This . . . is not a classic economic crisis," wrote Marchais, who was elected secretary general of the PCF in 1972. "It is a global crisis that touches at once economic and political life, ideology, and morality. It is the capitalist system itself, at its present stage, that is in question."[3] Both the PCF and the CPSU attacked the austerity measures promulgated in the fall of 1976 under the French government's plan to combat the high inflation, unemployment, and foreign trade deficit, for falling disproportionately on the workers. As Marchais declared in his Berlin conference address, as increasing numbers of people perceive the inability of state monopoly capitalism to solve any of the major problems confronting France, they are coming to question the very existence of the capitalist system itself.[4]

PEACEFUL VERSUS VIOLENT PATH TO POWER

The debate over peaceful versus violent paths to power, which crystallized during the Portuguese Communists' reach for power in late July and November 1975, derives from an ambiguity in Marxist-Leninist doctrine. Lenin's interpretation of Marxism denied the possibility of Communists attaining power exclusively by peaceful means. Parliamentary manipulation was a useful but limited tactic; ultimately, power could be won only by armed insurrection. In his speech to the 20th CPSU congress in 1956 Khrushchev resurrected the doctrine of the peaceful route, with an important caveat. According to Khrushchev, the peaceful path to Communist accession to power and the advent of socialism in Western European capitalist countries would be possible if a broad-based alliance of all the patriotic forces, led by the Communist party, obtained a parliamentary majority—provided the capitalists did not resist.[5]

The writings of contemporary Soviet authorities suggest that the likelihood of capitalist resistance blurs the distinction between peaceful and nonpeaceful forms of revolution. "It is expedient to bear in mind the division of 'paths of development of the revolution' into peaceful, that is, the unarmed path, and the armed path, civil war," wrote A. I. Sobolev, the influential editor of the journal of the Institute of the International Workers' Movement, *Rabochiy Klass i Sovremennyy Mir.*[6] "The concept of the 'path of the struggle' in the final analysis refers to the forms of the struggle, to tactics," he asserted, explaining that capitalist resistance makes some form of violence virtually inevitable.

> Revolutionary violence is the law of any revolution, since the deposed classes will not voluntarily and peacefully leave the historical arena. History knows of no social revolutions which have not been opposed in one form or another by counterrevolution. . . .
>
> The difference between the peaceful and the armed path to socialism is not the difference between evolution and revolution, but only between two forms of revolution. Peaceful and nonpeaceful forms of revolutionary struggle envisage the destruction of the state machine of the exploiting class, and the creation of a new system of state power.[7]

Peaceful coexistence and the increased strength of the Socialist community have improved the chances of success of the peaceful path. Parliament is to serve "not only as an arena of the class struggle but as a vehicle for the conquest of power by the proletariat."[8] As asserted in a Soviet book on the revolutionary movement published in 1976, however, "If the ruling classes resort to violence against the working class, the revolutionaries, no doubt, should likewise use nonpeaceful methods. This means that the Communist parties and the working class itself should always be prepared to employ any forms of struggle and mass action."[9]

The enunciation of the strategy of the peaceful path, which was confirmed at the International Conference of Communist and Workers' Parties in Moscow in 1969, contributed to the emergence of the PCF from its political isolation, its gradual assumption of the role of an aspirant governmental party, and its search for the means to broaden its base of popular support in the French electorate. Today all the major PCF documents explicitly endorse the primacy of the peaceful path. In his important monographic exposition of PCF strategy and objectives, Marchais unambiguously declared: " . . . we can so seriously envisage the possibility of a *peaceful* passage to socialism that our entire policy is henceforth founded on that perspective."[10]

The French road to socialism is to be a democratic road, down which progress is made by steadily expanding electoral support, with ultimate conquest of power by the ballot box. The actual strategy is divided into three stages: first, the political campaign to rally support for the Common Program of government subscribed to by the alliance of Communists, Socialists, and Left Radicals; second, following election of a government based on the Common Program, the enactment of its political, economic, and social provisions designed to accomplish the transfer of power from the bourgeoisie to the working class; and third, the eventual establishment of a Socialist state, based on the democratic expression of the majority popular will. The PCF does not aim merely for a few cosmetic or partial changes, such as it contends governing Socialist and Social Democratic parties have instituted elsewhere in Western Europe. The establishment of socialism is a "revolutionary goal," the PCF asserts, not in the sense of violence, but with respect to the total transformation of society, culminating in the transfer of power to the workers. "In this sense, the changeover to socialism, whatever form it takes, is a definite qualitative change, a revolutionary leap."[11] Thus, although the goal is revolutionary, the proclaimed means is democratic. As Marchais affirms, "In our view, there is today in France no other path leading to socialism than the democratic one which we have defined."[12]

One of the principal Soviet standard-bearers of the militant line of revolutionary strategy and tactics is the editor of the International Communist Journal *Problemy Mira i Sotsializma* (*World Marxist Review* in the English edition), Konstantin Zarodov. He rejects the notion that revolutionaries must abide by the will of the electorate. "Is the ballot box the best and most reliable instrument for determining the genuine will of the majority?" he asks.[13] The reply is negative, because the "political majority"—that is, the politicized workers and their allies—should prevail over the "arithmetic majority." In 1917 the conviction that they had the support of the revolutionary majority gave the Bolsheviks the green light to resort to armed uprising, Zarodov contends; and he castigates the "supporters of the 'wait and see' tactic" of that era—and perhaps inferentially supporters of the same caution today—as the "strike-breakers of the revolution."

Such views have provoked a storm of protest among certain Western European Communist parties, concerned about their negative impact on their own carefully nurtured relationships with their allies and studiously cultivated democratic image. The PCF vigorously denies that its espousal of the peaceful path is only a tactical accommodation to necessity, and insists that its commitment to democracy is sincere. Its newspaper, L'Humanité, published a blistering attack on the Zarodov thesis. The events of May-June 1968, wrote PCF Central Committee member and candidate member of the Politburo Jacques Chambaz, proved that advocacy of the concept of the revolutionary majority under contemporary French conditions would lead straight toward an active minority and destructive adventurism, rather than successful development of the revolution.[14] Marchais returned to this theme at the party's 22nd congress, reiterating the PCF's commitment to the achievement of socialism by the democratic expression of the majority popular will "through struggle and through universal suffrage." Whatever the path to socialism in France, he added (and it cannot be foreseen in detail), "at every stage the political majority and the arithmetical majority must coincide."[15]

The PCF is keenly aware of the dangers of a polarization of the French body politic into "enemy camps," which is why, it asserts, its goal is to rally a broad-based popular union. It calls "France's division into fairly equal halves" unacceptable "because to start the country on the road to democratic reform with the best chance of success requires a popular movement embracing a *large* majority of the people. Since we reject recourse to armed violence and repression, this is a requisite for victory."[16]

The Soviets have indicated by their selective reporting of PCF affairs their less than complete accord with the current PCF emphasis on ballot-box revolution. In a speech to the Japanese Communist Party, for example, Marchais specifically asserted that "struggle" does not mean "civil war" and "revolution" does not mean "violence"; Pravda's account of his speech several days later made no mention of these remarks. The CPSU newspaper's coverage of Marchais' speech to the 22nd PCF congress likewise completely ignored his emphasis on the democratic path, while reporting that he spoke of the necessity of class struggle to defeat reactionary attempts to resort to subversion and violence.[17]

Marchais' equation of "struggle" with "universal suffrage" in his party congress speech as dual means of democratic expression of the majority will is not mere happenstance. The peaceful path has two routes to its destination, and espousal of the electoral route in no way forecloses use of more pushful tactics. "The electoral process cannot be enough by itself to make the change effective if it is not preceded and backed up by permanent and extensive activity by the masses," the PCF leader has declared.[18] Mass mobilization is considered by both Soviet and French Communists to be a crucial complement to electoral activity, both to rally additional supporters to the party and to consolidate the gains achieved and prevent backsliding. Calling for "awakening such a majority movement of the people for socialism that the monopolies will be forced to surrender their entrenched positions without a chance to resort to civil war to thwart the people's will," the Champigny Manifesto, issued, as noted in Chapter 1, in December 1968, makes mass mobilization a crucial prerequisite of successful implementation of the peaceful path.[19] This idea is further developed in the PCF program prepared for and adopted by the 22nd party congress in February 1976:

> The Communists say it frankly to the workers: there is no means other than struggle for winning the immediate demands and imposing the thorough transformations which lead to socialism. The democratic path to socialism that we are proposing to the French people is a series of unyielding struggles —of mass struggle—to modify ever further the correlation of social and political forces for the benefit of the workers and all the people's classes. At every stage, these struggles will prepare the way for the democratic expression of the people's will through universal suffrage and will guarantee respect for that will.[20]

The Soviets have placed great emphasis on the incidence of strikes as a key indicator of the ripening of the revolutionary situation in individual capitalist countries. Strikes, they maintain, can be an especially important means of rallying large segments of the workers, encouraging militancy, and preventing the workers from being bought off by capitalist inducements, citing the political strike of October 1905 in Russia and the French general strike of May-June 1968 as effective examples of such consciousness-raising activities. CPSU General Secretary Leonid Brezhnev declared in his speech to the 25th party congress that "the strike wave . . . has risen to the highest level of the past several decades."[21]

The PCF has vigorously pushed the creation of additional Communist cells in enterprises and factories, in part to steal a march on the Socialists, who are challenging them there as elsewhere for primacy within the Left. It has also waged numerous strikes for both economic and political objectives. Joint action agreements have been concluded between the CGT and the Socialist-oriented *Confédération Française Démocratique du Travail* (CFDT), with a move to establishing a united labor front in opposition to the government.[22]

In March 1976 a 24-hour general strike by industrial workers and civil servants was called to dramatize dissatisfaction with the failure of wage increases to keep pace with France's inflationary spiral. In October 1976 the largest series of strikes and demonstrations since May-June 1968 took place in protest against the government's newly imposed austerity program, and in May 1977 moderate and anticommunist unions joined the Communist and Socialist unions for the first time in a decade in a 24-hour general strike. As Marchais has declared, "we will overlook nothing in order to put an end to the Giscard regime."[23]

ALLIANCE AND ELECTORAL STRATEGY

The PCF has progressively cast its alliance net in ever wider circles until today only a narrow group of "monopoly capitalists" is excluded from what the Communists expansively call the "union of the people of France" it seeks to rally under its banner. In his 22nd party congress speech, Secretary General Marchais defined this alliance in sweeping terms: "It is a union which is simultaneously *for* something and *against* something: It is an alliance of all the victims of the industrial and financial feudalities *against* the narrow caste which is dominating and suffocating the country and *for* a democratic change which will strike a serious blow against the caste by implementing profound democratic reforms."[24] Since, by the PCF's own calculation, workers constitute only about 44 percent of the French population, while the PCF share of the electorate normally hovers around 20 percent, the first step on the party's triptych path to power has been to build a broad, solid electoral alliance based on allegiance to a common governmental program. Unlike the Italian Communists, whose *compromesso storico* has meant an opening primarily to, and a willingness to share governmental power with, the Christian Democrats in a country where the Socialists are weak, the PCF has looked to the Socialists as their prime alliance targets, and has rejected entry into a bourgeois government.[25]

The first electoral cooperation between the Communist and noncommunist French Left occurred in the legislative elections of November 1962, in the form of mutual second-ballot withdrawals in favor of the best-placed candidates.[26] Electoral cooperation between French Communists and Socialists continued with PCF support of the presidential candidacy of Mitterand in 1965, and in the legislative elections of 1967. In February 1968 the Communists and Socialists issued a joint declaration which took note both of shared objectives and the persistence of areas of disagreement. A *premier bilan* (first summary) statement made public on December 22, 1970, outlined the considerable progress made toward formalizing a programmatic alliance with the avowed goal of establishing socialism in France. The PCF's first strategic priority was finally accomplished with the signing of the Common Program of government on June 27, 1972, by the PCF and the Parti socialists (PS), to which the small Radical-Socialist Left party subsequently adhered.[27] However, although the alliance did accomplish a near electoral upset in the 1974 presidential elections, and has continued to register gains, all has not proceeded according to the PCF plan, which was predicated on continuing Communist dominance within the Left alliance.

Since its 17th congress in 1964, the PCF had advocated the elaboration of a joint governmental program as a basis for united action by all leftwing parties. In its Champigny Manifesto of 1968, the party had called for the "union of all the forces of labor and democracy, regardless of their philosophical outlook, their religious beliefs, or their party affiliation, in the struggle to overthrow the monopoly government,"[28] and it had made numerous appeals urging the Socialists to undertake joint action. The International Conference of Communist and Workers' Parties held in Moscow in June 1969 had given the official imprimatur of the international Communist movement to the tactic of Communist parties joining in broad electoral alliances as a corollary of the strategy of the peaceful path to power. As the final document stated: "Communists, who attribute decisive importance to working-class unity, are in favor of cooperation with the Socialists and Social Democrats to establish an advanced democratic regime today and to build a Socialist society in the future."[29]

CPSU documents on strategy and tactics for coming to power also counseled the formation of broad alliances both in the current antimonopoly phase of the struggle and in the process of socialist transformation. As one of the principal treatises on the subject declared:

> In organizing and heading the masses' struggle against monopolies, the Communist parties create prerequisites for the formation of a political army of Socialist revolution and are laying the foundations for cooperation between the proletariat and its allies, not only in the overall democratic struggle, but also for the future—for society's Socialist transformation. It is becoming more and more obvious to such allies that their interests coincide with those of the proletariat. As a result, a temporary alliance may become permanent.[30]

Nonruling Communist parties were advised to make reciprocal concessions if necessary for the sake of reaching agreement with prospective allies on joint action programs, the conclusion of which the CPSU regarded as highly desirable.[31]

As seen in the previous chapter, however, the invasion of Czechoslovakia was a serious setback to the PCF's alliance aspirations. In the 1969 presidential election, following de Gaulle's unexpected resignation, the Socialists spurned the PCF's proposal to field a joint candidate, and the Left's vote was scattered among several candidates. On the first ballot, PCF veteran Jacques Duclos received 21.27 percent, far exceeding the total vote received by all other candidates of the Left; the Socialists' Gaston Deferre garnered only 5.01 percent. The PCF blamed the Socialists' lack of cooperation in naming a single leftist candidate for Duclos' failure to make the runoff.[32] On the second ballot the Gaullist Georges Pompidou was elected with 58.21 percent of the votes cast; however, the PCF was able to claim that 31.14 percent of the electorate had heeded its call for abstention.

The next opportunity for a test of PCF popular appeal came with the April 23, 1972, referendum called by President Pompidou on the issues of expansion of the European Economic Community (EEC) and French commitment to further European integration. Both the PCF and the PS opposed the referendum, which was inevitably depicted as a vote of confidence in the Pompidou regime. The PS, however, which basically favored European unity, advocated abstention, while the PCF called for an outright negative vote. The results encouraged both parties: although the referendum was approved, both the PCF and the PS could derive satisfaction from the high levels of "no" votes and abstentions. The mutual recriminations between the PCF and the PS did not cease, however, with Marchais ascribing to the Socialists' refusal to forge an alliance around the "no" vote the Left's inability to capitalize on the vulnerability of the Pompidou regime.[33]

Despite the persistence of such divisive issues as PS accusations of PCF acquiescence in the Czechoslovak "normalization"* and PCF recriminations about lingering rightist sentiments among the PS, leaders of the two parties did, as noted above, manage in June 1972 to affix their signatures to the historic Common Program of government. This document, the first such policy pact between Communists and Socialists since the days of the Popular Front in the 1930s, went considerably beyond a mere electoral alliance. It was, in effect, a statement of the kind of government the French people could expect if the Left alliance were voted into power.[34]

The first test of the voter appeal of the Left alliance following agreement on the Common Program came in the March 1973 elections to the National Assembly. The results launched a consistent trend: gains for the Left, but substantially greater gains for the Socialists than the Communists. For the PCF, elections pose the complex multiple challenge of convincing the general public of its reliability and commitment to play by the rules of the democratic

---

*"Normalization" is a standard term for the process of dismemberment of the Prague Spring reforms and restoration of Czechoslovak-Soviet relations to their prior status; it is always written in quotes.

game, convincing its allies of its loyalty to the program and goals of the alliance and curbing the Socialists' tendency to veer off to the right, on the one hand; and convincing its own militants that it has not sacrificed Communist principles on the electoral altar, on the other. Because of the peculiar French two-stage electoral system, and the electoral agreement between the PCF and its Socialist and Left Radical allies to withdraw in favor of the leading candidate in the second round, obtaining the highest vote on the first ballot was crucial. The PCF received 21.25 percent of the popular vote on the first ballot, virtually identical to its 1969 presidential election tally, and an increase over its 20.03 percent in the preceding legislative elections of June 1968. The Socialist-Left Radical ticket (which campaigned as the Union of the Socialist and Democratic Left—UGDS) garnered 20.36 percent, a healthy increase over the 16.53 percent the Socialist alliance had received in 1968, and an enormous improvement over Deferra's poor showing in 1969. Thus, while the PCF remained the "first party of the Left," its lead over the Socialist grouping was cut to less than 1 percent.

The PCF's electoral dilemma is compounded by the disparity between the two parties in control over their electorates. This characteristic was brought out by public opinion polls which showed that although more than 90 percent of the Communist first-round votes would go to the Socialists in the event of a Socialist-Gaullist runoff, only 50 percent of the Socialist electorate would back the Communist in a Communist-Gaullist contest.[35] The government capitalized on the public's distrust of the Communists, singling out the PCF for the brunt of its attacks on the opposition. The PCF responded by redoubling its efforts to clothe itself in the alliance mantle, campaigning under the slogan "the party of the outstretched hand, the party of alliance." Following the second ballot, the PCF had 73 deputies in the 490-member National Assembly, equal to the number elected in 1967, but an increase of 39 seats over its 1968 total, while the UGDS elected 100. However, while Communist voters generally followed the alliance directive to support the Socialists, Socialist voters, as the poll had predicted, failed to reciprocate.

In his extensive election postmortem, presented to the PCF Central Committee meeting of March 28–29, Marchais emphasized that the major achievement of the election was the fact that 11 million people had voted for the program of the united Left, despite the government's aggressive anti-Communist campaign.[36] Marchais complained, however, that the Socialists had exploited the government's anti-Communist campaign by pointed references to what had become in the French context anti-PCF themes, such as Czechoslovakia, "guarantees of freedom," and the necessity of restoring "balance" within the Left alliance; and that the Socialist-oriented labor confederation, the CFTD, had criticized the Common Program, urging its members to support it only at the last minute. Marchais also acknowledged that the party had encountered difficulties in getting its line accepted by its own militants, some of whom were unenthusiastic about the Common Program, and that it had had to "display particular insistence" in mobilizing grass-roots support for the alliance. Despite the acknowledged fact, however, that "the unification of left-wing parties was, for the first time, more advantageous to the Socialist party" than to the PCF, Marchais insisted that the PCF Politburo considered that both the party's general line and its implementation had been correct. He pledged continued PCF support for the Common Program, asserting that for the forthcoming period it was the best rallying point for all Frenchmen interested in thoroughgoing democratic change; but at the same time he urged renewed efforts by the PCF to mobilize mass support and increase party membership.

Soviet coverage of what were for the PCF events of capital importance is highly revelatory of two elements of CPSU policy which have direct bearing on PCF-CPSU relations. In the first place, the relative scantiness of Soviet media attention to the agreement on the Common Program, coupled with the simultaneous copious attention to Franco-Soviet relations, illustrates the delicate balancing act the Soviets constantly practice between relations with an important nonruling fraternal party, such as the PCF, and state-to-state relations with the country that was at the time the linchpin in the Soviets' detente strategy for Western Europe. This duality will be discussed in detail in Chapter 6. The other element concerns the Soviets' appraisal of the Common Program within the context of the CPSU position on alliances, which it is fitting to examine here.

The most striking aspect of the initial Soviet media coverage of the Common Program was the dearth of in-depth analysis of its content or its impact on the French political scene in the light of the forthcoming legislative elections. By restricting its coverage exclusively to factual reporting, the Soviets at first seemed to discount the likehood that the Common Program could indeed presage a proximate advent to power of a leftist government in France, while at the same time stressing the intrinsic importance of the unity move itself. Although an extensive extract of the PCF's own program had been published earlier in the year by the CPSU journal *Kommunist,*[37] the Soviets did not publish the Common Program. *Pravda* limited itself to publishing a terse TASS announcement on an inside page the day after the agreement, and a slightly longer TASS report following consideration of the Common Program by the PCF congress; *Izvestiya*'s coverage was similarly brief, while *Kommunist* published an abridged version of Marchais' report to the congress. The Soviet weekly *New Times* also published a generally descriptive article summarizing the principal provisions of the Common Program; significantly, however, the only section directly quoting the 150-page document concerned the signatory parties' commitment to continue the existing government's foreign policy based on peaceful coexistence.[38]

The Soviet attitude toward the Common Program and the Left alliance in France was clearly ambivalent. While taking satisfaction in the favorable development insofar as PCF-PS unity was concerned, the Soviets seemed to be particularly concerned with the question of how much the PCF had had to compromise its positions in order to reach agreement with the Socialists, and how much compromise would be required to maintain it. A TASS report on the resolutions adopted by the PCF Central Committee approving the signing of the Common Program placed special emphasis on the necessity for the PCF to maintain and strengthen its own influence, activity, and organization in order to accomplish a "swifter" transition to economic and political democracy and socialism.[39] In publishing another TASS report, *Izvestiya* omitted a section reporting the PCF's readiness to cooperate with "all Left, democratic forces of France. . . ."[40] The influence that the CPSU seemed to be telegraphing a warning to the PCF not to let infatuation with unity give rise to compromise of principles was substantiated by several pointed reminders on the subject in the speech delivered by CPSU Politburo member Suslov to the PCF 20th congress in December 1972. In an obvious warning against being outmaneuvered by a Socialist reversion to reformism, Suslov warned:

> . . . Communists never forget the final aims of their struggle—the liquidation of capitalism and the establishment of a new, just Socialist system. The ideas and policy of reformism and the theories of class cooperation with the exploiters have always been rejected and continue to be rejected by Communists. We learned with interest how your party combines the struggle for unity of actions with principled class positions and with the defense of the great teaching of Marxism-Leninsim.[41]

A *Pravda* report of Marchais' remarks to a mass meeting of supporters of the Common Program singled out for direct citation only his remark that "In this alliance . . . each retains and will continue to retain his convictions."[42]

As the campaign for the 1973 French parliamentary elections intensified, the Soviets began to present the elections as a test of the Common Program's appeal. The Soviet press portrayed the election results as a "major success" for the Left, and predicted that the Left's influence was "bound to grow."[43] The election results also produced the strongest Soviet endorsement of the Common Program to date. Terming it a "document of great strength, aimed far ahead and containing profoundly and comprehensively sound tenets," the Soviets went on record as stating the it "corresponds to the cherished aspirations of the working people of France."[44] Finally, Soviet analysts concluded that the elections demonstrated that the PCF was stronger than before, and that it continued to be the most influential party of the Left.

The Socialist-Communist alliance candidate in the 1974 presidential election following the death of President Pompidou was remarkably successful. On the first ballot, Socialist party chief Mitterand, whom the PCF had endorsed as the joint candidate of the Left, received the largest number of votes in the twelve-candidate field (43.35 percent versus 32.9 percent for the centrist Inde-

pendent Republican, Valéry Giscard d'Estaing, and 14.6 percent for the Gaullist, Jacques Chaban-Delmas). In the second round the PCF concentrated its
efforts on winning over the Gaullist vote, presenting itself as the genuine heir
of Gaullist dedication to French sovereignty and independent foreign policy,
and emphasizing the historical Communist-Gaullist cooperation in the Resistance.

The Soviets did not even try to disguise their preference for the candidate
they believed would best continue Gaullist policy toward the USSR—and that
candidate was Giscard d'Estaing. Moscow's flagrant disregard for the fortunes
of the PCF when these seemed in conflict with Soviet state interests was
dramatized by the well-publicized visit of the Soviet ambassador with Giscard,
discussed in Chapter 6, in the midst of a campaign in which the PCF was trying
to rally a broad alliance of French "patriots" against the allegedly pro-American Giscard.

Although Giscard was elected, the narrowness of the winning margin (1.4
percent) unquestionably established the Communist-Socialist alliance as na-
tionally viable, and left the two parties poised for the next elections. As
evidence of the CPSU's enhanced assessment of the standing of the Left
alliance following its strong showing, an article in *Kommunist* asserted that
"the 1973 parliamentary elections, followed by the 1974 presidential elections,
indicated that the strengthened and unified leftwing forces had become a
powerful factor of French political life which could no longer be ignored by
anyone."[45] In its offical greeting to the PCF on the occasion of its 21st party
congress in October 1974, the CPSU pointedly declared that the French Communist Party was the "leading and most authoritative force" within the alliance.[46] Mitterand's surprising showing, however, called attention to a shift
underway in the distribution of strength within the alliance. Legislative by-
elections in September 1974 confirmed this trend; both the Socialists and Left
Radicals scored gains in all six constituencies on the first ballot, while the PCF
suffered losses in all but two. Most disturbing for the PCF was the fact that
on the second ballot the sole PCF candidate still in the running failed to draw
the support of a significant segment of the allied parties' electorate and was
defeated. The same pattern was repeated in legislative by-elections in the
spring, summer, and fall of 1975 and the fall of 1976.

A public opinion poll published in February 1976 indicated that the
PCF's share of the electorate had declined from 21 percent in June 1974 to
20 percent, while the combined Socialist-Left Radical share had risen from 27
to 30 percent.[47] Cantonal elections of March 1976 reflected the trend in favor
of the Socialists. Again, the Left gained overall, compared with the comparable
elections of six years before, prior to the signing of the Common Program,
when the parties of the Left had been unable to reach agreement on an overall
electoral alliance. Within the Left, however, it was the Socialists who seemed
to be reaping the larger share of the benefits. The PS received 26.5 percent of

the total vote, the PCF 22.8 percent, and the Left Radicals 5 percent. A Soviet analyst, commenting on the election results, stated that they "gave a good idea of the public sentiment," testifying to the weakening of the government coalition's position, general popular dissatisfaction with the prevailing social and economic situation, and the "growing nationwide desire for far-reaching reforms."[48]

However, the elections also renewed the strains within the Left alliance. Marchais accused the Socialists of reneging in some cases on their commitment to support the Communist candidate against a Gaullist opponent. Public opinion polls conducted following the election indicated that if a national election were held at that time, the leftist opposition would win more than 50 percent of the votes; but within the alliance the distribution was probably about 30 percent for the Socialists and Left Radicals to 20 percent for the Communists.[49]

At their Dijon Congress in May 1976 the Socialists agreed to form joint lists with the PCF and Left Radicals from the first round in the municipal elections in March 1977. But the Socialist party's stipulations reflected its new sense of political muscle. Calling itself "the first party of France," the PS made it clear that it would refuse to accept PCF demands for representation that it considered excessive and disproportionate to the latter's actual strength. Marchais' reply was conciliatory, declaring that the PCF had "no excessive demands" and that minor matters could be easily settled.[50]

The agreement that was reached on June 28 prepared the way for what was a momentous leftist electoral victory. In the municipal elections of March 13 and 20, the Communist-Socialist-Left Radical alliance polled more than 51 percent of the national vote, giving the Left control of more than two-thirds of the 220 cities of over 30,000. Communists were reelected in 50 and elected in 22 additional of these largest cities, for a total of 72 and a gain of 22; Socialists were reelected in 41, elected in 40 additional, and defeated in 6, for a total of 81 successful candidates and a net gain of 35 (*Le Monde,* March 22, 1977). Of particular consequence for the future was the smooth functioning of the alliance. Socialist voters were as disciplined in supporting candidates of the opposite party as were the Communists. Although these results could not be considered a reliable prediction of the outcome in the ultimate contest—the 1978 parliamentary election—because of the Left's traditionally stronger showing in local elections, many observers of all political stripes considered them a harbinger of impending major changes in the French political scene. *Pravda* immediately hailed the Left alliance's "great success," and added the revealing observation that "it is noteworthy that the results achieved by the Left were positive both where the united lists were headed by Communists and also in cases where they were headed by Socialists."[51]

Under the French constitution, a leftist victory in the National Assembly in 1978 should result in the president naming a leftist—presumably Mitterand

—prime minister. Marchais has several times stated that he is "not a candi-date" for the prime minister's office.[52] But the PCF insists that if the Left wins a simple majority in the 1978 elections, the president must call on a leftist to form the government, and that the PCF would claim six or seven ministerial posts within it. Giscard, who has declared that the "chances of communism in France are nonexistent" (although admitting the possibility of a West German-type social-democratic orientation), has indicated that he might resign and call new presidential elections rather than name Mitterand prime minis-ter.[53] On other occasions, he has held out the possibility of enlarging the majority toward the Left, bringing the Socialists into the government. For the PCF, this is the most frightening nightmare—the possibility that the Socialists might join a government without the PCF, returning to their old pattern of "class collaboration," the Common Program and electoral alliance notwith-standing.

THE VANGUARD ROLE OF THE PARTY

Of the several serious issues that have threatened to split the PCF-PS coalition, perhaps none has been so divisive and intractable as that of the PCF's insistence, for both ideological and practical reasons, on maintaining its claim to and exercise of the "vanguard" role within the alliance. Moreover, as these pretensions to be the leader of and spokesman for the working class have increasingly abutted the tangible reality of the Socialist gains that were traced in the preceding section, the resurgent PS has responded with its own demands couched in terms of the need to restore "balance" within the alliance.

CPSU Insistence on Vanguard Role

The tug of war between the forces espousing the vanguard role of the Communist party and those insisting on balance has doctrinal as well as practical derivation. The period leading up to and including the signature of the Common Program coincided with the elaboration by the CPSU and the international Communist movement of several key documents on strategy and tactics for coming to power. These documents were directly relevant to the alliance tactics being pursued or contemplated by such European parties as the PCF and the Italian Communist Party (PCI), as well as by the Communist Party of Chile (PCCh).

The Kremlin's initial coolness to the signature of the Common Program and its warnings against excessive Communist concessions were described above. Moreover, it was surely no coincidence that the same issue of *Kommu-nist* that carried Marchais' report on the Common Program also contained an article setting forth the empirical justification for Communist party hegemony within the revolutionary movement.[54] For the CPSU there is no compromise on the role of the Communist party as the revolutionary vanguard. As *World Marxist Review* editor Zarodov wrote in his 1972 book, *Leninism and Contemporary Problems of the Transition from Capitalism to Socialism*, "Leadership by the Marxist-Leninist party is a mandatory condition of the victory of the socialist revolution and the building of Communist society. No sociopolitical, economic, or cultural changes can be effected without such a party, which knows and applies all the laws of the transition from capitalism to socialism."[55] The contemporaneous Soviet handbook of Communist party strategy and tactics edited by Zagladin, enjoined Communist parties that enter leftist alliances to work from within to convert their allies to the Communists' positions, while at the same time remaining vigilant against "unprincipled adaptation" to the allies' views.[56] The author cited approvingly the warning of the hard-line secretary general of the Portuguese Communist Party (PCP), Alvaro Cunhal, at the 1969 international conference, against "dissolution of Communist parties in the anti-imperialist front."[57]

The dual theme of positive assertion of the vanguard role of Communist parties and its negative counterpart of caveats against being submerged in the leftist alliance was well illustrated by a lengthy article in *Kommunist,* published in the immediate pre-Common Program period, which went far beyond its ostensible purpose of reviewing the Russian edition of the works of Chilean Communist leader Luis Corvalan. The reviewer reinforced Corvalan's stress on the leading role of the proletarian vanguard with the affirmation that "no reconciliation is allowed with alien views for the sake of unity."[58]

Soviet warnings to fraternal parties about the dangers of allowing themselves to be swallowed up in alliances multiplied after the September 1973 coup against Salvador Allende brought an end to the Chilean revolution. An article in *Kommunist*, for example, quoted from Marchais' book, *Le Défi démocratique,* to illustrate how the formation of a popular alliance contributes to the development of the revolutionary process. The *Kommunist* author warned, however, against sacrificing "working class hegemony" for the sake of the alliance, and against abandoning the party's "autonomy in directing the class struggle." No matter how broad the alliance may be, he declared, "the Communist party must not allow its role to be reduced to the status of an unequal partner."[59]

At a *World Marxist Review* symposium convened in April 1975 to commemorate the 40th anniversary of the seventh congress of the Comintern (which proposed the united front tactic), Zarodov rejected the demand that Communists relinquish the vanguard role of the party as a prior condition to entering united fronts; rather, tactical unity against "imperialism" should be combined with simultaneous struggle against the united front partners.[60] Zarodov's views received prominence by his publication in *Pravda* of an article in which he chastized Communist parties willing to "dissolve" themselves in alliances with social democrats, and stressed the continued validity of Communist party hegemony.[61] A subsequent Zagladin article also inveighed against compromise "to gain an extra ally or an extra thousand votes in elections. . . ."[62]

Publication of these articles placed the PCF and the PCI in an awkward position vis-a-vis their allies, who saw them as a signal of a Kremlin shift on the issue of alliances. After Zarodov's article appeared, PCF Secretary General Marchais felt compelled to call a press conference to reassure the Socialists about the PCF's loyalty to the alliance, and to assert that, at any rate, PCF policy was made in Paris and not in Moscow.[63] Chambaz published a point-by-point rebuttal of what he regarded as Zarodov's effort to impose Soviet prescriptions for the transition to socialism on France.[64] The PCI also refuted the applicability of the Soviet thesis to the Italian situation.[65] The publication of Zarodov's articles, coinciding with a high point of the Portuguese Communists' prospects for seizing power, may have reflected a Kremlin response to the ripening revolutionary situation and an endorsement of the PCP's revolutionary tactics. Moreover, with prospects for convening the long-planned conference of European Communist parties prior to the February 1976 CPSU congress rapidly fading, the Soviet leadership may have decided that there was less mileage to be gained by emphasizing a peaceful, gradualist approach attractive to the Western European parties which advocated this tactic then by propitiating domestic hard-liners who advocated a more militant stand.[66]

PCF Concept of the Vanguard

The PCF is careful not to predicate its claim to the vanguard role in the Left alliance on numerical superiority, and has conspicuously shifted its emphasis from earlier references to its strong electoral performance to more durable but less quantifiable qualities such as its being the sole possessor of a scientific revolutionary theory endowing it with superior lights to plot correctly the revolutionary course. At the 22nd party congress in February 1976, Marchais again attempted to assure the PCF's allies' concern that the vanguard concept implies their subordination to the Communists.

> The role of vanguard and driving force of the social movement played by the working class is not of an administrative nature. It implies no subordination. It cannot be decreed. It is merely being played now—and has proved correct—in the struggle against the big bourgeoisie and its reactionary policy and with a view to insuring the victory of the Common Program. In the near future it will become indispensable for the implementation of this program and beyond that stage, if the French people so decide, for building socialism.[67]

Marchais reiterated this position at the Conference of European Communist and Workers' Parties in Berlin in June 1976, saying, "We seek not to monopolize today's democratic movement and tomorrow's Socialist society but—and this is by no means the same thing—to play the role of vanguard of social and human progress."[68]

The PCF had interpreted the 1974 by-elections as an ominous bellwether of declining support in relation to its alliance partners. As the postelection PCF Politburo communiqué affirmed, "the fact that there has been a drop in the electoral influence of the Communist party . . . must be considered seriously by democrats."[69] The party upbraided its allies for having campaigned on themes blatantly detrimental to the Communists: ". . . the constantly repeated key phrase—the necessity for an alleged counterbalancing of the Left —takes on an increasingly pernicious character because it . . . implies the reduction of Communist influence. Moreover, the campaign aimed at giving credence to the idea that only a noncommunist candidate could defeat a government candidate can only compromise the essential regrouping of votes on the Left."[70]

The downward trend in PCF support had two immediate effects on the party itself. In the first place, it galvanized the PCF to move to the offensive, stepping up its polemic with the Socialists, and openly acknowledging its competition with its allies for influence among the electorate. The PCF immediately launched a recruitment drive, and set a goal of 600,000 party members and 10,000 cells in enterprises by the end of 1976 (the PCF claimed 500,000 members in July 1976 and 8,100 enterprise cells in January of that year[71]).

In the second place, the decline in PCF standing exacerbated dissension within the party itself and precipitated some jockeying for leadership. Alliance with the Socialists had never been popular with some PCF militants, who had found the *volte-face* on the Socialists hard to accept. Marchais had staked his personal prestige on the risky alliance course; it was because of his influence that the PCF Politburo had accepted the Common Program in June 1972, despite the compromises it had been obliged to make with its own program. And now, after several elections under alliance conditions, some local militants felt that alliance cooperation was yielding greater dividends to the Socialists.

An intense debate within the PCF Politburo preceded the 21st (extraordinary) congress in late October 1974, resulting in modifications in the conference draft resolution to rectify what was considered by a powerful faction within the leadership to be its excessive liberalism.[72] Capitalizing on grassroots dissatisfaction with the alliance strategy, it prevailed on the PCF federal congresses to adopt amendments changing the tone of the draft resolution, to stress the PCF's determination to remain the leader of the working class. In the opinion of PCF militants, there had never before been so genuine a discussion at all levels of the party organization. As one French political analyst observed, "In this case 'democratic centralism,' the alpha and omega of the party, operated from bottom to top—not a very frequent occurrence."[73]

One consequence of the internal PCF debate was the appointment, following the Central Committee meeting of November 14, 1974, of Roland Leroy, one of the leading critics of compromise for the sake of alliance, to the influential post of *L'Humanité* editor. Rumblings about an erosion of Marchais' leadership mounted following his heart attack in mid-January 1975, but he seemed to emerge with his leadership position secure. Reelected secretary general by the PCF Central Committee following the 22nd party congress, Marchais was specifically praised for having "decisively contributed to the development of a strategy in consonance with class realities and socialism's prospects in the France of our times."[74]

The PCF is clearly unwilling to be reduced to the status of an auxiliary party. As Neil McInnes rightly observed, "It would advantage the Communists nothing if in their effort to win power in the state they forgot their mission of half a century: to win power in the socialist movement."[75] Yet the cost of PCF persistence in its vanguard pretensions, despite the voters' expressed preference for the Socialists, could well be the elimination of any role for itself in shaping the future "socialism for France" for which it has so long labored. The reversal in party strength has also been reflected in a reversal in slogans. Now it is the PCF that is urging the restoration of "balance" within the Left, to guarantee that the Common Program will be implemented and that the PS will not succumb to the blandishments of class collaboration. One PCF spokesman said that 25 percent of the vote would constitute sufficient PCF influence,[76] but otherwise the party has been vague about how much is "enough." In June 1976 Marchais declared that the PCF was gaining 400 new members daily and in March 1977 the party indicated that it had reached its 600,000 goal.[77]

Clearly, the PCF's aspiration to play the vanguard role cannot be entirely divorced from its electoral standing. There is some irreducible minimum below which it cannot fall if its claim on the leadership position is to have any credibility. In the view of Ronald Tiersky, "the vanguard role is the essential 'face' or facet in the total visage of French communism, because it is that element which is directly concerned with the attainment of power, the continuing *raison d'être* of the movement."[78] But as the Socialists made clear in the joint list negotiations for the 1977 municipal elections, and as the electorate confirmed, the new correlation of forces within the alliance going into the 1978 parliamentary elections is in favor of the Socialists.

Soviet Attitude Toward the French Socialists

Moscow's attitude toward the French Socialists is ambivalent. On the one hand, it regards the PS as the most leftwing and least social-democratic of all Western European social democracy, while on the other hand it is wary of the strong reformist current within one of the party's factions.[79] The Soviets have sharply criticized PS alliance behavior, but they profess to regard the rejuvenation of the party as a positive development, despite the growing threat it poses to PCF leadership of the Left alliance. They describe the dominant Mitterand wing of the PS, however, as motivated to cooperate with the PCF by electoral necessity, not ideological conviction, and hence as permanently susceptibe to dispensing with the alliance when it is no longer expedient to maintain it. The more leftist and "dynamic" wing of the Socialist party, the group around the *Centre d'Etudes, de Recherches, et d'Education socialistes* (CERES), is, in the Soviet view, genuinely interested in cooperation with the PCF.

The CPSU has kept its options open by establishing a direct relationship with the PS. In April 1975 Mitterand was received by CPSU officials in Moscow, the first meeting between the two parties since Mollet's visit in 1963. The joint communiqué published following the visit asserted that "despite some divergence of opinions, the positions of the CPSU and the French Socialist Party coincide or have moved closer together" on the assessment of many international issues.[80] Upon his return to Paris, Mitterand attributed his "very cordial" reception by CPSU General Secretary Brezhnev to the fact that "the Soviets must believe that the PS is capable of governing France one day."[81] In December 1976, Supreme Soviet member Nikolay Inozemtsev visited Socialist party headquarters, and expressed "profound satisfaction" with the exchange of views between the two parties.[82]

IMPORTANCE OF CONSOLIDATING GAINS: LESSONS OF CHILE AND PORTUGAL

The revolutions in Chile and Portugal, although occurring under very different circumstances, each had a major impact on the elaboration of Communist strategy and tactics for coming to power, particularly on the assessment of the viability of two key elements: the peaceful path and the policy of alliances. It is therefore appropriate to examine the profound analysis of these events conducted by the Communist parties in both Paris and Moscow, and the lessons that were drawn.

The problem of how to consolidate the gains of the revolution, particularly following a peaceful conquest of power, was recognized and discussed in CPSU documents on revolutionary strategy and tactics. As Zarodov asserted, even though it may be possible to achieve power peacefully, "it will be much harder to retain this power peacefully."[83] The example of the 1956 Hungarian counterrevolution is cited in Soviet literature as indicative of what could happen when a peaceful conquest of power permits the survival of bourgeois elements opposed to the revolution.[84] Only a mobilized mass movement of the working class and its allies, led by the Communist party, the Soviets maintained, can ensure a preponderance of prorevolutionary forces capable of undermining the opposition's control over the army and police and thwarting an attempted counterrevolution. The CPSU therefore insisted on the necessity of coercion and sanctions to overcome the resistance of hostile vestiges of the old order. As an article in the party daily, *Pravda,* asserted, "the Socialist state cannot but adopt coercive measures and certain sanctions with regard to the remnants of the smashed exploiter classes when they resist the measures of the new power, and all the more so when they engage in hostile activities."[85]

From the Soviet perspective, Chile represented a hybrid form of revolution for which there was no ready-made formula. In the first place, the Chilean revolution had been accomplished by the ballot box, a unique case of the electoral path culminating in success. Second, the Communist party was only one of several equal partners in the *Unidad popular* (UP) coalition government. Because the CPSU rejected the possibility of geniune political pluralism in a socialist state, in the absence of Communist party hegemony the Soviets consigned Allende's Chile to the presocialist "national democratic revolution" stage.[86] For the transition from a national democratic revolution to a people's democratic revolution, the exercise of the vanguard role by the Communist party was *de rigueur.*[87]

Early Soviet judgments were tolerant of what was obviously regarded as an interesting and innovative experiment. Soviet commentators praised the UP government and Communist-Socialist alliance for opening up the possibilities for a peaceful transition to socialism, and lauded the action of the UP government in setting up local front organizations to rally grass-roots support (and as a counterweight to hostile elective bodies). During this period of apparent success of the Chilean experiment and of CPSU benevolence toward it, the Soviet party journal *Kommunist* devoted several articles to analyses of the Chilean experience, including one which presented in a favorable light the UP practice of "pluralism," which guaranteed freedom of expression to opposition views both within and outside the coalition.[88] The author made the telling observation, highly pertinent to the PCF, that, despite the basic agreement among the UP coalition partners on a governmental program, disagreements had arisen over its implementation. The inconsistency between this tolerance of opposition views and the author's assertion that the "working class already plays the hegemonistic role" within the UP coalition was apparently overlooked; only in retrospect would the CPSU seize on this PCCh failure to exercise hegemonistic control and the excessive tolerance toward the opposition as responsible for the defeat of the revolution.[89]

There is every indication that the CPSU believed the UP had only a relatively brief time in which to consolidate the gains of the revolution by peaceful means or risk its overthrow by the activist Right or Left opposition. The readers of *Kommunist* were informed that the Chilean revolution was being carried out within the framework of the existing constitution "at the current stage," and that adhering to the constitutional path alone was justified only if the UP, which then held only executive power, was able to gain the ascendancy in the legislature and judiciary as well.[90] However, they were also apprised of PCCh Secretary General Corvalan's assessment that, given the increasing counterrevolutionary activity of the "reactionary forces" in Chile, "the people may be forced to adopt one or another form of armed conflict."[91] The March 4, 1973, Chilean parliamentary elections, which happened to coincide with the first round in the French presidential election, were protrayed as part of an "acute class struggle" being waged between the pro- and antirevolutionary forces. Lenin's dictum that "the revolution is worth anything . . . only if it is able to defend itself" was cited in support of the UP's efforts to create a "total and absolute superiority of forces in favor of the revolution. . . ."[92]

The Soviets' postelection analysis of the Chilean results, in which the UP received 43.5 percent of the votes (up from Allende's mere 36 percent winning presidential tally), revealed the underlying uncertainty in their prognosis for Chile. While the deputy editor of *Pravda* seemed satisfied that the UP had successfully consolidated the gains of the revolution by means of mass mobilization and had definitively deprived the bourgeois opposition of its base of operations, the deputy director of the prestigeous Institute of World Economics and International Relations of the USSR Academy of Sciences disagreed.[93] "The reactionaries will now seek new methods of struggle against the Allende government," the latter prophetically predicted.

The Chilean experiment was also watched with a great deal of interest in France. Duclos visited Chile in December 1971 at the invitation of the PCCh, and returned praising the UP's unity on the basis of the common governmental program.[94] As PCF Central Committee member René Andrieu wrote: "Chile, of course, is not France; but what happens there is of concern to progressives throughout the world and perhaps to those in our country in particular. This is because the experience of the Popular Unity movement provides a number of lessons that could logically be of use to the French Left."[95] According to Andrieu, one of the principal obstacles the UP faced, in common with the French Left, was opposition control of the media. Moreover, the Chilean Right, supported by foreign capital and abetted by leftist excesses, was attempting to induce the UP government to step outside constitutional legality in order to justify a military coup. He believed, however, that the cohesion of the governmental alliance, plus the mobilization of the masses were successfully countering the opposition. Nevertheless, drawing a lesson for France, Andrieu asserted that, while the peaceful path is preferable, more forceful forms of struggle might be necessary: "Chile's example . . . confirms that the ballot by itself is not enough, and that it must be backed up by a mass political movement. . . ."

Perhaps because the Chilean experience never fit the orthodox mold, the overthrow of Allende initially gave rise to some diversity of interpretation among the CPSU's middle-echelon analysts concerning what lessons it conveyed for the nature and pace of future revolutions. The fundamental cleavage was between those who advocated a more aggressive revolutionary strategy and those who counseled restraint.[96] Not surprisingly, the harshest Soviet criticism was directed at the very innovations of the Chilean revolution that the Soviets had earlier observed with such interest, and is thus highly revelatory of Moscow's emerging prescriptions for revolution in Western European countries as well. Authoritative Soviet critics accused the Chilean leaders of having been excessively preoccupied with the individuality of the Chilean conditions at the expense of neglecting the accumulated international (Soviet, Eastern European, and Cuban) revolutionary experience.

More specifically, the UP leaders were censured, first, for not having respected the "law-governed necessity of the speediest demolition, rebuilding and transformation of the state apparatus in the process of the development of a revolution in any form."[97] Their misplaced trust that all classes of Chilean society would respect constitutional legality had led them to postpone the restructuring the state system that the consolidation of the revolution required. This excessive respect for constitutional legality was a fatal mistake.

> ... on the whole, the choice of the peaceful, constitutional way does not by itself serve as evidence of any worship of formal, legal norms. Everything depends on whether the situation and the constitution of a concrete country allow revolutionary transformations to be carried out and on what the leaders take as their paramount concern: formal observance of existing legal norms or their utilization in the interests of social change, the desire to maintain them inviolate or the aspiration to change them through the use of legal means.[98]

Second, again because the UP "absolutized the importance of bourgeois constitutional guarantees," and refused to go outside constitutional legality, the popular unity committees set up for the purpose of mass mobilization had not been allowed to play an active role. Third, the UP's belief in the apolitical, above-class nature of the Chilean armed forces caused it to neglect the necessary task of penetrating the armed forces and molding a prorevolutionary military force. As one Soviet analyst wrote, the lesson of Chile is that "there are no armed forces standing apart from politics and there can be none."[99] Finally, the insistence on equality of the six parties comprising the UP coalition deprived the revolution of the leadership and political consistency that the exercise of the vanguard role by the Communist party would have assured.[100]

Thus, the overriding Soviet theme was that every revolution, no matter how carried out, must know how to defend itself, with force if necessary. As

CPSU Central Committee Secretary Boris Ponomarev asserted at a high-level party conference, "the revolutionary class must always be prepared to defend its achievements from the attacks of counterrevolution, to change its form of struggle rapidly, and to reply with revolutionary actions to the reactionary violence of the Bourgeoisie."[101] The positive side of the Chilean experience, Ponomarev maintained, was the demonstration of the viability of the alliance strategy, including the feasibility of winning over a considerable portion of the peasantry and middle strata. On the negative side, he cited the UP's failure to consolidate the gains of the revolution by transforming the army and mass media into revolutionary agents. He contrasted the successful application by the Bolsheviks in 1917 of the lessons derived from the experience of the 1905 Russian revolution—a failed armed rebellion—with the unsuccessful Chilean attempt at "the first protracted experience of the 'peaceful' development of revolution."[102] The unmistakable conclusion, emphasized by a January Central Committee resolution on celebrating the 70th anniversary of the 1905 revolution, is that in order to succeed Communist parties must emulate Soviet revolutionary experience.

Another facet of the Soviet dissection of the Chilean experience concerned the lesson that a sharp move to the Left could precipitate a counterrevolution and a resurgence of fascism—not only in Chile, but in Western Europe as well. In fact, shifts in the Soviet position on the likelihood that the crisis of capitalism would eventuate not in triumph of the revolution but in a revival of fascism can be seen as a barometer of Soviet confidence in the permanency of the shift in the correlation of forces in favor of socialism. Thus, it is interesting to note that Soviet apprehensions about a resurgence of fascism, which were repeatedly expressed in the year following Allende's overthrow, were replaced in 1975 by confidence that heightened mass awareness made a "reactionary" denouement to the crisis of capitalism far less likely.[103]

Thus, while the defeat of the Chilean revolution did not cause the CPSU to abandon its endorsement of the peaceful path and the policy of alliances, it sparked a renewed emphasis on the overriding importance of mass action, speedy consolidation of the revolutionary forces' hold on the levers of political, economic, and military power, and willingness to resort to extraconstitutional means when the preservation of legality threatens the revolution itself. In his speech to the 25th party congress in February 1976 CPSU General Secretary Brezhnev summarized all of these threads of the Soviet analysis of the lessons of Chile.

> The Chilean tragedy has by no means invalidated the Communist thesis about the possibility of different ways of revolution, including the peaceful, if the necessary conditions exist for it. But it has been a forceful reminder that *the revolution must know how to defend itself.* It is a lesson in vigilance

against present-day fascism and the intrigues of foreign reaction, and a call for greater international solidarity with all those who take the road of freedom and progress.[104]

Like the CPSU, the PCF drew the conclusion from the Chilean experience of the necessity for renewed emphasis on struggle and mass action to supplement and, when necessary, supersede electoral activity. As an important PCF document setting forth the blueprint of "What the Communists Want for France" candidly declared:

> ... workers and the masses cannot be content to exercise their right to vote once every five or seven years. They must ... rally their forces at every stage and put forth a great deal of effort to put a stop to reactionary maneuvers, not only in the field of political struggle ... but also in the economic area, in order to paralyze or defeat possible attempts by the reaction to make use of illegality, subversion, and violence.[105]

According to Marchais, the lesson of Chile showed that "the exploitive capitalists will never willingly give up their domination and their privileges," but will use any means to keep or regain them. Under these circumstances the question arises, "How can we first win over the majority and then enforce a verdict for democracy and socialism?" The answer is "to respect and make others respect the people's verdict," by means of the electoral process combined with mass action: "Our wish is to ensure a peaceful changeover. But it must be said that we cannot rule out the case of reactionary forces resorting to subversion and violence against the majority of the people. The people should secure the means for themselves to prevent such attempts in time."[106]

The reassessment of Communist revolutionary prescriptions in the wake of the Chilean debacle was in full swing when the events unleashed by the overthrow of the Portuguese dictatorship by the Armed Forces Movement on April 25, 1974, presented another case study as grist for the analytical mill. The kaleidoscopic nature of the Portuguese situation throughout much of the period under review, as well as important Soviet foreign policy considerations connected with the Helsinki Conference on Security and Cooperation in Europe, contributed to the appearance of Soviet "groping for an integrated position"[107] on key issues of strategy and tactics. On the other hand, the situation in Western Europe demanded refinement of a coherent set of Communist guidelines. The near-upset victory of the PCF-PS presidential candidate in May 1974; the Italian Communists' successful opposition to a Christian Democratic proposal to abrogate the divorce law the same month; the collapse of the Greek military dictatorship; the increasingly unstable situation in Spain; and the deepening economic crisis throughout the capitalist world, all contributed to a picture of Western European Communist parties poised on the threshold of a new era. Thus, the analysis of the "lessons of Chile" and the attempt to keep pace with the onrushing events in Portugal and elsewhere became intertwined.[108]

The PCP had traditionally been a loyal ally of the CPSU, and in 1968 was the one Western European Communist party that had wholeheartedly applauded the Soviet-led invasion of Czechoslovakia. In 1974, on the occasion of the awarding of the Order of the October Revolution to PCP Secretary General Cunhal, CPSU Politburo member and Central Committee Secretary Suslov asserted that "unity of views exists between the CPSU and the PCP on all the fundamental questions of modern times"—an expression exceeding the customary description of cordiality between like-minded fraternal parties.

The alliance between the PCP and the Armed Forces Movement added a new element to the revolutionary outlook. The demonstration of solidarity with the Left by a significant segment of the Portuguese officer corps and forces was viewed as a particularly promising development in the wake of the rightist military putsch in Chile, leading at least one Soviet commentator to wonder if this leftward movement of the armed forces in Portugal would set a precedent for other Western European nations.[109]

Reasons of state interest generally dictated a low-profile Soviet posture toward the unfolding Portuguese revolutionary situation; an abrupt shift in the Soviet attitude, however, occurred around the time of the elections to the Portuguese Constituent Assembly in April 1975. It will be recalled that at precisely that time the influential *World Marxist Review* editor, Zarodov, published an article in which he rejected the notion of the supremacy of the will of the "arithmetical majority" expressed at the ballot box over the will of the "political majority" of mobilized workers and their allies.[110] Coming on the eve of elections in which the PCP was expected to—and did—suffer defeat, Zarodov's article seemed to suggest that Communists should not allow election results to vitiate their chances for success.[111]

The PCF had publicly supported its Portuguese comrades, despite the considerable strain on its domestic alliance that solidarity with a party closely identified with the strategy of Communist party hegemony produced. The week preceding the Portuguese elections Marchais had appeared to go out of his way to endorse the PCP's position, telling a PCF Central Committee meeting, ". . . insofar as we cannot rule out the possibility of reactionary forces resorting to subversion and violence against the majority of the people, it is the duty of the people to provide themselves in good time with the means to prevent such attempts and, if necessary, to deal a rebuff to them in order to frustrate them. This is what has happened in Portugal, and we understand it."[112] Aspects of the Portuguese situation, however, touched what were already raw nerves in the PCF-PS relationship. The PS was particularly affronted by Cunhal's bald assertion that "We Communists don't accept the rules of the election game!"[113]

The seizure of the Portuguese Socialist newspaper *República* on May 19, 1975, sparked an acrimonious debate between the PCF and its Socialist allies over freedom of the press in Portugal and in a future Socialist France.[114] The issue was further inflamed by the publication in the French newspaper *Le Quotidien de Paris* of a special edition of the suspended *República* containing what were purported to be Soviet instructions to the Western European Communist parties on how to go about seizing power.[115] The subsequent discovery that the "document" was a distillation of a previously published June 1974 Ponomarev article from the international Communist journal *Problemy Mira i Sotsializma* produced a most interesting revelation on the part of the PCF. Marchais called a press conference in which he asserted that the article merely represented the author's "personal reflections," which the PCF had chosen not to publish in the French-language edition of the journal *La Nouvelle Revue Internationale* for the simple reason that it seemed more likely to becloud than to illuminate the solution of current problems in France.[116]

The PCF continued to publicly support and defend the actions of its Portuguese counterparts even during the apex of the first threatened PCP power seizure in August. It denied that the PCP was attempting to bypass the electoral process by mobilizing pro-PCP grass-roots front organizations in order to implement "direct democracy." But at the same time the PCF took pains to qualify this solidarity. Virtually overlooked at the time of the *República* affair was the assertion by PCF Central Committee member Andrieu that "we do not feel responsible for all the decisions our Portuguese comrades could take completely freely."[117] No longer was it a question of "unconditional" solidarity or "alignment" with the PCP; rather, as Marchais made clear following the return of a PCF delegation from Lisbon, it was a matter of PCF support for the struggle to defeat reaction and fascism and ensure the survival of democracy in Portugal. The PCF disassociated itself from PCP tactics, reiterated its own commitment to abide by universal suffrage and its loyalty to the Common Program, and rejected the "Portuguese model" for France.[118]

The events in Portugal inevitably jeopardized the fragile PCF-PS alliance. Socialist fears about threatened loss of democratic freedoms in Portugal, on the one hand, and PCF accusations of PS foot dragging on formation of a common front to support the "antifascist struggle" in Portugal, on the other, naturally raised questions about the two leftist parties' ability to cooperate in a future French government which would inevitably have to confront similar problems. Moreover, the PCF's support of the PCP's aggressive strategy, and the CPSU's own apparent willingness to back such a strategy under favorable circumstances, highlighted the very aspects of Communist strategy and tactics that generate concern among noncommunist allies.

The playing out of the Portuguese drama produced "lessons" that reinforced those drawn from the Chilean experience. With Chile firmly in the grip of a rightist military junta, and the Communists effectively barred from the exercise of power in the Socialist-controlled government in Portugal following an anticommunist backlash in the wake of an abortive coup attempt by leftist military units linked with the PCP on November 25, the PCF reasserted its basic position: that only a correlation of forces favorable to the revolution, that is, overwhelming mass support, can thwart the "reactionaries' " resort to violence. The PCP's abortive August power play and the November misadventure, as well as the radical excesses of the Chilean ultra-Left, were undoubtedly on his mind when Marchais warned of the danger not only of failing to effect the necessary economic and political transformations in time, but also of hasty "adventuristic actions" designed to shortcut the revolutionary process, which end in "isolation and defeat." Thus, for the PCF, the critical lesson of these two experiences is the correctness of its own chosen path. As Marchais declared, "The decisive condition of success is the existence and assertion of a popular movement which is large enough to include a broad majority of the people firmly united around transforming objectives."[119]

The necessity for the thorough maturation of the "subjective factor" was also the CPSU theme after the late summer flurry of revolutionary activity in Portugal. Zagladin, Ponomarev's first deputy in the Central Committeee International Department section dealing with nonruling Communist parties, warned of the danger of sharp fluctuations in mass sentiment and of the risks inherent in a premature power bid.[120] He subsequently wrote in a lavishly enthusiastic report of the PCP's 8th congress that the Communists must deal with the problem of the inevitable *narrowing* base of support for the revolution as ever more radical measures are adopted. "It is futile to think that it is possible to avoid these processes with the aid of some kind of parliamentary or other type of framework or that arguments can persuade the opponents of progress to become its allies," he warned. Parliament alone can therefore not complete the revolutionary process, and must be regarded as only an adjunct of mass mobilization and armed forces support: "Revolutionary experience has confirmed the Portuguese Communists in their conviction that the revolution's gains must be defended in a revolutionary way—that is, by relying on the masses' activity and initiative and supplementing these actions with the tireless work in parliament and the other power organs."[121]

Furthermore, the Soviets may once again be reevaluating the necessity for a simultaneous peaking of all revolutionary preconditions. The author of an article in the first 1977 issue of the journal of the International Workers' Movement, for example, stated that the experience of all revolutions, including the Chilean and Portuguese, demonstrates that when nonsynchronization of the political parties' and masses' readiness for revolution occurs, such a discrepancy should not retard the revolution. "If the mass movement outstrips the development of the political parties" [France 1968?], he wrote, "it is important not to let slip the opportunities of this movement." On the other hand, "if the mass movement lags behind the development of the Left parties" [present-day France?] the latter should not be "held captive" either.[122]

NOTES

1. N. Inozemtsev, *Contemporary Capitalism: New Developments and Contradictions* (Moscow: Progress Publishers, 1974), p. 161.

2. "For Peace, Security, Cooperation, and Social Progress in Europe," final document adopted at the Conference of European Communist and Workers' Parties, Berlin, June 29–30, 1976, *New Times,* July 1976, no. 28.

3. Georges Marchais, *Le Défi démocratique* (Paris: Grasset, 1973), p. 30

4. *L'Humanité,* July 1, 1976.

5. *Kommunisticheskaya Partiya Sovetskogo Soyuza, S'ezd XX, Stenograficheskiy Otchet* (Moscow: Gosudarstvennoe Izdatal'stvo, Politicheskoy Literatury Moskva, 1956). In January 1977 the PCF Politburo published a communiqué which indicated that the traumatic impact of the secret portion of Khrushchev's report to the 20th CPSU congress in February 1956 and the PCF's hesitant de-Stalinization still haunt the party. According to the communiqué (*L'Humanité,* January 13, 1977), the PCF delegation, headed by Maurice Thorez, had a few hours' advance access to the Russian text of the speech, which it was told to keep in strictest confidence. The PCF claims that in June, following publication of the speech in the non-Communist French press, it reproached the CPSU for the way in which the matter had been handled and asked the CPSU Central Committee for a copy of the text. This request was never complied with. Only on July 6, 1956 did the PCF finally publish a resolution analyzing "the conditions under which some acts greatly harmful to socialism had occurred" (PCF Politburo Communique, January 12, 1977, "On a Point Relevant to PCF History Concerning the 20th CPSU Congress," *L'Humanité,* January 13, 1977).

6. A. I. Sobolev, "The Dialectic of the General and the Particular in the Development of the World Revolutionary Process," *Voprosv Istorii KPSS,* November 1975, no. 11.

7. Ibid.; cf. the assertion made in a textbook for party workers that "in all circumstances, even the relatively peaceful development of the socialist revolution takes place in conditions of an uncompromising class struggle. Sharp clashes with the class enemy, critical situations, and unexpected turns are inevitable along the peaceful road of development" of the revolution. V. V. Zagladin, ed., *The World Communist Movement* (Moscow: Progress Publishers, 1973), p. 142. This is the Soviet translation of Zagladin, ed., *Mezhdunarodnoye Kommunisticheskoye Dvizheniye: Ocherk Strategii i Taktiki (Moscow: Politizdat, 1972).*

8. Konstantin Zarodov, *Leninism and Contemporary Problems of the Transition from Capitalism to Socialism* (Moscow: Progress Publishers, 1972), pp. 177–79. The thesis of the peaceful path is advanced for tactical reasons, Soviet authorities admit, because it creates "better possibilities for cooperation with the Socialists, who recognize only the peaceful forms of struggle . . . ." Zagladin, *World Communist Movement,* p. 211.

9. V. V. Zagladin, A. A. Galkin, and T. T. Timofeyev, eds., *The Working Class—The Leading Force of the World Revolutionary Process* (Moscow: Progress Publishers, 1976), pp. 120–21.

10. Marchais, *Le Défi démocratique,* p. 181.

11. Georges Marchais, "Socialism for France, a French Path to Socialism," *France Nouvelle,* January 20–26, 1975.

12. *L'Humanité,* February 5, 1976.

13. Konstantin Zarodov, "Leninism on Consolidating the Victory of the Revolution," *World Marxist Review* 18, no. 4 (April 1975).

14. Jacques Chambaz, "Words and Facts," *L'Humanité,* September 4, 1975; Chambaz was promoted to full member of the PCF Politburo in 1976.

15. *L'Humanité,* February 5, 1976.

16. Jean Kanapa, "A 'New Policy' of the French Communists?" *Foreign Affairs,* January 1977, p. 287.

17. *L'Humanité*, April 9, 1976; *Pravda*, April 14, 1976; and *Pravda*, February 6, 1976.

18. Marchais, "Socialism for France."

19. "For an Advanced Democracy, for a Socialist France," *L'Humanité*, December 7, 1968.

20. "What the Communists Want for France," *L'Humanité*, November 12, 1975.

21. *Pravda*, February 25, 1976; cf. T. T. Timofeyev, "On Some Worker Movement Trends in the Contemporary Stage of Capitalism's General Crisis," *Rebochiy Klass i Sovremennyy Mir*, 1975, no. 5 (September-October), which depicts in tabular form the "unprecedented expansion" of the strike movement in capitalist countries; Yu. Vasil'chuk, "Main Production and Revolutionary Force," *Kommunist*, 1976, no. 10, which describes "new trends" in the strike movement; and Zagladin, Galkin, and Timofeyev, op. cit., pp. 95–114, which describes the strike movement as an "important form of class struggle."

22. For a discussion of the PCF-CGT relationship, see George Ross, "Party and Mass Organization: The Changing Relationship of PCF and CGT," in *Communism in Italy and France*, ed. Donald L. M. Blackmer and Sidney Tarrow (Princeton, N.J.: Princeton University Press, 1975), pp. 504–40.

23. *L'Humanité*, April 17, 1975. The so-called Barre Plan called for a price freeze, limitation of 6.5 percent on wage increases, and higher taxes on middle-level wages. In a related development, a report released by the Paris-based Organization for Economic Cooperation and Development (OECD), which pinpointed France as the Western nation with the greatest gap between rich and poor, became an additional source of contention between the unions and the government; New York *Times*, September 10 and 13, 1976.

24. *L'Humanité*, February 5, 1976.

25. The alliance aims of the PCF and PCI were sufficiently congruent, however, to permit the two parties to jointly declare at a meeting in Rome in May 1973 their willingness to work "with all proletarian and democratic forces" including those "representative of the popular masses of Catholicism"; *Le Monde*, May 12 and 13–14, 1973; see also Chapter 5.

26. For the history of cooperation between the Communist and noncommunist French Left, see Ronald Tiersky, *French Communism, 1920–1972* (New York: Columbia University Press, 1974), passim, and his "Alliance Politics and Revolutionary Pretensions," in Blackmer, and Tarrow, op. cit., pp. 420–55. For a discussion of the evolution of the noncommunist Left that made the alliance possible, see Nancy I. Lieber, "Politics of the French Left: A Review Essay," *American Political Science Review* 69 (December 1975).

27. *Programme commun de gouvernement du Parti communiste et du Parti socialiste* (Paris: Éditions sociales, 1972).

28. *L'Humanité*, December 7, 1968.

29. "Tasks at the Present Stage of the Struggle against Imperialism and for United Action of Communist and Workers' Parties and All Anti-Imperialist Forces," Final Document of the International Meeting of Communist and Workers' Parties, Moscow, June 17, 1969 in Richard F. Staar, ed., *Yearbook on International Communist Affairs: 1970* (Stanford, Calif.: Hoover Institution Press, 1971), p. 809.

30. Zagladin, *World Communist Movement*, p. 169.

31. Ibid., p. 151.

32. *L'Humanité*, June 11, 1969. The charge was echoed by Soviet correspondent Vladimir Volzhskiy, "France: The First Round," *Literaturnaya Gazeta*, June 4, 1969.

33. *L'Humanité*, April 24, 1972.

34. The following chapter, which discusses the Left's vision of the transitional state, will examine the provisions of the Common Program in detail.

35. Richard F. Staar, ed., *Yearbook on International Communist Affairs: 1974* (Stanford, Calif.: Hoover Institution Press, 1975), p. 137.

36. *L'Humanité*, March 30, 1973; also published (abridged) in *Kommunist*, May 1973, no. 7.

37. "A Program for a Democratic Government of Popular Unity—Fundamental Tenets," *Kommunist,* 1972, no. 2; the same issue carried an article by PCF Politburo member Kanapa, "The Government Program of the French Communist Party."

38. "Agreement Reached," *Pravda,* June 28, 1972; "The Common Program is Discussed," *Pravda,* July 10, 1972; "Program of Unity," *Izvestiya,* July 11, 1972; *Kommunist,* 1972, no. 11; and P. E., "France: Alliance of the Left," *New Times,* July 1972, no. 28.

39. TASS International Service in English, July 1, 1972. According to Neil McInnes, the CPSU dispatched an envoy to the PCF to warn against reformism and class collaboration; Neil McInnes, *The Communist Parties of Western Europe* (London: Oxford University Press, 1975), p. 198.

40. TASS International Service in English, July 10, 1972; and "Program of Unity," *Izvestiya,* July 11, 1972.

41. M. A. Suslov, speech delivered to PCF 20th party congress, *Pravda,* December 15, 1972.

42. *Pravda,* January 29, 1973.

43. A. Potapov, "France After the Election," *New Times,* 1973, no. 11; and S. Zykov, "France Wants Change," *New Times,* 1973, no. 15.

44. S. Zykov, "France After the Elections," *Izvestiya,* March 15, 1973.

45. B. Leybzon, "The Communists in the Struggle for a Unity of Democratic Forces," *Kommunist,* November 1974, no. 16.

46. *Pravda,* October 24, 1974.

47. The UDR (Gaullist) share had risen from 13 to 15 percent, the Independent Republicans (Giscard's party) had remained at 24 percent, and the centrist-reformist grouping had dropped from 12 to 8 percent; *Le Nouvel Observateur,* February 2, 1976.

48. Evgeny Babenko, "France: Signs of the Times," *New Times,* March 1976, no. 13; see also "French Communist Party Central Committee Plenum," *Pravda,* April 1, 1976.

49. James F. Clarity, New York *Times,* March 15, 1976.

50. Clarity, New York *Times,* May 17, 1976; see also Paul Winkler and Jean Brigouleiux, interview with François Mitterand, *France Soir,* February 19, 1977; "Our Only Will: To Unite," *L'Humanité,* June 29, 1976.

51. Yu. Kharlanov, "France: Success for Leftist Forces," *Pravda,* March 15, 1977.

52. See, for example, *L'Humanité,* April 19, 1974.

53. Giscard d'Estaing interviewed by Jacques Chancel, *Le Monde,* May 28, 1975. Never in the history of the Fifth Republic have president and parliament been in opposition; because of the constitution's inexplicitness as to the ultimate repository of political power, leftist control of parliament—bringing with it appointment of a leftist prime minister—could provoke a political crisis.

54. A. Chernayev, "The Continuously Growing and Developing Class, the Hegemonistic Class," *Kommunist,* July 1972, no. 11. The author also termed the PCF-PS agreement on a common governmental program one of the "major results" of the left-wing unity line endorsed by the 1969 international conference.

55. Zarodov, *Leninism and Contemporary Problems,* p. 131.

56. Zagladin, *World Communist Movement,* p. 239.

57. Ibid., p. 240.

58. I. Rybalkin, "The Chilean Experience: General Laws and Distinctiveness of the Revolutionary Process," *Kommunist,* 1972, no. 8, a review of Luis Corvalan, *Put' Pobedy* (Moscow: Politizdat, 1971). Ironically, the CPSU attributed the failure of the Chilean revolution precisely to the Chilean Communists' failure to exercise the vanguard role; Sobolev, "The Dialectic of the General and the Particular."

59. Leybzon, op. cit.

60. *World Marxist Review* 18, no. 8 (August 1975):108; the symposium was reported in the June, July, and August issues of the journal.

61. Konstantin Zarodov, "The Leninist Strategy and Tactics of the Revolutionary Struggle," *Pravda,* August 6, 1975. On September 17 Brezhnev received Zarodov and personally expressed satisfaction with the work of the *World Marxist Review* on the occasion of its anniversary, and Zarodov was accorded the honor of heading a separate *WMR* delegation at the 25th party congress.

62. V. V. Zagladin, "Changes in the World and the Communist Movement," *Rabochiy Klass i Sovremennyy Mir,* 1975, no. 5 (September-October).

63. *Le Monde,* August 10–11, 1975.

64. Chambaz, op. cit.

65. "Debate in USSR on Democracy and Revolution," *L'Unità,* December 9, 1975.

66. See Stephen Larrabee, "A Change in Soviet Policy?" Radio Liberty 399/75, September 23, 1975.

67. *L'Humanité,* February 6, 1976.

68. *Pravda,* July 3, 1976.

69. "In Order to Win, a Strong, Influential and Active Communist Party is Essential," *L'Humanité,* October 8, 1974.

70. Ibid.

71. A. Vieuguet, "French Imperialism on the World Scene," *World Marxist Review,* 19, no. 7 (July 1976):53; in *L'Humanité,* January 9, 1976, Marchais declared that he considered that the "formation of a Socialist section in an enterprise does not represent any progress for the workers' movement. What the working class needs is a revolutionary party. . . ."

72. Thierry Pfister, "New Leadership Balance Developing within French Communist Party," *Le Monde,* November 21, 1974.

73. André Laurens, "Communist Party Attempting to Regain Initiative within Left," *Le Monde,* December 1–2, 1974.

74. Report by Central Committee Secretary Gaston Plissonnier on the Central Committee meeting, *L'Humanité,* February 9, 1976.

75. McInnes, op. cit., p. 202.

76. Pierre Juquin, interview on Hamburg television, January 26, 1976.

77. *L'Humanité,* June 10 and March 28, 1977.

78. Ronald Tiersky, "French Communism in 1976," *Problems of Communism,* January-February 1976, p. 44.

79. See V. V. Gorelova and S. I Velikovskiy, "The Socialist Party of France: Renewal and Its Limits," *Rabochiy Klass i Sovremennyy Mir,* 1975, no. 5 (September-October).

80. *Pravda,* April 27, 1975 and *Le Monde,* April 29, 1975.

81. *Le Monde,* May 3, 1975.

82. "It Is Normal That We Soviets Should Feel an Obvious Sympathy with the French Leftwing Forces," *L'Unité,* December 24, 1976.

83. Zarodov, *Leninism and Contemporary Problems,* p. 181.

84. Zagladin, *World Communist Movement,* p. 151; and V. Gabuniya, "V. I. Lenin on the Class Struggle in the Period of Socialist Building," *Pravda,* February 28, 1970.

85. Gabuniya, op. cit.

86. The PCCh's advocacy of the peaceful parliamentary path to power predated Khrushchev's 1956 20th party congress endorsement of this policy. Its behavior as a UP coalition partner was a model of defense of pluralistic politics and the rights of the opposition as long as it remained within the law. The PCCh supported the unanimity principle in coalition decision making, according each partner equality, guaranteeing pluralism, and abjuring a Soviet-style vanguard role for itself. An innovative comparison of CPSU and PCI perceptions of the Chilean revolution is found in Joan Barth Urban's "Socialist Pluralism in Soviet and Italian Communist Perspective: the Chilean Catalyst," *Orbis* 18, no. 2 (Summer 1974).

87. V. Liusinov, "On the Forms of Revolutionary Transition to Socialism in the Developing Countries," *Mirovaya Ekonomika i Mezhdunarodnyye Otnosheniya,* 1973, no. 2.

88. Victor Diaz, "Fifty Years of the Communist Party of Chile: Results of the Struggle and New Tasks," *Kommunist,* January 1972, no. 1.

89. I. V. Danilevich, "The Revolutionary Vanguard and the Masses," *Latinskaya Amerika,* No. 3, May-June 1976.

90. M. Kudachkin, "Chile: Aggravation of Antagonism Between the Forces of Progress and Reaction," *Kommunist,* February 1973, no. 3; and Rybalkin, op. cit.

91. Rybalkin, op. cit.

92. Kudachkin, op. cit.

93. Vadim Nedrasov and Yevgeniy Primakov, respectively, on Moscow Radio, March 11, 1973.

94. *L'Humanité,* December 18, 1971. The UP experiment was not universally admired by French Communists, however; the dissident group organized around the bulletin *Unir-Débat* disputed the viability of the electoral path, and insisted on the inevitability of the armed struggle; see Jacques Courtois, "Concerning 'The Chilean Alternative,' " *Unir-Débat,* February 10, 1971.

95. *L'Humanité,* November 25, 1971.

96. See Joan Barth Urban, "Contemporary Soviet Perspectives on Revolution in the West," *Orbis* 19, no. 4 (Winter 1976) for an elaboration of this typology.

97. Sobolev, "The Dialectic of the General and the Particular."

98. Danilevich, op. cit.

99. Timur Timofeyev, "The Crisis of Capitalism and the Class Struggle," *New Times,* 1975, no. 39, p. 20.

100. Sobolev, "The Dialectic of the General and the Particular."

101. Boris Ponomarev, Report to the Scientific-Theoretical Conference of the Institute of Marxism-Leninism, the Academy of Social Sciences, the CPSU Central Committee Higher School, the USSR Academy of Sciences, and other party organs, January 18–21, 1974, in *Kommunist,* January 1974, no. 2.

102. Boris Ponomarev, "The World Situation and the Revolutionary Process," *Problemy Mira i Sotsializma,* 1974, no. 6; cf. Sobolev, "Revolution and Counterrevolution: the Chilean Experience and Problems of the Class Struggle," *Rabochiy Klass i Sovremennyy Mir,* 1974, no. 2 (March-April).

103. Ponomarev's speeches and writings reflect this shift; see his speech in the Kremlin on the 104th anniversary of Lenin's birth, Moscow Domestic Service, April 22, 1974; "Socialism's Role in the Present-Day World," *World Marxist Review* 18, no. 1 (January 1975); and "Communists in the Struggle against Fascism and War, for Peace, Democracy, and Socialism," address at a conference in honor of the 40th anniversary of the 7th congress of the Comintern, July 1975. See also Ernst Genri, "Why Do Dictators 'Command a Good Price'?" *Komsomolskaya Pravda,* January 26, 1974; and the same author's "On the Problem of Contemporary Rightwing Authoritarian Regimes," *Latinskaya Amerika,* no. 6, November-December 1975.

104. *Pravda,* February 25, 1976; emphasis added. International communism's continuing preoccupation with analysis of the lessons of Chile is evidenced by the announcement in the January 1977 issue of *World Marxist Review* of an agreement reached with the PCCh Central Committee for publication of a series of articles on this topic by leading Chilean Communists. The first of these, "Reflections on the 1,000 Days of Popular Unity Rule," by Volodia Teitelboim (*World Marxist Review* 20, no. 1 [January 1977]), discusses many of the themes in the present chapter, including the importance of mass action, the distinction between the political and the arithmetical majority, and the importance of resort to extralegal means when necessary.

105. *L'Humanité,* November 12, 1975.

106. Marchais, "Socialism for France."

107. Urban, "Socialist Pluralism," p. 495.

108. For background on the Portuguese revolution, and particularly on the role of the Portuguese Communist Party, see Arnold Hettinger, "The Rise of Portugal's Communists,"

Problems of Communism, July-August 1975; George W. Grayson, "Portugal and the Armed Forces Movement," *Orbis* 19, no. 2 (Summer 1975); Tad Szulc, "Behind Portugal's Revolution," *Foreign Policy,* no. 21, Winter 1975–76; and Eusebio M. Mujal-Leon, "The PCP and the Portuguese Revolution," *Problems of Communism,* January-February 1977.

109. Ernst Genri, "The Continents are Moving Toward the Left," *Literaturnava Gazeta,* November 6, 1974.

110. Zarodov, "Leninism on Consolidating the Victory of the Revolution."

111. The PCP received only 12 percent of the vote; see F. Stephen Larrabea, "Moscow, Portugal, and Detente," Radio Liberty 363/75, September 5, 1975; and "New Light on the Zarodov Controversy," Radio Liberty 413/75, September 29, 1975.

112. Georges Marchais, "There Will Be No Letup on Our Part," *L'Humanité,* April 17, 1975.

113. Interview with Oriana Fallaci, *Europeo* (Milan), June 15, 1975, reprinted in "A Talk with the Communist Leader," New York *Times Magazine,* July 13, 1975.

114. Particularly disconcerting was the attempt by the head of the CGT to portray the *República* affair as nothing more than "a classic labor dispute," since CGT control of printing in France is common knowledge; see Roy C. Macridis, "The French CP's Many Faces," *Problems of Communism,* May-June 1976; and René Andrieu, "Nostalgia for the Past?" *L'Humanité,* June 23, 1975, which also depicts the incident as a labor-management dispute. The explanation in *Pravda,* May 23, 1975, was that the labor-management dispute that provoked the *República* closure occurred because union members felt the paper was presenting only the point of view of the Socialist party.

115. "*Le Quotidien de Paris* Publishes Special Edition of *República.*" *Le Monde,* June 24, 1975.

116. Georges Marchais, "The 'Top-Secret Soviet Document' is a Crude Forgery," *L'Humanité,* June 27, 1975.

117. Andrieu, "Nostalgia for the Past?"

118. *L'Humanité,* August 19, 1975.

119. *L'Humanité,* February 5, 1976.

120. Vadim Zagladin, "The Preconditions of Socialism and the Struggle for Socialism," *Voprosy Filosifii,* 1975, no. 11.

121. Vadim Zagladin, "Portugal—the Poetry and Prose of Revolution," *Za Rubezhom,* no. 48, December 1976.

122. Yu. A. Krasin, "A Key Problem of the Communists' Strategy," *Rabochiy Klass i Sovremennyy Mir,* 1977, no. 1 (January-February).

3

THE TRANSITIONAL
STATE

PCF AND CPSU CONCEPTIONS OF THE ADVANCED
DEMOCRACY

The advanced democracy which the PCF-PS alliance is pledged to establish should it come to power in France is a transitional state which, while not Socialist itself, would "open the way to socialism."[1] As Secretary General Marchais declared in presenting the Common Program to party militants for ratification, "it would create the best possible conditions for a continuation of the struggle waged by the working people aimed at convincing the majority of our people of the need for a reorganization of society. This democracy would represent a form of transition to socialism."[2]

As defined by Marchais at the 22nd party congress, the *démocratie avancée* has the characteristics of a participatory democracy in which citizen involvement in economic and political decision making replaces what the PCF regards as the concentration of power in the hands of a monied elite caste. Reform of existing capitalist society can not substitute for socialism. As Marchais has written, "one cannot economize on revolution, that is, on profound economic and political transformations. . . ."[3] These transformations can be implemented "within variable time periods," and by a "succession of steps," but even from the first step they must be sufficiently far-reaching to constitute genuine progress toward the ultimate goal: socialism.[4] It is expected that the measures undertaken during this transition period will have broad popular appeal, generating a mandate for continued change in the direction of socialism. Although the duration of the Common Program is coterminous with that of the legislative session, no time limit has been placed on the transition stage itself. Three working groups established by the signatory parties to consider updating the Common Program in the areas of foreign policy, democratic freedoms, and the economy are to complete their work before the 1978 legislative election. Should the Left come to power, periodic revision of the Common Program to increase its Socialist content is the prescribed modality of the transition to socialism. As PCF Central Committee member Paul Courtiau wrote, "Our peaceful and democratic way is a relatively long and complicated revolutionary process in which partial qualitative changes will ultimately lead to socialism. It is not a strategy of sharp changes aimed at ending capitalism overnight."[5]

The Soviets also posit a period of transition to socialism during which the restructuring of society takes the form of bitter class struggle between "incipient socialism and dying capitalism."[6] In the period prior to the overthrow of the Allende regime, the CPSU accepted the notion that the installation of the new Socialist order might be a "relatively lengthy process which goes through successive stages," and which, taken together, would comprise "a transitional period from capitalism to socialism."[7] The concept of the "antimonopolistic or advanced democracy" embodied in the PCF Champigny Manifesto of 1968 was singled out as an example of such a stage as it might transpire in a developed capitalist country.[8]

The uncertain duration and possible reversability of the measures undertaken in the period of the advanced democracy, however, seem to have produced a CPSU reassessment of the nature of the transition period, particularly in the wake of the overthrow of the Allende regime. While acknowledging the necessity of an advanced democratic antecedent to the Socialist revolution in Western European democracies, Soviet writers seem to be promoting the idea that the briefer the stopover at this way station the better. One of *Izvestiya*'s most authoritative political commentators, for example, displayed considerable impatience with what he termed the "unsteady quagmire of half-measures" of the intermediary stages as opposed to the "firm soil of a policy according with the main trends of historical development" of socialism.[9]

The traditional communist view is that, in principle, the higher the level of economic development, the shorter the necessary transition stage.[10] Sobolev, the influential Soviet authority on the revolutionary movement in the West, probably expressed the position of the CPSU hierarchy when he implied that the transitional state is a necessary expedient of purely instrumental value; what matters, he declared, is the scope of the Socialist transformations "which are implemented less for the strengthening of democratic conquests . . . than for the consolidation of a new social system. . . ."[11]

Certain Soviet writers have expressed the view that the crisis of capitalism offers unique opportunities for communists to come to power and commence the transition to socialism, and therefore that the revolutionary timetable should be advanced. According to Soboley, the Leninist dictum calling for subordinating the struggle for democracy to the struggle for socialism is particularly apropos in the current situation.[12] Stepan Salychev, author of a major

Soviet study of the French Socialist party in the interwar period and of periodic articles in *Kommunist,* also stresses the "rapprochement between democratic and socialist tasks," and adds that "with the ripening of the objective and subjective conditions for the revolution ... an even greater percentage of democratic problems will be resolved on the basis of revolutionary programs."[13]

In the view of some observers, publication of such views calling for a speeding up of the transitional stage reflects a debate within the Soviet hierarchy over strategy and tactics for coming to power.[14] The Italian Communist party attacked Salychev for apparently advocating an acceleration of the revolutionary process and formulating an unacceptable "opposition between democracy and socialism...."[15] In a similar vein, the PCF, through its spokesman Chambaz, contested the propriety of Soviet publicist Zarodov's asserting the universal validity of conclusions drawn from Lenin's work which blatantly conflict with PCF strategy.

When Zarodov wrote in his August 1975 *Pravda* article that "the objectives of the two stages [democratic and social] are interlinked and can even be solved simultaneously," and that therefore the revolutionary party should not "overlook the importance of the indispensable temporary stages of the struggle, without dwelling on it," Chambaz inquired: Does this mean that "Zarodov proposes to take the necessary stages into account merely to pass them by more rapidly?"[16] Chambaz rejected this approach.

> This is not our strategy. Our strategy is founded on the concept developed in all party documents, especially the *Manifeste de Champigny* and *Le Défi démocratique,* that advanced democracy is both a necessary stage of and a possible way to progress toward socialism in France. This strategy ... is quite clear. It can be expressed in the slogan ... "nothing but the Common Program, the entire Common Program."[17]

The question of whether the transitional state is to be a period of progress along the path to socialism affording genuine opportunities for periodic stock-taking and possible termination or reversal, as the PCF professes to see it, or primarily as an unavoidable but preferably short-term concession to the traditions of Western democracy, as the CPSU seems to suggest, is obviously of more than academic interest. It is closely bound up with the PCF's professed commitment to political pluralism and alternation in power, cardinal features of the advanced democracy which will be discussed shortly. Suffice it to say that the PCF has always coupled its pledges to abide by the electoral will with expressions of confidence that the majority of the French people will identify their own self-interest with further progress toward socialism, and hence will vote their endorsement of continued steps in that direction.

POLITICAL POLICIES OF THE TRANSITIONAL STATE

PCF Acceptance of Political Pluralism

The plurality of political parties is clearly provided for in the Common Program, which states (p. 148): "Recognition of the role and the plurality of parties implies the guarantee of their rights. This plurality, which stems from freedom of association, is one of the elements that will permit the free exercise of the right to vote." All parties and groups will be able to function freely, provided they stay within the law and refrain from violence. The autonomy of the individual signatory parties is also spelled out in unambiguous terms. In contrast with the PCF's earlier aim of eventual merger of the Communist and Socialist parties, it now asserts that "fusion of the two parties is not on the agenda."[18] At the 22nd party congress Marchais explicitly refuted the charge that the PCF would seek to eliminate its coalition partners once the Left comes to power.

> Perhaps, certain people think, once we accede to power we Communists would intend to eliminate the others? Nothing in our practice can justify this fear. We have never eliminated anyone, either in the government in which we participated or in the numerous municipalities which we run. . . .
> As for the future, everything which we propose shows the falsity of that hypothesis. We want lasting cooperation among democratic parties—cooperation on an equal footing with the same rights and the same duties for each partner.[19]

The PCF has made its commitment to the principle of political pluralism a fundamental tenet of its proclaimed respect for democratic norms and civil liberties. The party's abandonment of the dogma of one-party rule is not new. Its endorsement of political pluralism for the period of "national and democratic renaissance" and for the "march toward socialism" actually dates from its 15th party congress in 1959, when it was enunciated as part of the party's campaign to elaborate proposals which could serve as negotiating positions with prospective allies. In 1961, at the 16th party congress, the PCF extended its acceptance of political pluralism to the period of the "realization of socialism," and in 1964 at the 17th party congress it completed the process by acknowledging the possibility of the existence of more than one party in a Socialist state.[20] The Communist-Socialist declaration of common aims in February 1968, which was the precursor of the Common Program, also explicitly guaranteed the "plurality" and "free activity" of political parties.[21] Moreover, the party has made much of what it regards as its responsible record of governmental participation in the immediate postwar period as testimony to its commitment to play by the rules of the democratic game in a coalition government.*

The place of the opposition is of course the true litmus test of a regime's commitment to genuine political pluralism. The PCF has asserted the right of opposition parties to continue to function even in a Socialist France. The Soviets, while professing to accept the existence of multiple parties in the transition period, define the concept of pluralism so as to preclude the existence of a genuine opposition. They denounce "so-called 'pluralism,' i.e., the existence of different political parties," as "nothing but a reflection of the different social contradictions in capitalist society. . . ."[22] Conceptions of political pluralism (like that of the PCF) "under which the working class and its party are accorded solely the role of an equal partner with other social forces," and introduction into the transition period of the "free play" of political forces or abandonment of the leading role of the Communist party are likewise condemned.[23]

PCF COMMITMENT TO ALTERNATION IN POWER

There is no way of ascertaining in advance, of course, the sincerity of the PCF's commitment to political pluralism. Neither its three-year record of postwar governmental participation, nor its local government experience, are analogous to the situation of a government formed on the basis of a leftist electoral victory at the national level. Asked whether they thought the PCF would try to eliminate its partners once the Left came to power, 46 percent of the respondents said "yes," and only 31 percent said "no"; the rest were undecided.[24]

In order to overcome this lingering image problem, the PCF has made its pledge to abide by the rules of the electoral game and accept the principle of alternation in power the touchstone of its commitment to democracy. The Common Program provides that if the signatory parties, after having formed a government, are subsequently defeated in national elections, their ministers would resign from the government and return to the opposition: "If the nation's confidence were denied the majority parties, they would give up power and take up the struggle again in the opposition," is the Common Program formulation (p. 149). This is precisely the language used in the statement of the Socialist position in a December 1970 Communist-Socialist status report on the progress of their negotiations prior to reaching agreement on the

---

*Publication of Billoux' book, *Quand nous étions ministres,* was part of this campaign to project the image of a responsible governmental party.

Common Program. The PCF, conversely, at that time refused to admit the possibility of electoral defeat.[25] Thus, the Common Program represents a PCF concession on this crucial point. Its following sentence, however, records the PCF's confidence that such an eventuality will not occur: "But the democratic power, whose existence implies the support of a popular majority, will have as its principal task the satisfaction of the working masses, and thus will be strengthened by the ever more active confidence that they will bring to it." The Left Radical party, junior partners in the alliance, has demanded that the acceptance of alternation be made more explicit in a revised Common Program, and the PCF agreed.[26] As Marchais asserted, "democracy commands respect for the popular verdict *by all and in all circumstances.* This responds most clearly to the question of 'alternation.' " The PCF "will respect *in all cases* the verdict expressed by direct, secret, and proportional universal suffrage, whether favorable or unfavorable to us," he declared.[27] But, he maintains, if the Left comes to power and implements the Common Program, the French people will not want to "turn back the clock."[28]

In the event the Left wins a legislative majority under a nonleftist president, as would be the case in 1978, appointment of a government not reflective of the legislative profile is supposed to be precluded by the device of the legislative contract provided by the Common Program. Under its terms the elected deputies of the governmental parties must give the government a vote of confidence and a commitment of the funds required to implement its program (pp. 153-54). Should the government receive a motion of censure, the president may either dissolve the National Assembly and call new elections or appoint a new prime minister and government. The latter must then present its program for legislative approval, failing which, dissolution and new elections become mandatory. The PCF regards the legislative contract as its guarantee, first, that even a hostile president could appoint only a government based on the elected majority, and second, that the PCF can not be frozen out of a leftist government against its will by a Socialist deal with a bourgeois president.* The PCF has indicated its willingness to settle for six or seven ministerial portfolios in a possible leftist government of approximately twenty positions, and that these would most likely be ministries concerned with the economy and public services rather than the sensitive areas of defense, interior, or foreign affairs.[29]

Elections conducted on the basis of proportional representation, as the Common Program provides, would obviously immediately enhance the PCF's strength in the legislature. The Common Program also proposes about a dozen

---

*The effectiveness of this provision, however, depends on the PCF's numerical strength in the legislature.

constitutional amendments to correct the unbalanced accretion of presidential power under the Fifth Republic (including repeal of Article 16, which gives the president extraordinary emergency powers).

Political activity in the advanced democratic state, however, is not to be restricted to electoral and parliamentary activity alone. In addition to retention of the referendum (although not as a plebiscite for presidential policies), a kind of vast mobilization society seems to be envisioned. The French people will be called upon to exercise their rights of citizenship on a "permanent" basis, "not solely at election time," and will have the right to "intervene in all domains of political, economic, social, and cultural life of the country, and to oversee the manner in which their elected representatives accomplish the tasks with which they have been charged."[30] Political parties (which will be authorized to organize at work sites), labor unions, and a vast array of cultural and social associations will provide additional forums for political activity. This active participation of the masses in political life thus becomes an important means of mobilizing support for the regime and thereby of securing the gains of the advanced democracy.

In the Communist-Socialist declaration of February 1968, the two groups agreed to "examine together the measures to be taken to stop all efforts to impede a government of the Left from putting its program into practice."[31] The phrase "to stop all efforts" became known as the "terrible little phrase" and required considerable explanation on the part of the parties to counter the impression that they were advocating repression of the opposition. What was intended, they insisted, was the prevention of antigovernment economic activity. The PCF has made it clear that the kind of "economic sabotage" that helped bring down the Allende regime will not be tolerated. A powerful mass movement and implementation of the Common Program, the PCF believes, will prevent the "big bourgeoisie from resorting to economic disorder and violence against the democratic government."[32] The inescapable question, however, is what constraints a leftist government would be willing to impose if confronted with the high rate of inflation and flight of capital that contributed to undermining the Allende regime.

PCF Abandonment of the Dictatorship of the Proleteriat

The third foundation stone in the PCF's political edifice of the advanced democracy, following logically from its acceptance of political pluralism and alternation in power, is its abandonment of the Marxist-Leninist principle of the dictatorship of the proletariat. Because this represents an undeniable repudiation of Marxist-Leninist doctrine, it is the most portentous of the three. Still present in the Champigny Manifesto of 1968, the concept of the dictatorship of the proletariat underwent considerable mutation and attempted redefinition before being scrapped entirely at the 1976 party congress as inappropriate for contemporary France.

The question of dropping the phrase from the party statutes surfaced publicly for the first time at the 17th party congress in 1964. Despite PCF endorsement of political pluralism both during and after the construction of socialism, uncertainty persisted over how much and what kind of opposition would be allowed in a future Socialist state. In addition, it was pointed out that public confusion over the difference between dictatorship of the "majority" as Marx and Lenin had used the term and the dictatorship by a "minority" such as imposed by Franco and Hitler had made the term itself a barrier to Communist-Socialist cooperation. Rather than eliminate it, however, the party initially decided to demystify the term by giving it a French connotation. Marchais was assigned the task of explaining that eliminating the phrase entirely would be a "grave political error." He rejected the suggestion of one local cell to replace "dictatorship of the proletariat" by the phrase "political power," because, he said, that would vitiate the class content of the state and too closely resemble bourgeois democracy.[33]

Over the next few years such euphemisms as "the Socialist regime of the working class and its allies" (19th party congress, 1970) continued to replace or qualify the contentious phrase. An article on the lessons of the French Commune for the contemporary transition to socialism, for example, defined in convoluted terms one of the main requirements of the Socialist revolution as the "establishment of the dictatorship of the proletariat under one form or another, understanding thereby the government of society by the working class and its allies and the extension of democracy to all workers as well as the people overall."[34]

The overriding significance of the formal abandonment of the outmoded term is not in that action itself, which was the culmination of the long preparatory process just described, but in the context in which it occurred. Taken together with the endorsement of pluralistic democracy within the framework of the French *path to socialism* and the French *practice of socialism,* and the mounting campaign to disassociate itself from aspects of Soviet and Eastern European socialism which it regards as undemocratic (see Chapter 4), the PCF's renunciation of proletarian dictatorship marks its strongest declaration of "independence" from the CPSU to date. On the one hand, it represents a forceful statement of determination to pursue a course of action which assigns a higher priority to domestic electoral aims than to solidarity with the CPSU. On the other hand, it aligns the PCF with the Communist parties of Italy, Spain, and Japan in their support of political pluralism, the existence of opposition parties, and alternation in power (see Chapter 5). As PCF Politburo member Jean Kanapa was later to write: "This decision caused quite a storm in France and elsewhere, because it was quite evident that this was not a question of a mere change in terminology, but of an entire political approach."[35]

The PCF leadership went out of its way to convey the impression that the dropping of the dictatorship of the proletariat had been the subject of extensive free debate within the 98 regional congresses, which had thereafter endorsed it overwhelmingly. Opposition to the move was duly reported in the party press. Ultimately, as Kanapa told the delegates to the 22nd party congress, only 113 of the 22,705 delegates to the regional congresses voted against the move, with 216 abstentions.[36]

The CPSU has vigorously opposed this PCF breach of Marxist-Leninist doctrine. Using the convenient technique of selective reporting, it glossed over the portions of Marchais' speech to the 22nd party congress which outlined the PCF decision. *Pravda*'s cryptic report stated only that "Marchais set forth the essence of the discussion in the PCF on the draft document, including the issue of the dictatorship of the proletariat."[37] It then quoted directly from Marchais' speech the wording of the draft congress document on the new PCF formulation of the exercise of political power in the transition to socialism: "The power which will lead to the Socialist transformation of society will be the power of the working class and of other categories of working people. . . . of the overwhelming majority of the people. This power will be created and will operate on the basis of the choice freely expressed by universal ballot, and its task will be to implement the broadest democratization of the country's entire economic, social, and political life."[38]

Conspicuously absent from this *Pravda* version is the following final sentence of the document's statement on this subject: "Its duty [i.e., the duty of "the power"] will be to respect and to ensure respect for the people's democratic choices."[39] Omission of this key expression of the PCF's commitment to democratic alternation in power, the complement to the party's rejection of the "dictatorship" concept, is evidence of the CPSU's disapproval of these far-reaching PCF departures from official Marxist-Leninist ideology.

For the CPSU, the dictatorship of the proletariat is a sine qua non of the construction of socialism, although prominent Soviet writers have acknowledged that the issue is a contentious one. As Zarodov asserted, the dictatorship of the proletariat is "prominent among the problems of the transition period over which the ideological struggle is particularly sharp." But on this point he gives no ground: "The dictatorship of the proletariat is the chief instrument for carrying out all the tasks of the transition period," he declares; furthermore, "socialism cannot be built without such a dictatorship."[40]

The CPSU offers the Western European parties the example of the Eastern European "peoples' democracies" as models of acceptable variations in the implementation of the dictatorship of the proletariat. Such examples of the "multiparty form" of proletarian dictatorship in which "independent democratic parties" are united in popular or national fronts which "recognize the leading role of the Communist parties," are said to be of enormous significance for future revolutions.[41] The Soviets suggest that this model is particularly relevant for Communist parties in capitalist countries in their effort "to draw nonproletarian masses and their political parties into the struggle for socialism."[42]

The kind of antimonopolistic or advanced democracy outlined in the Champigny Manifesto, the Soviets state, is an example of a revolutionary-democratic state in which the power of the monopolies will have been broken, and the "guiding role" of the working class established. Establishment of such a state is therefore undoubtedly a great victory for the revolutionary forces. Continued forward progress toward socialism, however, requires a higher level of working-class awareness and a "close unity" of the workers' and democratic movements. The outcome of this process is far from certain because, "as experience has shown, acute class clashes flare up in the transitional stage to the dictatorship of the proletariat."[43] Therefore, after the emergence of a "revolutionary regime of the transitional type," Communist parties and other "democratic forces" must increase their efforts to heighten mass awareness in order to arrive at the point where this transitional state form develops into one of the forms of the dictatorship of the proletariat.[44]

The Soviets have, however, demonstrated some flexibility on the matter of terminology. "Absolutely new designations may also appear to define the rule of the working class and its allies," Zagladin predicted.[45] In what appeared to be a harbinger of an attempted terminological compromise on the issue of proletarian dictatorship in order to minimize differences with the Western European Communist parties, various other formulas, including "power of the working class"[46] were assayed. As CPSU Central Committee member Alexei Rumyantsev candidly acknowledged to an Italian journalist: "I am well aware that this word ['dictatorship'] scares a lot of people. So let us rather say: 'the leadership of the proletariat and its theory.'" However, he stipulated, "since this theory is scientific and corresponds to the interests of all humanity, it must be accepted and followed by whoever calls himself a Communist."[47] Such an assertion must be read as a warning—to the leaders of the Italian, French, Spanish, Japanese, and other Communist parties—that one can not reject the *essence* of the dictatorship of the proletariat and still remain a Communist.

Thus, one must ask whether the much-heralded PCF abandonment of the dictatorship of the proletariat represents anything beyond a superficial semantic adjustment for tactical electoral advantage. Is it, as former Prime Minister Jacques Chirac, leader of the reincarnated Gaullist *Rassemblement pour la République* (RPR) and one of the foremost adversaries of the Left alliance, has claimed, merely a tactical ploy?[48] Or is it, as the PCF insists, a genuine commitment, from which there is no turning back? What, after all, is the real import of such a step in the light of the party's persistence in its doctrinaire vanguard pretensions? The key question, of course, is the locus of power in the state: the degree to which it is shared, and the ability of competing groups to aspire to, attain, and exercise it. Only the advent of the Left to power could answer the question of how the PCF would reconcile these seeming irreconcilables, in order to achieve "a pluralistic concept of French political life . . . naturally associated with the idea of the struggle for a guiding PCF influence in the popular movement."[49] This is not, however, to minimize the importance of the move. For any party that relies so much on communication of verbal cues and is so much a product of its ideology, any change of this nature inevitably entrains significant consequences—both domestic and international.

ECONOMIC POLICIES OF THE TRANSITIONAL STATE

The core of the advanced democracy program for the transition to socialism is a series of nationalizations of banks and key industries. This is, in fact, the only section of the document besides the preamble which specifically mentions socialism. The Common Program asserts that transfer of the center of production activity from private to public ownership and installation of democratic management structures permitting an expansion of the power of the workers will "shape the real transformation of society and open the way to socialism" (p. 112). Public ownership would eliminate the ability of what the Common Program signatories label a small group of powerful monied interests to frustrate governmental programs for the sake of maximizing private profit, and make a crucial financial contribution to the implementation of the expensive health, education, housing, and other social programs the Common Program proposes.

The economic section of the Common Program is also the most precise with respect to timetable and content. A minimum nationalization threshold is to be crossed in the first three months of the legislature, consisting of the entire banking and financial sector and a selected list of industrial groups and enterprises occupying "strategic positions" within the economy. Included in this list (p. 116) are nine named groups: Thomson-Brandt (electronics), Pechiney Ugine Kuhlmann (chemicals and metals), Saint-Gobain-Pont-à-Mousson (glass and building materials), Compagnie Générale d'Electricité, Rhône-Poulenc (chemicals), Dassault (aircraft), Roussel-Uclaf (pharmaceuticals), Honeywell-Bull (computers), and ITT-France. According to *The Economist,* this would mean nationalized firms accounting for 18 percent of the GNP (on a value-added basis) and give France one of the largest nationalized sectors in Western Europe.[50] In addition to the industries that are to be entirely taken over by the public sector, another group will enter the public sector by means of state financial participation ranging as high as the majority interest.

The Common Program is vague on the subject of compensation. Indemnification of stockholders "will be equitably resolved," it blandly states (p. 116). Compensation is one of the subjects discussed in the Common Program update negotiations carried out by the signatory parties in preparation for the 1978 legislative elections. The Communists advocated compensation for all stockholders (for major stockholders on a case-by-case basis) by conversion of shares into government bonds repayable over 20 years by constant annual installments on the basis of the average price of shares during the 3 years immediately preceding nationalization. Assuming a stock value of the designated firms of $6 billion, and also assuming that the major holders would not be fully compensated, the PCF calculates the annual interest and amortization would amount to only $580 million.[51] The Socialists, on the other hand, proposed that compensation be achieved by the legal conversion of existing stock into nonvoting prefereed stock which would be traded on the exchange. The government would guarantee a minimum dividend, but the full dividend would be pegged to company profits. Thus, under the Socialist scheme, "nationalization" would mean government securing control over companies by eliminating their shareholders' voting rights. The firms themselves would remain in private hands, the government's financial obligation would be minimal, and the nationalized firms would retain their incentive to increase productivity and profits.[52] The Communists adamantly rejected these proposals, which they regarded as scarcely disguised perpetuation of the market economy, and therefore as a betrayal of the Common Program.

The extensive nationalization program and the designation of targets by name represented key Socialist concessions: the Common Program also leaves open the possibility of additional nationalizations if the workers in a given industry so desire. As Marchais declared in his candid report to the PCF Central Committee, what was the minimum threshold of nationalizations for the PCF was the maximum threshold for the Socialists.[53] Conversely, the PCF had to lower its nationalization sights for the sake of Common Program agreement. It lost the most bitter battle of the entire negotiation process when it failed to achieve inclusion of the metallurgy industry on the immediate nationalization agenda, an issue it again raised in the course of the Common Program revision negotiations: metallurgy and oil are among the sectors in which governmental financial participation is the mechanism provided for entry into the public domain. Only in the case of the automobile industry, however, did the PCF fall short of achieving the substance of its own nationalization program, and even here the Common Program provides for preferential treatment for the existing nationalized segment (Renault). The PCF has pressed for an enlargement of the nationalized sector, while the Socialists in early 1977 indicated opposition to exceeding the original nationalization program "during the coming five years."[54] If the Left comes to power, the Communists would mobilize union pressure to overcome Socialist resistance to securing majority government financial participation in additional industries, particularly metallurgy.[55]

Under the Common Program the objective of the state's industrial policy would be to "insure national independence" within the context of the development of international trade and "balanced international cooperation" (p. 121). With respect to international agricultural policy, the government would press for a "profound modification" of the price supports and market structure of the Common Market (p. 127). In terms of economic philosophy, the Common Program speaks of "balanced growth" benefiting the largest number of people (p. 139). To this end, state intervention would be used to foster regional economic balance, giving special assistance to depressed areas (p. 119). State-controlled financial institutions would employ their credit policies to promote the expansion of needed infrastructure and agricultural development (pp. 122 and 126). All new foreign investment would be required to contribute productive capacity and new technology to the French economy, within guidelines established by the economic plan; adoption of similar provisions would be recommended to the other members of the Common Market (p. 123). Taxes on consumer necessities and on incomes at the bottom rung of the economic ladder, as well as for small businessmen and artisans, would decline, while those of the wealthy would rise (p. 131).

The concept of worker initiative permeates the Common Program's economic provisions. Economic management in the advanced democracy would be decentralized and autonomous, not "authoritarian and bureaucratic."[56] Twice the Common Program asserts that "nationalization will not mean state control" (pp. 110, 114). The entire economy would be knit together by a "democratic plan," with large input by worker organizations, regional and local collectives, and consumer organizations. The nationalized enterprises would be administered independently, by a board of directors, consisting of selected worker representatives, consumers, and government-appointed representatives, the latter not constituting a majority (pp. 110–11). These boards would be responsible for setting policy with respect to their production program, budget, and markets, and for entering agreements with other nationalized enterprises and with the private sector.

Believing that "economic democracy and political democracy are inseparable" (p. 105), the drafters of the Common Program have provided for major expansion of worker and union powers. Worker committees in enterprises would have broad prerogatives pertaining to working conditions and hiring practices; any dismissal without reassignment to an equivalent job would be prohibited (p. 106). The Common Program leaves unresolved, however, the contentious issue of worker self-management. Here no compromise formula could be found to encompass the signatory parties' divergent views. Thus, a provision for the possibility of the development of "new forms" of worker intervention in the management and control of industrial enterprises resorts to the awkward explanation (p. 111) that the Socialist party views these within the context of worker self-management (*autogestion*), while the Communist party (which rejects that term) envisions them as "the permanent development of democratic management."[57]

Although the public sector will be paramount, neither the Common Program nor the PCF's own program calls for the elimination of private property in the transitional state. The PCF has repeatedly disavowed any aim to impose Soviet-style collectivism in France, and has unequivocally assured that "even in a Socialist France, private property will have its place." Small industrial, commercial, and agricultural enterprises will continue to coexist with the steadily expanding state sector, and the assets of small depositors will be excluded from nationalization (p. 116). The PCF denies that these are tactical moves designed to neutralize the opposition of the middle class; rather, it insists, they are pragmatic moves dictated by considerations of efficiency.[58] Without collectivizing these enterprises, however, the PCF does raise the possibility of linking them to the national economy by means of new forms of cooperation. The Common Program speaks of agricultural cooperation tied to production and marketing, and in a government of the Left the PCF could be expected to work for the expansion of agricultural cooperatives. In an article written for the Soviet journal *Rural Life,* Marchais termed agricultural cooperatives "the most acceptable means of managing agriculture" under present economic and technical conditions. Based on voluntary participation, he asserted, government-supported cooperatives would render technical and financial support to farmers.[59]

At the heart of the Common Program's economic policies is the expectation that merely eliminating waste, reducing military expenditure, curbing the flight of capital, and mobilizing extensive underutilized productive capacity and human resources would somehow generate the means to realize the Common Program's ambitious economic and social goals. The PCF's assumption is that increased governmental control over the economy would itself correct what Marchais has labeled a 30 percent underutilization of France's productive capacity.[60] The five-year budget presented by PCF and PS economists in January 1973, which was designed to show how the increases in social security, public services, and nationalizations would be financed, was predicated on a continuing 8 percent growth rate, which critics correctly saw as unrealistic. What might have been feasible under an expanding economy such as existed when the Common Program was drawn up is clearly beyond the means of an economy in the grip of recession and inflation.

Joint working groups of the signatory parties were empowered to make the necessary revisions in keeping with the altered economic circumstances, but the PCF, for its part, has insisted that these will be minor. Its solution to the economic crisis is to increase the purchasing power of the workers in order to stimulate domestic consumption, concentrating on enlarging the domestic market rather than emphasizing export promotion, for which it criticizes the Giscard regime. Furthermore, the party asserts, the prices of industrial goods and the value-added tax on consumer products must be reduced, tax privileges enjoyed by the large corporations eliminated, and public credits made available for investment to create jobs.[61] The fact remains, however, that the prospect of coming to power in a period of economic crisis poses a dilemma. Demanding sacrifices by supporters, as the Italian Communists learned, entails serious risk, which the PCF, after having led the attack on the Barre Plan and witnessed the PCI's difficulties, may be unwilling to incur.

FOREIGN AND DEFENSE POLICIES OF THE TRANSITIONAL STATE

Defining the foreign and defense policies of the *Union de la gauche* government proved to be one of the most difficult tasks of the Common Program negotiators. This is also the area in which the PCF, in order to prevent the complete rupture of the negotiations, was forced to accept the greatest compromise with its own positions.[62]

Entering the negotiations, the PCF had three foreign policy objectives: to secure the best external conditions for the implementation of the Common Program, a consideration that dictated rejection of any supranational institution which would infringe on French independence; to "disengage" (the word used in the PCF program) France from the Atlantic Alliance; and to oppose the monopolistic character of the European Common Market as presently constituted.[63] Despite the PCF's consessions on important foreign and defense policy issues, Marchais claimed that the PCF had succeeded in keeping out of the Common Program anything that would compromise the Party's program and principles, in particular because Common Market membership had not been designated as one of the fundamental principles of the government's foreign policy.[64] PCF hostility toward both NATO and the Common Market has common roots: "Both strike at the independence of France. Both constitute class alliances, having as their nature and function the chaining of our country to the imperialist system, under the direction of the United State."[65]

The preservation and enhancement of French independence is the keynote of the foreign and defense policy sections of the Common Program, although its provisions are often contradictory. The PCF did not gain a commitment to outright withdrawal from the Atlantic Alliance. The Common Program asserts, however, that the government "will demonstrate its desire to engage the country on the path of independence with regard to all politico-military blocs" (p. 175). The government's intention to pursue a policy of independence from all military blocs "in all circumstances" is to be incorporated in its statement of investiture. The Common Program signatories are on record as favoring replacement of France's membership in NATO with a European collective security system, the reduction of military budgets, and the conclusion of nonaggression treaties and defensive alliances. While pledging to work for the mutual and simultaneous phased dissolution of NATO and the Warsaw Pact (a move initially advocated by the USSR in the Warsaw Pact declaration of July 1966 and endorsed by the Berlin Conference of European Communist and Workers' Parties in 1976), however, pending the creation of a European collective security system, the government will maintain "respect for France's existing alliances" (pp. 172 and 175). The magnitude of this major PCF concession is tempered by the qualification that any problems posed by the obligations deriving from France's membership in the Atlantic Alliance will be resolved in the spirit of total independence from all political and military blocs. Moreover, the Common Program specifies that the policy of independence from military blocs will govern French participation in international conferences and negotiations (p. 175).

In practice, this programmatic legerdemain would seem to mean French reversion to the policy of total estrangement from a unified NATO defense system in peacetime. PCF and PS thinking on this point, however, is not in complete harmony. For the PS, military strength at present remains the best deterrent. Peace, it says, "rests on the military balance," and France must be part of the Western deterrent: "That is why, in affirming its independence, France must continue to belong to its own camp and to defend it against possible future pressure or aggression from the other camp. This attachment to one of the two existing camps is all the more important in a period marked by an intense Soviet military buildup...."[66] The PCF, on the other hand, while professing to see no incompatibility in having Communist ministers in a government of a France which belonged to NATO, would react favorably if the NATO partners themselves "in this new situation, considered it necessary to renegotiate the terms of the Alliance...."[67]

In the view of the PCF, "a detente and disarmament policy and the conclusion of friendship treaties would be a responsible way to insure France's security and independence."[68] The party has strongly criticized the revisions of French military doctrine under post-de Gaulle governments which replaced the previous *tous azimuts* (omnidirectional, that is, with no declared adversary) strategic targeting doctrine with a posture of defense against a hypothetical attack from the East alone. On this point the Common Program echoes the precise language used by Marchais at the PCF 21st party congress in defining a military strategy which would be aimed at opposing "any eventual agressor, whoever it might be" (p. 172). Finally, PCF acquiescence in present French membership in NATO implies no more than acceptance of its mutual defense provisions: ". . . NATO must not go beyond the obligation of mutual assistance in the event of an external threat or pressure," PCF spokesmen insist.[69] This would preclude French participation in a NATO defense effort on behalf of third countries, such as in the event of a new Middle East war.

Universal and controlled disarmament is termed the principal goal of the Union de la gauche government, and the signatory parties pledge to initiate French participation in the Geneva disarmament conference. The Common Program endorses outright "renunciation of the nuclear *force de frappe* under any form whatsoever" (p. 171); immediate cessation of nuclear testing; and the conversion of the French nuclear weapons industry to the peaceful uses of atomic energy. France under a Common Program regime would adhere to the nuclear test ban and nonproliferation treaties, which the present French government has spurned, and would seek the creation of a denuclearized zone and controlled and balanced force reductions in Europe. The exclusion of a ban on France's tactical nuclear weapons, like the Common Program's silence on existing nuclear weapons stocks, were grudging but necessary PCF concessions. The PCF claimed to suspect the PS of harboring intentions to include French nuclear weapons in a Western European defense community (with implied West German access to nuclear weapons), to which it, like the USSR, is adamantly opposed. PCF failure to obtain Socialist consent to the liquidation of the existing nuclear stockpile was balanced, Marchais told the Central Committee, by Socialist acceptance of return to the tous azimuts doctrine. Moreover, Marchais stated in his report to the Central Committee that the PCF intended to pursue its drive for total liquidation of French nuclear weapons.

In contrast to the PCI, which has hinted at an appreciation of the role of the NATO shield in helping assure Italian independence under an eventual government with Communist participation, the PCF has stepped up its attacks on NATO. During the preparatory sessions which preceded the Berlin Conference of European Communist and Workers' Parties in June 1976, the PCF delegation pressed, unsuccessfully, for a denunciation of Western imperialism and the Atlantic Alliance; and in his conference address Marchais condemned the French government's decision to deploy its forces, along with those of the "imperialist" West German Bundeswahr, in a "forward battle" posture facing the borders of the Socialist countries.[70] In an October 1976 press conference, Marchais indicated that the PCF is cleaving to its militant line on NATO.

> We want to have a completely independent defense. We believe that France should be kept outside NATO, which it has rejoined in various ways. We support General de Gaulle's decision to insure that France does not take orders from any military organization—whether NATO or the Warsaw Pact. This does not mean that we should withdraw from the Atlantic Alliance.... A left government will have to take initiatives with a view to dissolving military blocs and pursuing a policy of disarmament and peace.[71]

The Common Program signatory parties shared the apprehension that the most probable source of military threat to France under a leftist government would come in the form of pressure to prevent its implementation. The text endorses the principles of peaceful coexistence and the renunciation of the use or threat of force, "including to impose on a country the choice of its alliances [or] . . . a political or social system against the will of the majority of its inhabitants" (p. 169); and it affirms that the government "will oppose any interference, pressure, or external reprisals intended to jeopardize the realization of the objectives of economic and political democracy inscribed in the governmental program" (p. 170). The PCF strongly condemned former Secretary of State Henry Kissinger's expressions of U.S. opposition to Communists gaining political power in Western Europe as interference in French domestic affairs, and also attacked what it interpreted as moves by the Atlantic Alliance, led by the U.S. and West Germany, to block a governing role for the PCI. Although the fact that the United States has been "compelled" to accept peaceful coexistence makes its overt interference in the internal affairs of another country more difficult, Marchais has written, "it would be foolish to depend on the support or goodwill of imperialist America" in building a Socialist France.[72] However, the PCF insists that it is "unreasonable" to assume that the advent of Communist ministers means the rupture of the complex web of economic and other relations built up between France and the United States. Moreover, any attempt to isolate France economically would result not in destabilizing the new French government but in creating an imbalance in Europe, PCF spokesmen insist. What the PCF seeks, therefore, is to establish relations of "friendship and cooperation" with the United States, "based only on mutual respect, reciprocal advantage, and equal rights."[73]

The PCF contends that, under present allied doctrine, French strategic nuclear weapons serve not the needs of France but the global military strategy of the United States and the NATO Alliance, that is, as a deterrent to attack by the Soviet Union, and that France's own defense needs have been sacrificed. As a consequence of the priority status accorded the force de frappe, the PCF Politburo declared, the Giscard government was increasingly "diverting the army from its mission of national defense to place it at the service of foreign strategic requirements; it is sacrificing its modernization to nuclear armament. . . ."[74] According to Marchais, a government of the Left "would immediately put an end to the production of the *force de frappe.*"[75]

Subsequent to the original Common Program agreement some socialists began reappraising their visceral rejection of nuclear weapons, eventually coming to regard positively the Gaullist idea of an independent defense system based on a nuclear deterrent.[76] A series of PCF statements in the spring of 1976 prompted speculation concerning a similar PCF shift toward accepting the nuclear deterrent as an asset in assuring French independence and in wooing Gaullist voters.[77] In April 1976 Louis Baillot, a Communist National Assembly deputy from Paris and the party's leading military specialist, was reported to have acknowledged saying at a meeting of the Foundation for General Defense Studies that "the nuclear force presents itself as a fact, and it is impossible not to recognize this."[78] He was also said to have declared that "nuclear weaponry can be considered as an element of political independence." Several days later Marchais stated that "France must have a national defense system to insure its independence. . . . It must acquire appropriate political means—it already has the necessary technical means—for this, that is, conclude nonaggression treaties with specific countries."[79] The PCF policy shift on the subject of nuclear weapons was officially confirmed by Marchais' assertion at a Central Committee meeting on May 11, 1977 that the PCF now believed that the nuclear strike force should be maintained at its present level. In the light of governmental neglect of France's conventional forces, he declared, the PCF considered it mandatory to retain the force de frappe as the only means of providing a credible deterrent. However, if the PCF has reappaised its policy regarding nuclear weapons for the short term, this does not mean it has abandoned its opposition to such weapons in the long term. Marchais' position on the future of France's nuclear submarine base in Brest under a leftist government reflects the party's longer term objectives:

> We are in favor of an active disarmament policy leading to the destruction of nuclear arms. The role of the Brest base should be seen against the background of a general defense policy which should not be based merely on military means. . . . No one will convince us that the national interest depends on the force de frappe.[80]

For the PCF the important immediate emphases are the cessation of the nuclear *priority,* return to the tous azimuts targeting doctrine, and disassociation from all military activities of the Atlantic alliance. As Jean Kanapa wrote in the January 1977 issue of *Foreign Affairs,* ". . . France must make absolutely certain that her security is assured. In this respect, a government which includes the Communists will guarantee this security through the *up-to-date defense policy using all the necessary means at its disposal,* a security which would be genuinely national, one not integrated into NATO (in accordance with the provisions adopted in 1966), and ready to face *any* eventual aggressor."[81]

The question of the structure and mission of the armed forces in a France governed by the Left is complicated not only by divergences between Communist and Socialist views on the subject of defense, reflected in the Common Program's reticences and compromises, but also by the state of flux within the French military itself. Debate on the utility of the armed forces and their relationship to NATO has ranged from the antimilitarist campaigns of the extreme Left to the official reassessment of military doctrine and force structure undertaken by the Giscard government.[82]

The PCF views the new strategic concepts elaborated by the Giscard regime as representing a shift from deterrence to a war-fighting posture, and as sacrificing the autonomy of French decision making to the exigencies of NATO solidarity—opinions shared by Gaullist critics. While it eschews the antimilitarism of the radical Left, the PCF supports "those who want to preserve the independence of our army and the free determination of its missions within the sole framework of the defense of the national territory."[83] In April 1975 it brought a motion of censure against the government for refusing a general policy debate in the National Assembly on the issue of French reintegration into the NATO alliance.[84]

The three Common Program signatory parties in December 1975 issued a joint communiqué in which they reaffirmed their commitment to a "strong modern army capable of facing any potential aggressor," but at the same time also stressed their intention to reorganize the army to ensure that it is "democratically based" and integrated into the French nation.[85] Because the PCF is convinced that the allegiance of a considerable part of the military is essential to successful pursuit of the peaceful path to socialism, it considers the "democratization" of the armed forces an important priority. As part of this effort, the PCF has called for the military establishment to make Communist publications available to all personnel, and has urged young communists serving in the armed forces to seek promotions to officer ranks.[86]

On the subject of European integration, the Common Program represents a compromise between the Socialists' traditionally strong integrationist orientation and the PCF's suspicion of any hint of supranationalism that would restrict France's independent domestic and foreign policy decision making or facilitate the exertion of international pressure to impede the progress toward socialism. The government of the Union de la gauche, the Common Program asserts, will "participate in the construction of the EEC ..." (p. 177). However, this participation is to be directed to freeing the community from the domination of U.S. multinational corporations, democratizing its institutions, establishing policies which serve the interests of the workers, and preserving French freedom of action to implement the Common Program. French participation is additionally qualified by the document's pointed statement that the government will preserve the right to invoke the safeguard clauses of the Treaty of Rome, enlarge the public sector of the economy, define and apply its own credit policies and employ other measures to promote democratic planning, and engage in economic cooperation with other countries irrespective of their socioeconomic systems. The Common Program specifically notes that the government will seek diversified and expanded industrial, scientific-technological, and cultural cooperation between the EEC and Comecon (pp. 180–81).

The fact that the signatory parties were able to reach agreement on the section of the Common Program dealing with European integration is in part a reflection of a certain convergence of the positions of the PCF and the Socialists on the Common Market and the relationship of Europe to the United States. Following the CPSU's example, the PCF has in recent years come to accept the existence of the EEC and to concentrate on shaping it to serve its interests (see Chapter 5). In 1967 the PCF decided "not to deny or to liquidate the Common Market, but to transform it," based on the position that the "ties established between our country and our partners could not be broken unilaterally without damage to the national economy."[87] As an illustration of the changed PCF position, in 1973 it decided to seek representation in the European parliament and the consultative assembly of the Council of Europe, which it had previously shunned.

The Socialists, originally ardent supporters of European economic and political integration, but now strongly influenced by the minority leftist CERES faction within their ranks, have increasingly manifested an aversion to the economic penetration of the Common Market by U.S. multinational corporations and disenchantment with the failure of its technocratic institutions to respond to the needs of Europe's workers. Today, the prevailing Socialist view is that the most immediate danger to a France under the Common Program is not Soviet military might but U.S. economic and political hegemony. As Socialist leader Mitterand is reported to have declared in his conversations with Soviet officials in Moscow in April 1975, U.S.-dominated "multinational capitalism poses the Common Market problem in new terms. We must deal with the problem of Europe in a different way from how some of us dealt with it ten or fifteen years ago."[88] The Socialists still support the Common Market, he asserted, but only as long as it doesn't interfere with the nationalizations and other measures envisioned by the Common Program. As a leading Socialist declared: "We share with our Communist partners . . . the refusal to abandon our sovereignty under the false pretext of building Europe."[89] While the Common Program does not aim to exclude U.S. investment from France or Europe, the PCF and the PS would work to modify the EEC's antitrust rules so as to regulate more strictly such investment on a Europe-wide level and in France.

Unlike the Socialists, and also contrary to its Italian Communist counterparts, the PCF long opposed the idea of direct elections to the European parliament in Strasbourg. The French Communists fear that as a result of such elections a leftist French government could find itself confronting a European majority opposed to its policies and fortified by the legitimacy deriving from a popular mandate. The Socialists, conversely, have defended this increase in the EEC's supranationality as a means of democratizing the Community by increasing the control of a popularly elected parliament over its technocratic and bureaucratic executive institutions. However, the PS Common Program negotiators acceded to the PCF insistence on continued appointment of the French representatives to the European parliament in proportion to their respective parties' membership in the National Assembly. Then, as in the case of maintaining French nuclear weapons, the PCF adroitly dropped its opposition to direct elections to the European parliament in May 1977 when continued opposition appeared futile and conciliation offered the prospect of wresting concessions from the Socialists on other issues under discussion in the Common Program revision negotiations. Interestingly, the changed PCF position was announced following a Marchais-Berlinguer conference in Italy in which direct election to the European parliament was among the topics discussed. But practical problems of European integration, particularly the issue of direct elections, continue to divide the PCF and the PS. PS advocacy of such far-reaching supranational measures as a common European citizenship, including the right to vote in the country of residence, and a common civil code, exceed PCF intentions. The proximity to the French legislative contest of the European parliamentary elections scheduled for spring 1978 is certain to heighten tensions within the Union de la gauche (as well as between the Gaullists and Giscard's pro-European, rechristened Republicans within the governmental coalition).

Factional disputes within the Socialist party over European integration, plus the history of differences with the PCF over the admission of Britain in 1972, direct elections to the European parliament, defense policy, and NATO do not augur well for smooth functioning of a leftist government. There is continuing friction over the effort to pin down foreign policy planks that were intentionally left vague in the Common Program platform. One of these is the timing of the withdrawal from NATO. The Socialists have made it clear that abandonment of NATO is predicated on successful construction of an alternative European collective security system. The Communists, conversely, by their emphasis on bilateral non-aggression pacts, appear once again to be pressing for unilateral initiatives on the part of France that would effectively nullify French membership in NATO. The PS has rejected PCF proposals for extensive revision of the foreign policy section of the Common Program on the grounds that such revisions risk destroying the delicate balance among the three signatory parties.

Relations between a France under the Union de la gauche and its NATO and Common Market partners will almost inevitably be brittle, no matter how the latter cope with French *démarches* in defense and European community affairs. Both the PS and the PCF have advocated much closer cooperation with the Soviet Union, and have pledged that the leftist government will seek to orient the EEC member country's "political cooperation" toward implementing the foreign policy positions expressed in the Common Program. The Soviets may view the prospect of a leftist victory in 1978 with less disfavor than in the past, when a Gaullist foreign policy was more compatible with their own (see Chapter 6). In many areas policies sketched out by Mitterand as a presidential candidate in 1974 conform to Soviet prescriptions with respect to peaceful coexistence and European cooperation. As Mitterand himself pointedly reminded his Soviet interlocutors, he was the "first French politician" to approve the Soviet proposal for convening the European security conference. A prime consideration of French foreign policy under a leftist government, therefore, is likely to be the avoidance of actions that would jeopardize the chances for construction of a European collective security system, which both the PCF and the PS support.

NOTES

1. Preamble, *Programme commun de gouvernement du parti communiste et du Parti socialiste* (Paris: Éditions sociales, 1972). The present discussion draws on this edition, published by the PCF, as well as on other PCF formulations of its conception of the advanced democracy contained in party documents and leaders' writings and speeches.

2. Georges Marchais, Report to the National Conference of the PCF, July 9, 1972, in *Kommunist,* July 1972, no. 11. According to the PCF, with the sole exception of its failure to call for the immediate withdrawal of France from NATO, there is "absolute conformity" between the Common Program and the PCF definition of the advanced democracy outlined in the Champigny Manifesto. See Marchais' report to the Central Committee, June 29, 1972, in Étienne Fajon, *L'Union est un combat* (Paris: Éditions sociales, 1972), p. 112.

3. Georges Marchais, *Le Défi démocratique* (Paris: Grasset, 1973), p. 174.

4. Ibid.

5. Paul Courtieu, "Communists in the Struggle for Democratic Unity," *World Marxist Review* 18, no. 8 (August 1975):80–81.

6. Konstantin Zarodov, *Leninism and Contemporary Problems of the Transition from Capitalism to Socialism* (Moscow: Progress Publishers, 1972), p. 227.

7. V. V. Zagladin, ed., *The World Communist Movement* (Moscow: Progress Publishers, 1973), p. 153. This is the Soviet translation of Zagladin, ed., *Mezhdunarodnoye Kommunisticheskoye Dvizheniye: Ocherk Strategii i Taktiki* (Moscow: Politizdat, 1972).

8. Ibid., p. 165.

9. A. Bovin, "Europe: The Distribution and Dynamics of Social Forces," *Izvestiva,* July 24, 1976.

10. See, for example, Zarodov, *Leninism and Contemporary Problems,* p. 227.

11. A. I. Sobolev, "The Dialectic of the General and the Particular in the Development of the World Revolutionary Process," *Voprosy Istorii KPSS,* November 1975, no. 11.

12. A. I. Sobolev, "Questions of Strategy and Tactics of Class Struggle at the Present Stage of the General Crisis of Capitalism," *Rabochiy Klass i Sovremennyy Mir,* no. 1 (January-February 1975).

13. S. Salychev, "Revolution and Democracy," *Kommunist,* November 1975, no. 17; also published in Moscow in the quarterly journal of the USSR Academy of Sciences, *Social Sciences* 7 no. 4 (1976). Salychev is the head of the History of the International Revolutionary Movement Section of the Institute of World History of the USSR Academy of Sciences. It is noteworthy that a reviewer criticized Salychev's book for "inadequate treatment" of the question of "transitional forms of power"; cited by Joan Barth Urban, "Contemporary Soviet Perspectives on Revolution in the West," *Orbis* 19, no. 4 (Winter 1976). Urban notes that Salychev, whom she categorizes as an exponent of the "revolutionary" view among Soviet political analysts, was no longer

appearing in print in the major Soviet journals by late 1974, perhaps indicating official disfavor. If so, his reappearance in *Kommunist* in late 1975 suggests the possibility of renewed interest within the Soviet hierarchy in airing this viewpoint.

14. Urban, op. cit. For a Soviet denial of the existence of any such debate, see Boris Vesnin, "The Calculations of Anticommunism and the Realities of the Communist Movement," *Novoye Vremya*, no. 50 (December 1975).

15. "Debate in the USSR on Democracy and Revolution," *L'Unità*, December 9, 1975.

16. Jacques Chambaz, "Words and Facts," *L'Humanité*, September 4, 1975.

17. Ibid.

18. Marchais, *Le Défi démocratique*, p. 133. As Marchais asserts, "to make the existence of a single party the condition for the passage to socialism would not correspond to our traditions [or] to our political habits" (ibid., p. 128). Contrast this with the declaration of Maurice Thorez to the *Times* of London on November 17, 1946: "The French Worker party which we propose to constitute by the fusion of the Communist and Socialist parties would be the guide of our new popular democracy"; reprinted in François Billoux, *Quand nous étions ministres* (Paris: Éditions sociales, 1972), p. 188.

19. *L'Humanité*, February 5, 1976.

20. See Ronald Tiersky, *French Communism, 1920–1972* (New York: Columbia University Press, 1974), pp. 276-82 and 292-304. The PCF's commitment to political pluralism in a Socialist state will be discussed in the following chapter.

21. *Le Monde*, February 25-26, 1968.

22. Zagladin, *The International Communist Movement*, p. 88.

23. Zarodov, *Leninism and Contemporary Problems*, pp. 228, 233.

24. *Le Nouvel Observateur*, February 2, 1976; cited by Kevin Devlin, "The PCF's Turning-Point Congress," Radio Free Europe Report, February 4, 1976.

25. "First Summary Declaration of Communist and Socialist Parties," *Le Monde*, December 24, 1970.

26. *L'Humanite*, August 17, 1976.

27. Marchais, *Le Défi démocratique*, p. 116.

28. "No Major Plan for France without National Independence," report of Marchais' press conference, *L'Humanité*, June 10, 1976.

29. *Le Monde*, May 16, 1974.

30. Marchais, *Le Défi démocratique*, pp. 118–24 passim.

31. *Le Monde*, February 25–26, 1968; cited by Arthur P. Mendel, "Why the French Communists Stopped the Revolution," *Review of Politics* 31, no. 1. (January 1969):10–11.

32. *France Nouvelle*, December 19–25, 1973.

33. Tiersky, op. cit., p. 293.

34. Lucien Mathey, "The Commune and the Transition to Socialism in our Time," *Cahiers du Communisme*, March 1971. The PCF program issued in 1971 omitted all reference to proletarian dictatorship; see *Programme pour un gouvernement démocratique d'union populaire* (Paris: Éditions sociales, 1971).

35. Jean Kanapa, "A 'New Policy' of the French Communists?" *Foreign Affairs*, January 1977, p. 282.

36. "A Debate of Unprecedented Breadth," *L'Humanité*, February 8, 1976.

37. "Comrade G. Marchais' Report," *Pravda*, February 6, 1976. The Soviet journal *New Times* similarly merely noted that the issue "was raised"; Evgeny Babenko, "The French Communist Congress," *New Times*, 1976, no. 7, p. 7.

38. *Pravda*, ibid.

39. *L'Humanité*, February 5, 1976.

40. Zarodov, *Leninism and Contemporary Problems*, p. 229.

41. Zagladin. *The World Communist Movement*, p. 163.

42. Ibid.

43. Ibid., pp. 165 and 166.

44. Ibid., p. 166. During the period in which the draft document for the PCF's 22nd party congress was under discussion, *Kommunist* published an article which strongly intimated that without resolution of the question of the transfer of full political power to the "masses" the PCF program would be no better than that of the social democratic parties. This proposition is all the more interesting because it was advanced by an author who had earlier denounced the "ideological concessions" being demanded by the "right wing" Social Democrats in capitalist countries— including the abandonment of the dictatorship of the proletariat—as a precondition for the establishment of alliances. This pressure is unquestionably directly related to the "appearance of revisionist groups within some Communist parties," he declared; S. Salychev, "Revolution and Democracy," and Salychev, "On the Characteristics of the Contemporary Class Struggle in Capitalist Countries," *Kommunist,* 1973, no. 6.

45. Zagladin, *World Communist Movement,* p. 163.

46. A. I. Sobolev, "The Revolutionary-Transforming Activity of the Working Class," *Rabochiy Klass i Sovremennyy Mir,* no. 2 (March-April 1976).

47. Gianni Corbi interview with Alexei Rumyantsev, "CPSU and Dictatorship of the Proletariat—on This Point We Split," *L'Expresso,* December 7, 1975. In a major *Kommunist* article then Soviet President Podgorny refuted the contention that proletarian dictatorship is incompatible with democracy, and insisted that "the historical experience of the USSR and the other fraternal countries confirms that the consolidation of power in the hands of the working class and its allies . . . is an objective law of the transitional period from capitalism to socialism, and an inviolable prerequisite for building socialism. . . ." N. Podgorny, "The 25th CPSU Congress and Development of Socialist Democracy," *Kommunist,* November 1976, no. 17.

48. *Le Monde,* February 22-23, 1976.

49. *L'Humanité,* October 22, 1976.

50. *The Economist,* February 19, 1977. The Common Program's nationalizations would add to what is already a substantial public sector share of the French economy; see Henry W. Ehrmann, *Politics in France* (Boston: Little, Brown, 1976), p. 37.

51. Georges Marchais, in *L'Humanité,* February 14, 1977, and *The Economist,* op. cit. Experts, however, regard these figures as far too low.

52. François Mitterand, interview in *France-Soir,* February 19, 1977; *The Economist,* op. cit.

53. Georges Marchais, Report to the Central Committee, June 29, 1972; Marchais' report was not made public until its publication in 1975 in Fajon, op. cit.

54. Mitterand interview, op. cit.

55. Marchais report, in Fajon, op. cit., pp. 105–06.

56. Marchais, *Le Défi démocratique,* p. 71.

57. The importance the PS attaches to "autogestion" was well illustrated by PS secretary Michel Rocard, in "French Socialism and Europe," *Foreign Affairs,* April 1977, in which he credits adoption of this concept with the renaissance of the Socialist party. By contrast, Kanapa, in his own article in the previous issue of the same journal, completely ignored the self-management theme. Two Soviet authors attribute this disagreement to fundamental differences in the two parties' conceptions of the organization of the economy and society, and state that it reflects their "different evaluation of the experience of building socialism in different countries." V. V. Gorelova and S. I. Velikovskiy, "The Socialist Party of France: Renewal and its Limits," *Rabochiy Klass i Sovremennyy Mir,* no. 5 (September-October 1975).

58. Marchais, *Le Défi démocratique,* pp. 55–56, 61, and 69.

59. Georges Marchais, "For a Better Life and a Bright Future," *Selskaya Zhizn,* February 28, 1973; cf. Marchais report, in Fajon, op. cit., p. 59.

60. Georges Marchais, interview on the program "Ten Questions—Ten Answers," Paris Radio, December 13, 1976.

61. Ibid.
62. Marchais report, in Fajon, op. cit., p. 95. This section outlines the foreign and defense policy provisions of the Common Program and other PCF and PS statements bearing on the foreign policy of a future Union de la gauche government; the impact of international relations on the PCF-CPSU relationship is discussed in Chapter 6.
63. Ibid., p. 96.
64. Ibid.
65. Ibid., p. 95. In his report to the Central Committee, Marchais followed this statement with the unflattering observation that "It is for this fundamental reason that the Socialist party is profoundly attached both to the Atlantic Alliance and to the integration of *La petite Europe occidentale*." He also declared that the PCF would strive to implement a foreign and defense policy that would "no longer be subjected to the world imperialist class system" and would no longer be part of the "global strategy of imperialism" (p. 95).
66. Rocard, op. cit., p. 556.
67. Kanapa, op. cit., p. 291.
68. Georges Marchais, *L'Humanité*, October 9, 1976.
69. Martin Verlet, member of the foreign policy department of the PCF Central Committee, "French Imperialism on the World Scene," *World Marxist Review* 20, no. 1 (January 1977):100.
70. *L'Humanité*, July 1, 1976. The PCF strongly criticized former Prime Minister Chirac for raising the possibility of French first use of tactical nuclear weapons and installation of French tactical Pluton missiles on West German soil: *Le Monde*, May 9, 1975. PCF and PCI views are compared by James E. Dougherty and Diane K. Pfaltzgraff, *Eurocommunism and the Atlantic Alliance* (Cambridge, Mass.: Institute for Foreign Policy Analysis, 1977).
71. *L'Humanité*, October 9, 1976.
72. Georges Marchais, "Socialism for France, a French Path to Socialism," *France Nouvelle*, January 20-26, 1975; conversely, Marchais had earlier declared that "Soviet military strength constitutes a safeguard for peace": *L'Humanité*, April 15, 1971.
73. Kanapa, op. cit., pp. 293-94, citing PCF declaration on the occasion of Secretary of State Henry Kissinger's visit to Paris, May 1976.
74. PCF Politburo statement, "In Favor of a Democratic Solution to the Army's Problems," *L'Humanité*, December 6, 1975.
75. Georges Marchais, report to the Central Committee, April 8, 1974, in *L'Humanité*, April 9, 1974.
76. See Michael M. Harrison, "A Socialist Foreign Policy for France?" *Orbis* 19, no. 4 (Winter 1976):1488.
77. James F. Clarity, "French Reds Shift Stand on Defense," New York *Times*, April 25, 1976.
78. *L'Humanité*, April 23, 1976.
79. "Georges Marchais on the 'l'Événement Program,'" *L'Humanité*, April 30, 1976.
80. *L'Humanité*, October 9, 1976.
81. Kanapa, op. cit., p. 292; first emphasis added.
82. See, in particular, speeches of Giscard d'Estaing and Chief of Staff General Méry at the Institute des Hautes Etudes de Défense Nationale, reprinted in *Le Monde*, June 4, 1976, and *Défense Nationale*, June 1976, respectively; see also P. J. Friedrich, "Defence and the French Political Left," *Survival*, July/August 1974; and Jean Klein, "France, NATO, and European Security," *International Security* 1, no. 3 (Winter 1977).
83. PCF Politburo member Guy Hermier, cited in "An Army: Why and How?" *L'Humanité*, February 27, 1975; see also PCF Politburo statements, *L'Humanité*, December 6 and 9, 1975; the PCF denied that it was involved in the unionization efforts among the military.
84. See Louis Baillot, "The Reinsertion of France into NATO is a Fact," *Le Monde*, May 2, 1975.

85. *L'Humanité,* December 6, 1975.

86. Jacques Isnard, "Revival of Political Agitation in the Barracks," *Le Monde,* November 7, 1975; *Le Figaro,* May 27, 1974, estimated that almost 50 percent of the military voted for the PS-PCF presidential candidate, François Mitterand, in the March 1974 presidential election because of their low morale and financial grievances; cited by Friedrich, op. cit., p. 171.

87. Georges Marchais, report to the Central Committee, *L'Humanité,* January 22, 1974.

88. Report based on notes by Claude Estier on François Mitterand's April 24-25 Moscow talks: "Nine Hours of Talks," *L'Unité,* May 2-8, 1975; see also Sue Ellen M. Charlton, "European Unity and the Politics of the French Left," *Orbis* 19, no. 4 (Winter 1976).

89. Rocard, op. cit., p. 558.

4

THE SOCIALIST STATE

The fundamental doctrinal innovation enunciated at the PCF 22nd party congress, the abandonment of the dictatorship of the proletariat, not only marked an important clarification of the party's position with respect to the advanced democratic transition state which would follow a leftist electoral victory. It also completed an important installment in the evolution of PCF doctrine on the future Socialist state, reconciling it with the party's shibboleth that socialism is the ultimate democracy. Although awkward vestigial references to proletarian dictatorship had gradually disappeared from the PCF lexicon, the proposal for its official expurgation lent credibility to the party's professions of respect for political pluralism and individual and collective liberty in a Socialist France.

The broad outlines of the PCF conception of the future French Socialist state have been publicized in such party documents as Marchais' book, *Le Défi démocratique,* and the important Declaration on Freedoms, issued in 1975. In contrast to the fairly specific blueprint for the transitional advanced democracy contained in the Common Program, however, the nature of the eventual Socialist state remains vague. What is certain, as the PCF frequently reminds the French public, is that the Common Program itself does not inaugurate socialism in France. Even less is said in PCF writings and statements about an ultimate construction of communism. As Marchais himself observed, "I seldom mention a Communist society—it is so far away...."[1]

PCF REJECTION OF THE SOVIET MODEL

Because the Soviet experience is inscribed in a particular historic context, the PCF asserts that it would be "absurd" to convert it into a binding model for the construction of socialism elsewhere.[2] This rejection of the Soviet model of socialism as unsuitable for the specific French traditions and contemporary conditions is an extension of the party's insistence on a uniquely French path *to* socialism. As Marchais proclaimed from the platform of the 22nd party congress, "An unquestionable diversity of Socialist reality already exists, and it would take the dishonesty of anticommunism to deny this. . . . There is not, nor can there be, a 'model' of socialism which can be transported from one country to another or which can be reproduced."[3] Moreover, he predicted, as the number of Socialist countries multiplies, the more pronounced the diversity will become. On other occasions Marchais has argued that more, not less, emphasis should be placed on such existing features of Socialist diversity as the contrast between the comprehensive agricultural collectivization in the Soviet Union and the very small collectivized sector in Poland. He has taken the Eastern European countries to task for their excessive adherance to the Soviet model and for not paying greater attention to the unique circumstances of their own Socialist construction. Just as it rejects the Soviet model, he has declared, the PCF also does not intend to "pour Socialist France . . . into the mold of . . . the peoples' democracies."[4]

The PCF has engaged in verbal sparring with the CPSU and its surrogates in the Eastern European Communist parties over the issue of the universal applicability of the Soviet model. PCF Politburo member Plissonnier, who headed the party's delegation to the CPSU 25th party congress, ostentatiously declared at a Moscow press conference that the party's abandonment of the dictatorship of the proletariat and its position on a specifically French form of socialism were not negotiable. Shortly thereafter, in direct refutation of a reported statement by the secretary general of the Czechoslovak Communist Party that "Soviet communism represents the best model of communism," the PCF issued a reminder of its opposition to the idea of universally valid models and, for added emphasis, reprinted three paragraphs from Marchais' 22nd congress speech on Socialist diversity.[5]

Perhaps in no area is there greater uncertainty in attempting to translate present words into future policy, however, than in the effort to extrapolate the characteristics of a putative future French Socialist state from what has been said about it by responsible PCF officials. Even the party's rejections of the Soviet model are often accompanied by praise for what it terms the positive aspects of Soviet-style socialism—greater mass participation in political and economic affairs, expansion of the powers of elected officials, economic growth, and a "permanent effort to develop the material conditions for the exercise of true liberty."[6] The negative features of the Soviet experience are explained as "difficulties and errors" due mainly to the unfavorable material and historical conditions under which socialism was established in the USSR, and the conclusion is reached that "an eminently positive balance sheet should not be eradicated or underestimated because of this."[7]

The problem is compounded by a deliberate PCF effort to project a nondoctrinaire image. "We have a living, flexible, inventive concept of the

Socialist system which we want for our country . . ." Marchais declared to the assemblage of party militants, and beyond them to the French electorate, from the rostrum of the 22nd party congress.[8] In considering PCF declaratory positions, therefore, it should naturally be borne in mind, first, that only the party's advent to power could confirm the degree of conformity with or divergence from Soviet and Eastern European models; and, second, that the characteristics of any actual French Socialist regime would reflect the correlation of political forces within the Left alliance at the time of its establishment.

SOCIALISM IN FRENCH COLORS

What, then, has the PCF said about the future Socialist society it advocates for France, which it calls *socialism aux couleurs de la France*?[9] It begins with the affirmation of the basic attributes of a Socialist state: collectivization of the principal means of production and exchange, exercise of political power by the working class, and the leading role of the Communist party. The implementation of these principles differentiates a Socialist country from the Social Democratic parties' conception of socialism, the PCF asserts, while at the same time providing opportunities for national innovation.

In a future French Socialist state, private ownership of both consumer and durable goods and the right of inheritance would continue. What the PCF advocates is not "collectivism" or "barracks communism," Marchais explained in his party congress speech. Taking account of "international experience," small-scale private ownership in commerce, industry, and agriculture —which makes it possible to better satisfy consumer demand—would persist. The various forms of social ownership would range from cooperative or municipal to national, and would enjoy considerable management autonomy. The PCF has also said, however, that "interested parties themselves will be able to introduce rapidly new and original forms of management,"[10] suggesting the kind of economic and social experimentation that frightens the middle class.

Political Pluralism in a Socialist France

Socialist France, the PCF asserts, will have "varied original forms of democratic life."[11] Parliament, elected by universal suffrage on the basis of proportional representation, will "become an effective tool of the will of the people and the nation." Elected officials at all levels will see their prerogatives enhanced. Religious freedom will be guaranteed, and there will be no official state philosophy. Unions will have increased rights and functions, and worker participation and control over elected officials will be encouraged. The practice of political pluralism will continue, including the existence of "several demo-

cratic parties" associated in the exercise of political power. Opposition parties
will be free to try to form a new majority and will enjoy the same access to
the media as the governing parties—corresponding to their influence in the
country. Only parties advocating violence will be proscribed. The PCF professes no concern about the consequences of guaranteeing the right of the
opposition to regain the majority legally because of its confidence in the
continuing popularity of the leftist government's policies. Yet the question of
the authenticity of the political pluralism the PCF intends is inevitably raised
by its exclusive reference to Eastern European examples. Moreover, its coop-
tion of the role of vanguard casts a shadow over its commitment to abide by
democratic norms of alternation in power. In the final analysis, how the PCF
would react if confronted by electoral defeat once socialism had been established in France can only be conjectured.

Of perhaps more relevance is the opposition's ability to muster sufficient
strength to challenge seriously the governing parties. The PCF believes that
mass mobilization and the use of the "democratic" power of the police and the
mass media would prevent reconquest of power by the bourgeoisie. The problem is not to deprive the reactionary minority of its freedom, Marchais declared at the 22nd party congress. "Will the reactionaries be able to organize
themselves into a reactionary party?" he rhetorically asked. "They are doing
so today: it will be nothing new," was the somewhat ambivalent answer. Given
the workers' extensive powers in industry, the access of their representatives
to the mass media, and the "democratization" of the police, however, they will
have "effective means of fighting against the economic sabotage of reaction."
Thus, the working people "will develop their struggle and force the big bourgeoisie into retreat and defeat. Supported by this broad struggle, Socialist
power will be in a position to make reaction respect the choices freely expressed by the vast majority of the people."[12]

It is important to stress that the PCF is in a period of profound evolution,
in which the 22nd party congress was a major benchmark but by no means
a final destination. One of the most revealing indicators of the direction of the
party's development was the June 1976 party rally in Paris attended by PCI
Secretary General Enrico Berlinguer, which marked a continuation of the
rapprochement between the two parties begun at their historic November 1975
meeting in Rome. In the joint declaration issued at the November meeting, as
well as in the speeches of the two parties' leaders on both occasions, the PCF's
alignment with the PCI on the fundamental issues of democratic pluralism,
alternation, and respect for individual liberty is pronounced (see Chapter 5).
This declaratory identification with the Italian positions, accompanied by an
increasing tendency to criticize Soviet practices, undoubtedly serves the party's
electoral strategy by projecting an image more compatible with Western European and specifically French conditions. It may also represent a sincere
commitment; yet similar statements by Eastern European Communists in the

early postwar period suggest that any judgment on this question would be premature.

Individual and Collective Liberty in a Socialist France

The PCF conception of French socialism envisages an expansion of the basic civil and religious liberties enjoyed by the French people, including freedom of speech, the press, and association. This commitment was spelled out in detail by Marchais at the June rally when he linked the PCF's policies with those of the Italian Communists, endorsing principles in obvious conflict with Soviet and Eastern European practices.

> Together we say: All the freedoms which our peoples have gained must be guaranteed, developed, and extended—be it a question of the freedom of thought and expression, publication, creation, assembly and association, the movement of people at home and abroad, and religious freedoms; be it, also, a question of pluralism, respect for universal suffrage and the possibility of democratic alternation and the independence of trade unions; or finally, be it a question of the development of the rights of workers in enterprises.[13]

In May 1975 the PCF issued its monumental Declaration of Freedoms, which it proposed be added as a preamble to the French constitution.[14] In this document the PCF sets forth in detail the basic freedoms essential for the implementation of the political and economic democracy to which it is committed. Many of the freedoms refer to economic issues, reflecting the PCF's tenet that political democracy is not complete without economic security. The 89 points include such collective rights as the guarantee of the existence of cooperatives and injunctions on democratic planning, as well as a guaranteed minimum wage for farmers. Individual rights such as freedom of speech and assembly, freedom from arbitrary arrest and imprisonment, and the right of habeas corpus are also spelled out. Torture, the use of hospital detention for political purposes, deprivation of citizenship, and the identification of party and state are specifically condemned. Such an enumeration constitutes the strongest possible implicit repudiation of Soviet practices; the fact that the PCF considered it necessary testifies to its continued sense of vulnerability on this issue.

PCF-CPSU DEBATE OVER SOCIALIST DEMOCRACY

The Soviets have shown increasing irritation over the efforts of the Western European Communist parties to devise alternative models of socialism. Articles excoriating "national models of socialism" and asserting the law-governed nature (*zakonomernost*) of the content of socialism appear with increasing frequency in the Soviet press. A typical article blamed "bourgeois ideologists and affiliated reformists and revisionists" for "highlighting the multiplicity of paths to socialism."[15] Some diversity in the paths to and construction of socialism is natural and acceptable, the Soviets assert, but this diversity is limited and temporary:". . . the quite tangible differences which sometimes extend beyond the framework of purely national characteristics constitute a temporary rather than a permanent factor of the new system and the fact that this system is still in the formative stage in a number of countries. Socialism's common features will be displayed increasingly graphically as it assumes its mature form."[16]

The Soviet delegate to the PCF 22nd party congress extolled existing socialism as a "treasure house" of "unquestionably great value" for all those seeking to build a new society. Speaking at a meeting of French workers and party members in the Paris suburb of Nanterre, Andrei Kirilenko declared, "The successes of socialism are an important external factor which promotes the achievement of new successes in the struggle of the working people in the capitalist countries. . . . The successes of real socialism serve as an inspiring stimulus for all peoples seeking social and national liberation."[17]

The PCF reacted angrily to this Soviet pressure. Referring to the emphasis on the general laws of socialism at the 25th CPSU party congress, Marchais retorted: "We are told that you cannot cut up socialism into national slices. I say that you do not build socialism by dogmatically repeating a quotation made some 15 or 20 years ago."[18]

Perhaps on no issue has the PCF crossed swords more frequently with its Soviet counterpart in recent times than that of liberty. The polemic has been surprisingly public, no doubt due in large part to the PCF's manipulation of the issue for domestic image-building purposes and the CPSU's great sensitivity in the wake of the Helsinki conference to criticisms of its treatment of Soviet citizens. The PCF campaign to focus attention on the issue of liberty as a means of asserting its independence from the CPSU was particularly intense in the period around the convening of its congress in February 1976. In his September 1975 critique of the Zarodov article published in *Pravda,* Chambaz seemed to go out of his way to reiterate the PCF's commitment to individual and collective freedoms, both in the advanced democracy and in a Socialist France.[19] The following month, the PCF seized on the issue of Soviet treatment of dissidents. Stating that the party had "long tried to get information" about the case of Soviet mathematician Leonid Plyushch, a *L'Humanité* editorial asserted that if it were true that he had been interned in a mental institution because of his dissident views, the PCF would express "total disapproval."[20] Then in mid-November 1975 PCF Politburo member Kanapan criticized the refusal of the Soviet authorities to grant Andrei Sakharov permission to travel to Sweden to collect his Nobel Peace Prize as an abridgment of the freedoms of travel and publication.[21]

A French television documentary on Soviet prison camps in December 1975 produced an immediate PCF Politburo communiqué describing conditions in the camps as "intolerable." Noting that "trials are in fact proceeding in the Soviet Union in which citizens are being prosecuted for their political beliefs," the statement continued:

> In these circumstances, the PCF Politburo declares that if the facts agreed with the pictures televised and if they were not publicly refuted by Soviet authorities, it would express its profound surprise and most formal reprobation. Such unjustifiable circumstances can only be harmful to socialism. . . . Furthermore, the PCF Politburo reaffirms that it opposes all repression affecting human rights, especially freedom of opinion, of expression, and of publication.[22]

On December 19, 1975, *Pravda* struck back, attacking those who had "objectively aided" anti-Sovietism by being taken in by the "crude falsification" of the television film.[23] Far from retreating, the PCF immediately counterattacked on several fronts. While it has always fought and will continue to fight anti-Sovietism, it declared, recourse to administrative measures and repression are incompatible with the democratic road to socialism the PCF pursues.[24] *L'Humanité* editor René Andrieu followed with the next salvo:

> . . . even though we are aware of the Socialist countries' immense contribution to the progress of history and of the need to insure the workers' solidarity throughout the world, we are not prepared to approve blindly of everything that takes place in the Socialist countries. Let us repeat—for this does not seem unnecessary—that as far as we are concerned, there exists no Socialist model which it would suffice to copy mechanically. Especially when errors are involved.[25]

This position is not merely tactical, Andrieu added, nor is it adopted for opportunistic reasons aimed at fostering a more credible image; it is a matter of consistently followed PCF principles.

At the time of this exchange over the Soviet prison camps, PCF Secretary General Marchais was attending the first congress of the Cuban Communist party, where he presumably heard CPSU hard-line theoretician Suslov expound on the necessary unity of all revolutionaries on the basis of Marxist-Leninist doctrine. While in Havana, Marchais fully endorsed the Politburo's stand on the camps and Andrieu's rebuttal of *Pravda*.[26] On his return he further animated the controversy by declaring: "Socialism is synonymous with liberty. This idea is valid in all countries, under all circumstances. . . . There is a divergence between us and the CPSU with regard to Socialist democracy."[27]

Marchais renewed his criticism of Soviet repression in his opening address to the PCF party congress, specifically naming the USSR as the target of his attack. In an angry reply. Soviet delegate Kirilenko assailed the campaign "in defense of human rights" in the Socialist countries being waged—he said—by the "reactionary press."[28] As a testimony of the depth of the PCF-CPSU breach, Marchais did not attend the CPSU 25th party congress later that month. His replacement, Politburo member Plissonnier, pointedly reminded the delegates that the PCF's commitment to "see democracy through to the end," that is, to socialism, "implies a guarantee for all individual and collective freedoms."[29]

The internecine conflict was again ignited by the appearance of PCF Central Committee member Pierre Juquin at a meeting of the French Com- mitte of Mathematicians, a lobby which had been instrumental in gaining the release of the interned matematician Plyushch. Juquin's speech infuriated the USSR by coupling a call for the release of dissidents imprisoned in the Soviet Union and Czechechoslovakia to a plea on behalf of those interned in several Latin American nations. "We will never accept that, in whatever country it may be, people resort in the name of socialism to methods which infringe the rights of the individual," Juquin declared.[30] In a scathing denunciation of the "anti-Sovietism" exhibited by the participants in the meeting, a Soviet writer declared:

> ... it is difficult to understand why representatives of the French Communist Party were among the participants in the meeting. . . . It is perfectly self- evident that, whatever considerations guided them, the PCF representative's speech . . . rendered a service to reactionary forces organically hostile to the ideals of freedom, democracy, international detente, and socialism, for whose implementation the party of the French working class has always struggled.[31]

The PCF rejected the Soviet complaint and ordered seven million copies of Juquin's speech printed for general distribution to call attention to the party's struggle for liberty.

As the PCF has come to take its right to criticize internal Soviet affairs for granted, it has also grown intolerant of Soviet and Eastern European attempts to suppress such criticism. Thus, when CPSU Central Committee member Ponomarev chastized "bourgeois propaganda" for undermining the Communist parties' ties with the masses in capitalist countries by "weakening the magnetic forces of socialism," Kanapa retorted that it is the existence of Socialist shortcomings and not PCF criticism of them that weakens socialism's appeal.[32] Reflecting the party's sensitivity to the domestic ramifications of the issue of liberty in the USSR and Eastern Europe, Kanapa asserted:

> We . . . cannot let people believe that it [socialism] would tolerate repressive measures against either freedom of opinion and expression, or freedom of artistic creation or freedom of movement of people. Whenever we can ob-

> serve the continuance of such measures in any Socialist country, we say that
> there is . . . a very serious difference of opinion between ourselves and the
> Communist party of the country concerned with respect to the question of
> democracy and the question of socialism. . . .[33]

Because of the "continuing deficiencies in the democratic progress of several
Socialist countries," Kanapa continued, the PCF is obliged to differentiate its
own objective by the appellation "democratic" socialism.

Kanapa also expressed the PCF's indignation at the circulation in France
of an article by Czechoslovak Communist official Alois Indra which unfavor-
ably compared elections in capitalist countries with those in Socialist regimes.
Indra's offering the Czechoslovak electoral system as an exemplary model, he
declared, shows that a "profound political disagreement exists in this
sphere. . . ."[34] On January 25, 1977 the PCF Politburo issued a communiqué
condemning the actions of Czechoslovak party and government authorities
with respect to the signatories of a human rights declaration known as Charter
77:

> We cannot regard the exercise of the right of petition, the dissemination of
> pamphlets, and a demand for dialogue as offenses. . . . We cannot permit
> practices which imply that with socialism any discordant voice would be
> condemned either to silence or to repression. The French Communists cate-
> gorically exclude these attacks on individual and collective rights and free-
> doms. . . . They declare them to be alien to the ideal of socialism.[35]

The PCF also bitterly condemned the banishment of Soviet dissident Vladimir
Bukovskiy in exchange for the imprisoned Chilean Communist leader Corvalan. The party "considers it intolerable that a man struggling for ideas which
he regards as just should be faced with the intolerable alternative of prison or
exile," the Politburo communiqué declared.[36] Respect for the principles on
which socialism is based, it added, would avoid situations permitting "the class
enemy" to equate the actions of a Socialist country with the practices of a
fascist one. At a January 7 press conference, Marchais again assailed repression in the Soviet Union, and refused to back down from the Politburo's
statement.

The Soviets have suggested that Western European Communists who
criticize the Soviet Union are actually harming their own efforts to raise the
political consciousness of the masses. The fact that certain people who favor
socialism are taken in by the "totally fabricated yarns" in films and articles
by "unconscientious 'eye-witnesses' " merely testifies to their own naïveté and
ignorance of the real situation in the USSR, a *Pravda* author charged.[37]

A comparison of Soviet and Eastern European constitutional guarantees
with actual practice in the areas of political pluralism and protection of rights
would obviously raise more questions than can be answered about future PCF

behavior. The basic Leninist premise that there is no democracy in general, but only bourgeois or Socialist democracy, obviously colors such words as "pluralism" and "liberty." As Soviet Politburo member Kirilenko assured his audience of French Communists: "The laws of the Socialist state clearly define and guarantee such rights of the individual as the freedom of speech, press, and assembly, the freedom of conscience and religion, and the inviolability of the individual and home."[38] The Soviets readily acknowledge that their system does not recognize pluralism in the Western sense, that it does not allow "freedom of action for reactionary forces hostile to socialism."[39] In the present world which is divided into antagonistic classes, the Soviets assert, "there is no extraclass democracy, no extraclass freedom . . ." and the state "punishes enemies of the Socialist revolution."[40] This reasoning is exemplified by the explanation of freedom of the press in a Soviet brochure on the rights and duties of Soviet citizens: "From the very first days of its existence, the Soviet state took away from the bourgeoisie and turned over to the working people the printshops and stocks of newsprint, thereby effectively securing freedom of the press."[41]

The issue of liberty remains one of the PCF's greatest domestic vulnerabilities. Commenting on the Soviets' treatment of Alexander Solzhenitsyn, French Communist dissident Pierre Daix, who charged that Soviet pressure had forced the closing of his journal, *Les Lettres français,* declared that freedom of the press would not survive long in France either if the PCF came to power.[42] Yet there are few relevant examples of PCF behavior that can serve as guideposts to the party's likely future behavior with respect to democratic rights if socialism were established in France. For the most part, one must rely on frustratingly inadequate present words to provide clues to future actions.

One exception, which should not be overlooked despite being dated and not entirely analagous to a potential French situation, concerns PCF actions in the unfolding drama of the Dubcek regime. In July 1968, it will be recalled, a PCF delegation headed by Secretary General Rochet traveled to Prague in an effort to convince the Czechoslovak Communists to curtail the domestic liberalization that was threatening to cause an irreparable breach between themselves and the CPSU. The essence of the PCF message was that opposition activities permitted by the Dubcek regime in the name of freedom of the press and abolition of censorship were not being countered with sufficient forcefulness by the Czechoslovak Communist Party, thereby risking a "shift to the right which could endanger socialism. . . ."[43] With so much "democratization," Rochet warned, noncommunists hostile to socialism were free to deny the party its leading role and attack its policies. "Certainly, we understand well that with freedom of the press, noncommunist journals can publish things which are erroneous," he declared. The solution was a reassertion of strong party control over its own information media and the waging of an active struggle against the antisocialist forces: "That is why there are the party press, trade unions, and also the state radio to provide an answer in a fundamental way, so that these false ideas would be refuted and would not be able to influence the masses," Rochet asserted.

Thus, doubt persists whether to give more credence to PCF behavior of a decade past when confronted with the possibility of the overthrow (or even transformation) of established socialism, or to current verbal assurances which totally contradict that past behavior.

NOTES

1. "Georges Marchais on the 'L'Événement Program," *L'Humanité*, April 30, 1976.

2. Georges Marchais, *Le Défi démocratique* (Paris: Grasset, 1973), p. 127.

3. *L'Humanité*, February 5, 1976.

4. Georges Marchais, report to the PCF Central Committee, *L'Humanité*, May 29, 1975.

5. *L'Humanité*, March 17, 1976. The PCF also polemicized with the Hungarian Communist party over assertions by its Politburo member Dezso Nemes (*Problemy Mira i Sotsializma*, September 1976), that the East European model—and particularly the dictatorship of the proletariat—is universally valid; see Jean Kanapa, "Socialism: The Past Does not Have the Answer for Everything," *France nouvelle*, October 5, 1976.

6. Marchais, *Le Défi démocratique*, p. 127. Marchais also wrote that the Soviet worker is "much more free than his French comrade" because he does not have to worry about unemployment, sickness, or the education of his children (p. 163).

7. Georges Marchais, "Socialism for France, A French Path to Socialism, *France nouvelle* January 13-19, 1975.

8. *L'Humanité*. February 5, 1976.

9. Marchais, *Le Défi démocratique*, p. 180. According to PCF Politburo member Kanapa, when Gaston Plissonnier referred to "socialism in French colors" at the CPSU 25th party congress, it caused "something of a stir" (Agence France Presse, February 28, 1976). Marchais has also stated that communism, when it comes "in the distant future," will also be a "French communism."

10. Marchais, "Socialism for France."

11. Ibid.

12. *L'Humanité*, February 6, 1976.

13. Georges Marchais, "Change: The Big Question on the Agenda," *L'Humanite*, June 4, 1976. Marchais, however, did not go as far as his Italian counterpart at this rally in specifically criticizing Soviet and Eastern European socialism; cf. Enrico Berlinguer's speech, "For a Democratic Alternative to the Crisis," *L'Humanité*, June 4, 1976.

14. *L'Humanité*, May 16, 1975.

15. G. Shakhnazarov, "The Socialist Future of Mankind," *Pravda*, July 23, 1976.

16. Ibid.; see also P. N. Fedosesv, "Urgent Problems of the Social Sciences," *Kommunist*, 1975, no. 5; and A. I. Sobolev. "The Dialectic of the General and the Particular in the Development of the World Revolutionary Process," *Voprosy Istorii KPSS*, 1975, no. 11.

17. "A Demonstration of Solidarity," *Pravda*, February 7, 1976.

18. *Le Figaro*, February 28-29, 1976.

19. Jacques Chambaz, "Words and Facts," *L'Humanité*, September 4, 1975.

20. Reported by Kevin Devlin, "The PCF's Turning-Point Congress," Radio Free Europe Report, February 4, 1976. After pressure from the French, Italian, and British Communist parties, Plyushch was released.

21. *L'Humanité,* November 13, 1975.

22. *L'Humanité,* December 13, 1975.

23. V. Alekseyev, "A Crude Falsification," *Pravda,* December 19, 1975.

24. *L'Humanité,* December 20, 1975.

25. René Andrieu, "A Question of Principle," *L'Humanité,* December 22, 1975.

26. *L'Humanité,* December 27, 1975.

27. *Le Monde,* January 9, 1976.

28. "A Demonstration of Solidarity," *Pravda,* op. cit.

29. Moscow broadcast in French to Europe, February 28, 1976.

30. *L'Humanité,* October 22, 1976.

31. Grigoriy Kozlov, "Provocation at 'La Mutualité,' " *Literaturnaya Gazeta,* October 27, 1976.

32. Ponomarav, "The International Significance of the Berlin Conference," *Kommunist,* July 1976, no. 11; and Kanapa, in *France nouvelle,* October 18, 1976, cited by *Le Monde,* October 20, 1976.

33. Kanapa, ibid.

34. The article, which appeared in *Temps nouveaux,* 1976, no. 38, was also published in the corresponding *New Times,* the English-language version of the Soviet Journal, under the title "Democracy of a Higher Type." The PCF harbors no fondness for Indra since his revelation in January 1970 that a PCF delegation to Prague in November 1969 had handed over to Czechoslovak party leaders the minutes of Rochet's July 1968 meeting with Dubcek, an action that proved to be highly embarrassing to the PCF.

35. *L'Humanité,* January 25, 1977.

36. *L'Humanité,* December 20, 1976. The PCF also criticized the East German regime for depriving protest singer Wolf Biermann of his citizenship after allowing him to leave the country.

37. I. Alexandrov, "On Genuine and Imaginary Freedoms," *Pravda,* February 20, 1976. But the harshest criticism was reserved for PCF historian Jean Ellenstein for accusing the Soviet Union in his book *Le PC—Le Parti communists* of violations of democracy, suppression of freedom, and repression of dissidents; Yu. Sedov, "Falsification instead of Objective Study," *New Times,* January 1977, no. 5.

38. "A Demonstration of Solidarity," *Pravda,* February 7, 1976.

39. Vadim Zagladin, "Architect of a New Civilization," *New Times,* 1976, no. 18.

40. Zagladin, "Portugal—the Poetry and Prose of Revolution," *Za Rubezhom,* 1976, no. 48.

41. V. Koldayev, *Soviet Citizens: Their Rights and Duties* (Moscow: Novosti Press Agency Publishing House, 1976), p. 42.

42. *Le Nouvel Observateur,* May 28, and July 14, 1973.

43. Report based on notes taken by PCF Politburo member Jean Kanapa, *Politique aujourd-'hui,* May 1970.

CHAPTER

5

PROLETARIAN
INTERNATIONALISM

As noted in the previous chapters, the PCF-CPSU doctrinal disputes over strategy and tactics for coming to power and conception of the future French society stem from the PCF's deliberate projection of an image of autonomy from Soviet control, dating from its disapproval of the invasion of Czechoslovakia in August 1968. The decision to support Mitterand in the 1965 presidential election (despite the Soviets' preference for General de Gaulle) and *L'Humanité*'s publication of a protest against the trials of Soviet writers Sinyavsky and Daniel in 1966, while significant earlier exceptions to the PCF's customary unconditional fealty to the CPSU, did not in themselves constitute such a decisive watershed in the relationship. After August 1968, however, the PCF—at one time the most loyal of the Western European parties—reserved the right to criticize any domestically embarrassing aspects of the practice of socialism in the Soviet Union and Eastern Europe. This reservation of the right of critical judgment inevitably came into conflict with the Soviets' equation of solidarity within the international Communist movement with unconditional support for the fountainhead of communism itself as a fundamental requirement of proletarian internationalism.

PCF NATIONALIZATION OF PROLETARIAN
INTERNATIONALISM

Unlike its unceremonious shedding of the dictatorship of the proletariat, the PCF has not relegated proletarian internationalism to the dustheap of antiquity. Disavowal of this fundamental Marxist-Leninist doctrine would isolate the party from its historical and ideological heritage and the support it receives from identification with an international movement it believes to be on the ascendant worldwide, as well as alienate many of its own pro-Soviet militants. Rather, through deliberate selective practice, it has transformed and

103

"nationalized" proletarian internationalism, tailoring a kind of proletarian internationalism "in French colors." This has involved an uneasy delineation by both the PCF and the CPSU of the boundaries of permissible deviation, increasingly strained by the PCF's insistence on expanding the scope of its autonomy and the CPSU's perceived need to restrict it. The heretical assertion of the primacy of the national over the international is, of course, not a new phenomenon for the international Communist movement. What is new is the recent addition of the PCF to the ranks of such "autonomists" as the Yugoslavs and Romanians among the ruling parties, and the Italians, Spanish, British, and Japanese among the nonruling parties.

A clear-cut division between autonomists and loyalists is actually too rigid to account accurately for the complexity of the crosscutting issues that confront the international Communist movement. No party better illustrates the necessity for this caveat than the PCF, whose basic support of CPSU foreign policy (see Chapter 6) contrasts with its disagreements over the construction of socialism. For if the insistence on party autonomy can be regarded as detracting from proletarian internationalism, PCF practice also emphasizes features which, it believes, reinforce it. As PCF Politburo member Plissonnier declared at the 25th congress of the CPSU: "The close links of brotherhood and solidarity which unite the PCF and the CPSU, steeled in difficult trials, are based on the two indissociable principles of proletarian internationalism and independence."[1] The PCF denies any weakening of solidarity with other communist parties, frequently praises the economic achievements and foreign policy of the USSR, and vigorously condemns anti-Sovietism. PCF spokesmen readily profess the party's support for all national-liberation forces, illustrated by its campaigns in the early 1970s in behalf of the "anti-imperialists" in Vietnam and the anti-Francoists in Spain. Significantly, however, the PCF advocates the establishment of new forms of interparty relationships, which it exemplifies by forging closer ties with European parties of similar disposition. Lest there be any doubt that its version of "international solidarity" represents a break with its past docility, however, Marchais has made it clear that the party "cannot adopt a formula used a long time ago under completely different conditions and according to which support for anything pertaining to the Soviet Union is the touchstone of internationalism."[2] And the PCF demands that the solidarity be reciprocal, involving commitments and obligations on the part of the ruling as well as the nonruling parties, the neglect of which will no longer be endured in silence.

PCF INSISTENCE ON PARTY AUTONOMY VERSUS CPSU EMPHASIS ON UNITY

The PCF is no stranger to verbal declarations of party autonomy, although a skeptic questioning the sincerity of the party's professions of independence can validly point out that Thorez' famous 1946 statement about national paths to socialism did not presage an immediate alignment with the PCI when Palmiro Togliatti proclaimed his doctrine of polycentrism a decade later. However, one can say that Marchais' syllogism in 1968 that there is neither one single nor several heads of the international Communist movement— which at the time represented primarily an attempt to circumvent a direct confrontation with the Chinese—did correctly indicate the evolution in party policy, which the events of August 1968 brought to the fore. As PCF Central Committee member Billoux commented on the PCF's reaction to the invasion of Czechoslovakia, the party's "unconditional attachment" to the CPSU, which had been an historical necessity, had already been refined to a "conditional attachment based on the PCF's own critical judgment."[3]

The insistence on party autonomy concerns above all the independent elaboration of the path to and the form of socialism in France. The PCF has gone so far as to contend that the greatest contribution it can make to internationalism is successfully to implement its program leading to the establishment of its own style of socialism in France. As Politburo member and Central Committee secretary Laurent declared to the assemblage of foreign party delegates at the PCF's 22nd party congress, ". . . we feel deeply that it is primarily by advancing on the democratic path to socialism in our own country, preparing the victory of a specifically French socialism and taking full responsibility for all aspects of the policy . . . that our party will make its essential contribution to the implementation of genuine internationalism."[4] Thus, it is the coupling of the demand for autonomy, equality, and noninterference in the party's internal affairs with the intention to continue criticizing Socialist regimes that constitutes the crux of the PCF's challenge to Soviet authority.

The Soviets' consternation over the increasing centrifugal tendencies in the international Communist movement is evident in the vigor of their reassertion of their leadership role. This has typically been expressed in a summons to "fidelity to proletarian internationalism," any deviation from which, "irrespective of the form it takes," is said to be "fraught with serious failures for revolutionaries."[5] Correct practice of proletarian internationalism, the Soviets make clear, includes recognition of the USSR as primus inter pares in the international Communist movement.

Writing in the pivotal period of preparations for the PCF 22nd party congress, a *Pravda* commentator seemed to suggest that those European communists who were advocating independent policies were inadvertent agents of imperialism. After pointedly praising by name those communist parties which follow the correct proletarian internationalist line, he called on the errant parties to mend their ways. Implying a kind of doctrine of "limited sovereignty" for communist parties, he approvingly cited the statement of the Norwegian Communist Party chairman that Norwegian Communists "consider it their duty to heed the opinion of fraternal parties . . . when something we do seems wrong to them." Criticizing Soviet practices, the author suggested, means adding "grist to the mill of anti-Sovietism and anticommunism," and is therefore incompatible with proletarian internationalism. The several forthcoming Communist party congresses, he declared, would provide a timely opportunity to "raise still higher the banner of proletarian internationalism. . . ."[6] Ironically, the banner under which the first of those congresses was held proclaimed not proletarian internationalism but "A Democratic Path to Socialism—a Socialism for France."

The Soviets would have liked the public disagreements over strategy and tactics, not to mention the public criticisms of the Soviet system, which underlie the argument over fidelity to proletarian internationalism, to terminate with the enunciation of the official Soviet position at the 25th CPSU party congress, if not before. Brezhnev's affirmation of the necessity of unqualified support for proletarian internationalism is unequivocal.

> We should like to place special emphasis on the importance of proletarian internationalism in our time. . . . to renounce proletarian internationalism is to deprive Communist parties and the working class movement of a mighty and tested weapon. It would work in favor of the class enemy who . . . actively coordinates anticommunist activity on an international scale. We Soviet Communists consider defense of proletarian internationalism the sacred duty of every Marxist-Leninist.[7]

Paradoxically, the Soviets' predicament derives from the fact that some of the nonruling Communist parties are taking too literally the pledges of party autonomy which have been inscribed in the documents of the international Communist movement since Khrushchev's pathbreaking June 1955 agreement with Tito guaranteeing noninterference in other parties' affairs.[8] Among the subsequent official meetings issuing statements pledging respect for party equality and autonomy the following stand out: the 21st CPSU party congress in 1959, which declared that "there are 'superior' and 'subordinate' parties in the Communist movement"; the 23rd CPSU congress in 1966, which asserted that "the CPSU is against any hegemonism in the Communist movement and for genuinely internationalist equal relations among all parties"; and the June 1969 International Conference of Communist and Workers' Parties, which affirmed that "all parties have equal rights" and "there is no leading center of the international movement. . . ."[9]

For the Soviets, independence and proletarian internationalism are merely two sides of the same coin, and the autonomist parties have been pushing party independence beyond the acceptable limits. What the founders of Marxism-Leninism meant when speaking about the independence of Communists, the CPSU Central Committee journal declared, was "independence from class enemies, from opportunists and revisionists of all hues." In other words, "the independence and autonomy of Marxist-Leninist parties ... is expressed in their independently drawn policies directed toward defending the interests of each detachment of the working class ... and toward developing to the utmost cooperation between Communists the world over."[10] To the Soviets, therefore, the PCF's insistence on its right to criticize certain aspects of existing socialism and to elaborate its own model of socialism constitutes a breach of proletarian internationalism. In a hard-hitting speech delivered to the 1976 meeting of the Soviet Academy of Sciences, party ideologue Suslov reiterated the CPSU's rejection of "everything the opportunists present as some 'regional' or 'national' versions of Marxism [which] have nothing in common with revolutionary theory and do harm to the cause of the working class."[11] Thus, behind the Soviets' attacks on bourgeois Socialist theoreticians and such critics as ex-PCF member Garaudy for espousing "nationalistic corruptions of Marxism" designed to drive a wedge between the Communist parties in Socialist and capitalist countries, is an unmistakable warning to the leaders of the wayward parties, whose heresies are far more portentous for international communism, not to push the limits of divergence too far.[12]

CONDEMNATION OF ANTI-SOVIETISM

The PCF's practice of proletarian internationalism includes vigorous opposition to criticism of the Soviet Union that it considers unwarranted. This visceral defense of the first Socialist country persists despite the party's own increasing tendency to criticize individual features of the socialist regimes. As French publicist André Wurmser succinctly stated in an article published in *Pravda*, "... there is no genuine Communist party in the West which, irrespective of its views about this or that aspect of Soviet life, can tolerate any form of anti-Sovietism whatever."[13] The party's rationale for this stance is well illustrated by the expression of loyalty articulated by the PCF representative on the international Communist journal, *World Marxist Review:* "We are aware that it is thanks to the existence, development, and influence of the Socialist countries that we can elaborate our advance to socialism in France along the democratic way. We shall strive to develop that solidarity and resolutely oppose anti-Sovietism and the lies and slanders to which the Socialist countries are constantly subjected."[14]

The combination of criticism of Soviet repression with vigorous attacks on anti-Sovietism has created the impression of opportunistic pandering to two constituencies with conflicting demands—the domestic and the international. The PCF retreat from its original harsh criticism of the Soviet-led action in Czechoslovakia is a case in point. Another example is the party's reaction to the Leningrad trial of accused Jewish hijackers in 1970. While questioning the holding of the trial behind closed doors and the imposition of the death penalty for the abortive attempt, the PCF nonetheless condemned the "strident anti-Soviet campaign launched primarily by Zionist circles."[15] And it dismissed the charges of Soviet anti-Semitism as unsubstantiated, since, it observed, "racism" is proscribed by Soviet law.

One of the most sustained PCF campaigns against anti-Sovietism coincided with the publication of Solzhenitsyn's book *The Gulag Archipelago* at the end of 1973. Solzhenitsyn's receipt of the Nobel prize in 1970 had elicited from the PCF an expression of hope that the Soviets would eventually permit publication of his works in the USSR. While reaffirming the party's position on freedom of the press in a Socialist France, Marchais said that what was at issue was not freedom of creative expression but a "book so manifestly at variance with the laws and sensibilities of the Soviet people."[16]

Such PCF knee-jerk defensiveness regarding the Soviet Union contributes to the impression of a dual standard: only criticism of the USSR by those whose fundamental loyalty is above question (that is, the PCF itself) is permissible. Criticism from other sources, be they French Socialists or Chinese Communists, is denounced. The PCF has undeviatingly taken the Soviet side in the Sino-Soviet dispute, accusing the Chinese of nationalism and of "playing the game of imperialism."[17] As a consequence of the absence of party-to-party relations with the PCF, the Chinese Communists have gone so far as to deny entry to French Communist deputies who were to participate in French parliamentary delegation visits to China in 1971 and 1974, and to refuse a visa to the *L'Humanité* correspondent assigned to cover the visit of French President Pompidou to Peking in 1973. Following Pompidou's visit, the PCF charged that the Franco-Chinese communiqué demonstrated that Peking, because of its "anti-Sovietism carried to absurdity," shared the French government's desire for a political and military coalition of European capitalist states.[18] Speaking to the Brussels meeting of European Communist parties in 1974, Marchais declared that the Chinese Communist Party's support for the transformation of the EEC into an "expanded Atlantic Alliance" testified to its "desertion of the principles of proletarian internationalism."[19]

The PCF's own coming of age as a proponent of party autonomy, however, has been reflected in growing opposition to formally excommunicating the Chinese. This evolution in the PCF attitude was responsible for its decreasing enthusiasm for the Soviet proposal to use a world Communist conference as a forum for reading the Chinese Communists out of the international Communist movement, which would have enhanced the Soviets' ability to impose their orthodoxy on the other independent-minded parties.

The death of Chinese Communist Party Chairman Mao Tse-tung provided additional evidence that the PCF, along with other "autonomist" parties, has increasingly come to regard the Sino-Soviet schism as an asset with respect to its own freedom of maneuver. Marchais referred to Mao as "one of history's greatest figures," whose death evoked feelings of "sadness and respect." Continuing the conciliatory tone, he recalled the PRC's accomplishments under Mao, and added: "Whatever the problems that have divided us, concerning inter alia the very concept of socialism, no French Communist can forget or neglect this prodigious achievement."[20] In its condolence message the PCF Central Committee stated that it "profoundly regretted" that the "grave divergences" that had arisen between the two parties over international problems and the concept of socialism had "changed our relations"; this was not the PCF's doing nor its desire, the statement declared.[21] The PCF accepted the Chinese Communist Party's rejection of this message with notable restraint, a further indication that any overtures to Peking are primarily motivated by a desire to reinforce its own autonomy.[22] Although the PCF expressed the hope for more friendly relations in the future, an indication of the unlikelihood of any rapprochement was the Chinese decision in late 1976 to receive representatives of the small group of French Maoists, who are a constant source of criticism of the PCF from the extreme Left.

TOWARD A EUROPE OF THE WORKERS

A marked upsurge in the PCF's interaction with other Communist parties of the European capitalist nations has accompanied its emergence from its domestic ghetto and the shadow of the CPSU. Carrying out its policy of seeking new and more effective forms of interparty relations, it has systematically engaged in bilateral contacts and promoted increased coordination of the activities of the Western European Communist parties. At the same time, it has spearheaded an effort to apply its own alliance strategy to the European arena, urging the exploitation of areas of agreement with Socialists and Christians in a common effort to replace the present "monopoly-dominated" Europe with a "Europe of the workers."

The PCF's growing sense of regional identification was apparent in the foreign policy report presented at its Central Committee meeting in May 1973, in which it asserted that the time was ripe "to seize the initiative with a view to developing the unity of class struggles on the scale of capitalist Europe."[23] Previously there had been several regional conferences of Western European Communist parties, including those in Brussels in June 1965 and Vienna in 1966; two meetings of "solidarity with the Indochinese peoples" jointly sponsored by the PCF and PCI in Paris and Naples in 1970; and a 1971 parley on united antimonopoly action in London. But the real impetus for joint action by the Communist parties within the Western European context was provided by the January 1974 Brussels conference of Communist parties of the European capitalist countries.

Declaring that such a convocation "could not be more opportune or more necessary under the present situation" of the crisis of European capitalism, Marchais applauded the moves toward coordinated European trade union action, and expressed the PCF's readiness to open a dialogue with Socialist and Christian forces. The PCF does not spurn European solidarity, Marchais told the conference participants; but the solidarity it seeks is the joint struggle of the "working people and democrats against the policy of big capital which assails them in the same way throughout Western Europe." Strengthening the unity of the Communist parties of capitalist Europe contributes to strengthening the unity of the international Communist movement, he said. And the PCF, he concluded, while highly aware of its national responsibilities, considers the implementation of proletarian internationalism in all circumstances to be the condition of its own success.[24]

Summing up the party's position on Europe in the light of the Brussels conference, foreign policy expert Kanapa declared:

> For years now our country's grand bourgeoisie has tried to make believe that only one Europe was possible—the Europe of the monopolies, the Europe of blócs, including military blocs, the Europe of a Common Market subjected to the law of big capital. The greatest merit of the Brussels conference is to make perfectly credible in the eyes of the great masses that another Europe is possible and that it is necessary. . . . a democratic, peaceful, and independent Europe: the Europe of the workers.[25]

The role of the PCF as a catalyst for unity among the Western European parties was highlighted by the attendance of leaders of six of the participating parties at a follow-up conference in Lyons in March 1974 and at a working session attended by representatives of 13 parties at PCF headquarters in Paris in December 1975.

While the PCF's activities have become increasingly Eurocentric, it denies that it is pursuing a policy of European exclusivism, and pointedly eschews the term "Eurocommunism." Proletarian internationalism is "indivisible," Marchais asserted in his 22nd party congress address. "We would no more recognize any form of internationalism superior to it than we would want to see it carved up into regional slices," he affirmed.[26]

The avoidance of the term "Eurocommunism" and the continued use of "proletarian internationalism" are two superficial differences between the PCF and the European party with which it has become most closely aligned, the Communist Party of Italy (PCI). This alignment is one of the most striking phenomena in the evolution of the PCF during the period under review, since the two parties had traditionally represented opposite poles of Western European communism—the PCF upholding the CPSU's unitary policies in the face of PCI advocacy of autonomy and polycentrism.[27]

Even after the PCF had abandoned its posture of uncritical support for the Soviet Union and placed its alliance strategy at the top of its list of priorities, differences in strategy, tactics, and attitude toward international communism remained. The two parties disagreed over the normalization in Czechoslovakia and over Communist tactics in Portugal. With respect to domestic strategy, the compromesso storico advocated by the PCI calls for Communists to enter the bourgeois government led by the Christian Democrats, while the PCF has consistently attacked its own Socialist allies for harboring precisely such "collaborationist" aspirations.[28] For a long time the two parties also differed in their positions on European unity. A meeting between Marchais and the Italian party leadership in Rome in May 1973, however, produced an important shift in the PCF approach, bringing its position more into line with that of the PCI. Together they appealed for the elaboration of a common policy on European questions by Communists, Socialists, leftist Catholics, and other "democratic" forces, aimed at "democratizing" the European community from within, and at fostering closer EEC cooperation with the Socialist countries. Following the meeting, the PCF also announced a reversal of its policy of nonparticipation in the European Parliament, joining the PCI which had been represented in the EEC since 1970.

On the key issues of acceptance of political pluralism, alternation in power, and advancement toward socialism via extension of democracy and liberty, the positions advocated by the PCF coincide with those long espoused by the PCI. This convergence of views was dramatically documented in a joint statement issued by the two parties culminating a series of discussions in the fall of 1975. In this statement, which Marchais said provided "the basis for an unprecedented development of their fraternal cooperation," the two parties strongly affirmed their commitment to work toward the building of a Socialist society "within the framework of a continuous democratization of economic, social, and political life."[29]

The statement pledged their guarantee of freedom of thought and expression, the press, assembly and association; freedom to demonstrate, to travel at home and abroad; the inviolability of private life, religious liberty, and "the complete freedom of expression of currents of thought and of every philosophical, cultural, and artistic freedom." It endorsed political pluralism, democratic alternation in power, the rights of opposition parties, and the independence of the judiciary. It reaffirmed the two parties' commitment to implement the decisions of the Brussels conference, and reiterated their intention to work to unite all the leftist forces in Europe in support of democratic transformation of the EEC. With respect to foreign policy, the two parties endorsed detente, with the proviso that peaceful coexistence does not mean preservation of the social and political status quo, but rather provides the most favorable conditions "for the struggle against imperialism and for democracy and socialism." Declaring themselves "opposed to all acts of foreign interference" (i.e., Soviet as well as U.S.), they pledged to work for arms reduction and eventual disarmament and dissolution of military blocs. Finally, "confirming the principles of the autonomy of every party, of respect and nonintervention and of internationalism," the PCF and PCI expressed their intention to further strengthen their fraternal cooperation. Emphasizing the significance of the statement, Marchais declared that, "far from being a tactical agreement of limited importance, this is a fundamental agreement" which could serve as a catalyst for joint action among all Communist parties and progressive democratic forces.

At a mass rally in Paris organized by the PCF in June 1976 as a public demonstration of its rapprochement with the PCI, Marchais and PCI Secretary General Berlinguer reaffirmed their basic agreement on the substantive issues of strategy and tactics, the pluralistic nature of an eventual Socialist society, and party autonomy.[30] Their speeches also revealed interesting differences in approach. While Berlinguer used the occasion to criticize the practice of socialism in the Soviet Union and Eastern Europe, for example, Marchais chose not to mention it. For his part, Marchais spoke directly of the PCF's deep attachment to proletarian internationalism, while Berlinguer spoke of "Eurocommunism" and referred more abstractly to the "international spirit" that motivates the PCI's support for the global national-liberation struggle. Berlinguer also noted that the PCI does not "call into question" Italy's continued membership in NATO, while Marchais excoriated the Giscard government for reintegrating France into the NATO military structure. And Marchais significantly modified the thrust of the November declaration by adding to its expressed opposition to "all" foreign interference (which Berlinguer repeated verbatim) a specific injunction against intervention by the "imperialist leaders of the United States" in France.

Coming as it did after a similar joint statement issued by the Italian and Spanish Communist parties on July 11, 1975, the November PCF-PCI declaration seemed to concretize a new strategic relationship forming among the Western European Communist parties. A PCF delegation visited Spain for the first time since the 1930s in February 1975 and again in January 1976, on the latter occasion reaching an "identity of views" with the leaders of the Spanish Communist party.[31] Then in March 1977 a meeting of great significance for Western European communism took place in Madrid between Marchais, Berlinguer, and the secretary general of the Spanish Communist party (PCE), Santiago Carrillo. In the joint communique following their meeting, the leaders of three of Western Europe's major Communist parties called for the development of democracy and advance toward socialism based on political pluralism and the guarantees of "all collective and individual liberties. . . ."[32] The top leaders of the PCF and the PCI met again in Rome from April 28 to May 3, 1977. The major innovation of this session was its emphasis on strengthening Franco-Italian relations at the state-to-state level, going beyond the two parties' previous concern chiefly with interparty affairs. Their objective clearly was to help make the European environment more hospitable for eventual Communist governmental participation in France and Italy, specifically by forging a Franco-Italian alliance to offset expected West German opposition.

Thus, although the PCF disavows any desire for the establishment of a formal communist organizational structure at the regional level, just as it opposes any attempt to reimpose a centralized direction at the international level, its involvement in Western Europe-centered activities will undoubtedly increase. While not in itself amounting to a diminution of its allegiance to proletarian internationalism, this trend does represent a significant shift in focus which could have a major impact on both interparty and interstate relationships in the Communist world and beyond.

MEETINGS AND GREETINGS

Because of the significance of verbal cues in Communist party relationships, the statements and joint communiques following bilateral meetings, salutations addressed to party congresses, and speeches at international conferences can be excellent barometers of the status of interparty comradeliness. In its greetings to the 19th PCF congress in February 1970, for example, the CPSU Central Committee lauded the PCF as a "profoundly internationalist party," stated that Soviet Communists "highly value" the traditional bonds of friendship and cooperation existing between the two parties for a half-century, and wished the PCF "new successes" in its efforts to unify the French Left.[33] Soviet correspondents described the congress as "taking place under the banner of proletarian internationalism" and as having "convincingly confirmed the unshakable loyalty of French Communists to the principles of Marxism-Leninism and proletarian internationalism. . . ."[34] The following year the PCF reciprocated, telling the delegates to the 24th congress of the CPSU: "Every new achievement of the Soviet Union in the economic, political, scientific, technical, or cultural fields is an important contribution toward further strengthening the might of the world anti-imperialist front."[35]

In July 1971, an important meeting took place in Moscow between top-ranking officials of the two parties. Participants included Brezhnev, Kirilenko, Ponomarev, and Zagladin on the Soviet side, and Marchais, Leroy, Billoux, and Kanapa on the French side. The ensuing joint communiqué, to which the Soviets have frequently referred with approval, was a marvel of dialectical interweaving of affirmation of proletarian internationalism and endorsement of party autonomy.[36] In his address to the PCF's 20th congress in December 1972, CPSU Politburo member Suslov lauded the French comrades for "consistently and resolutely" fulfilling their proletarian internationalist duty, particularly the French Communists' "multifaceted work in disseminating the truth about the achievements of the Soviet people. . . ." He recalled the "profound unity of views of the PCF and the CPSU on all basic questions of modern times" that had been confirmed in the July 1971 communiqué, and expressed unqualified confidence that the friendship between the two parties —based on the immutable principles of Marxism-Leninism—would continue to strengthen.[37]

In June 1974 Ponomarev led a delegation to Paris in order, according to *Pravda*, "to learn about the French Communist Party's work experience" and probably to prepare for the forthcoming Brezhnev-Marchais meeting. TASS specifically noted that the subjects discussed included the international situation and the unity of action of the world Communist movement, in addition to the two parties' domestic activities. It is likely that the import of the decisions reached by the European Communist parties in Brussels for the international Communist movement figured on the agenda. The PCF may also have raised the issue of the Soviet ambassador's intervention in the French electoral process the month before (see Chapters 2 and 6). An aura of uncordiality during the Soviets' five-day stay was conveyed by *Pravda*'s reference to these as "businesslike conversations." This impression of disharmony was strengthened by the following statement: "Confirming the loyalty of the CPSU and of the PCF to the ideas of Marxism-Leninism and proletarian internationalism, the delegations reached an understanding about further measures aimed at the development of cooperation between both parties."[38]

The joint communiqué issued following the Brezhnev-Marchais meeting in Moscow gave no overt indication of discord. According to the statement, "both leaders warmly congratulated each other on the creative activity and the successes of both parties."[39] Since it noted that the PCF particularly stressed the importance of Soviet achievements for the workers' and liberation movements, however, one may wonder whether the absence of any corresponding specific favorable assessment by the CPSU side of the PCF's endeavors reflected disapproval of its alliance tactics.

The deterioration in the relationship emerges most sharply from a comparison of the upbeat language of the CPSU greetings to the 21st PCF congress in October 1974 with the tone of the corresponding message to the 22nd congress in February 1976.[40] On the key issues of strategy and tactics, model of socialism, and proletarian internationalism, the 1976 message conveys a mood of coolness toward the PCF and aggressive defensiveness about Soviet achievements totally absent from the preceding communication. In 1974 the CPSU praised the PCF for its "consistent struggle" to satisfy the needs of the French workers and for the "genuine democratization of all public and political life," which were said to have contributed to the growth of the party's influence and prestige. The 1976 message, conversely, restricts itself to the less flattering appraisal that the PCF, together with all French democratic forces "is striving for" major successes.

The defensive tone is particularly apparent in what is and is not said about the USSR's accomplishments. With respect to its own achievements, the CPSU takes credit in the 1974 message only for the progress of detente, credit which it shares with the other detachments of the revolutionary movement. In 1974 it is the PCF that is praised for working for "democratization," whereas two years later the Soviets self-justifyingly point out that the CPSU, "as it creates a Communist society, steadfastly develops Soviet socialist democracy. . . ." The subject of the road to socialism is completely passed over, whereas in 1974 the PCF's "consideration for France's specific conditions" was placed in a favorable context. In the one area in which there is no change, it is interesting to note that on the subject of foreign policy the identical language is used to commend the PCF's efforts to strengthen Franco-Soviet relations. Finally, on the litmus test of proletarian internationalism, in 1974 the CPSU unstintingly praised the PCF. In 1976 a far more hortatory tone is conveyed: "We express our confidence that the French Communist Party, proceeding from the principles of revolutionary proletarian solidarity and internationalism, will continue to play an active part in the common struggle for the cohesion of the international Communist movement."

The message delivered by Soviet Politburo member Kirilenko, one of the several foreign delegation heads who addressed an evening meeting of communists and workers in Nanterre—the first time the Soviet delegate did not address the congress itself—reinforces this analysis. Kirilenko pointedly reminded his audience of the fact that when he spoke from the rostrum of the 19th party congress, the slogan was "Fifty Years of the PCF's Fidelity to Leninism." Much of his speech was devoted to a recitation of Soviet economic, social, and foreign policy achievements, for which the CPSU and Brezhnev "personally" were praised. The PCF's current domestic activities were mentioned briefly and in general terms, but noticeably without enthusiasm. What were specifically singled out, however, were the strong statement condemning anti-Sovietism adopted by the PCF Central Committee plenum in January 1974, and Marchais' similar statement back in 1971 in his speech to the 24th CPSU congress, which Kirilenko called manifestations of class solidarity and proletarian internationalism. As if to ensure that his listeners grasped the message in his reminder to the PCF of its own past positions, he made his point directly.

> You, comrades, should find it understandable why the Soviet people are so steadfastly devoted to the cause of Lenin's party, why they welcome and support its policy so warmly. . . . You probably also understand why we hold

the achievements of socialism so dear and give such a resolute rebuff to all
its opponents. At the same time, you should know that we have a fraternal
attitude toward genuine friends, friends who understand us, friends who are
in solidarity with us both in the hour of grim ordeals and in the joyful days
of victories.[41]

The PCF was highly critical of the proceedings of the CPSU 25th congress, particularly the lack of public debate on the issue of freedom in the
USSR, the effort to discredit the PCF in the eyes of the Eastern European
parties, the exaltation of Russian nationalism, and what it termed the "surprising phenomenon" of the Brezhnev personality cult.[42]

THE JUNE 1976 CONFERENCE OF EUROPEAN COMMUNIST PARTIES

Soviet pronouncements on proletarian internationalism sometimes suggest a recurrent wistful longing for the days when an institutional mechanism
for the exercise of tighter Soviet control over the fraternal parties existed in
the Comintern. To some extent, the periodic international Communist conferences act as a surrogate for the absent institutional structure. As political
analyst Kevin Devlin makes clear in his study of the exercise of "conciliar
communism," however, the convening of such conferences by no means guarantees that Soviet views will prevail. Devlin contrasts the adoption of the 1960
international conference documents with apparent monolithic and binding
unanimity with the nonbinding and nonunanimously adopted document of the
1969 Moscow conference, which included a last-minute Soviet concession
denying the existence of a "leading center" in the international Communist
movement. As Devlin asserts, "the 1969 conference, and the precedents it
established, marked the institutionalization of diversity and dissent in the
world Communist movement."[43]

The Soviets had originally wanted to convene another worldwide Communist meeting, similar to that held in 1969, for the principal purpose of
expelling the Chinese from the international Communist movement. Throughout the spring of 1974, and particularly on the occasion of the fifth anniversary
of the 1969 meeting, the Soviets mounted a campaign in favor of a world
conference. When the extent of resistance to an anti-Chinese conference
became apparent, however, Soviet sights shifted to an all-European parley on
the model of the 1967 Karlovy Vary conference. At the first consultative
meeting to launch preparations for the conference, held in Warsaw in October
1974, representatives of 28 Eastern and Western European Communist par-

ties* fixed the approximate date—no later than mid-1975, the place—East Berlin, and the agenda—"the struggle for peace, security, cooperation, and social progress in Europe." Ponomarev conveyed the Soviets' view that in order to make detente "irreversible," an "even closer and more organic" interaction of the Socialist states and the working class in European capitalist countries was necessary.[44] He further outlined the Soviets' conception of the conference products, namely, two documents comprising a concrete political platform which would link the question of peace with the tasks of social progress. The first document would be the common action platform, based on the participants' assessments of the changes that have occurred in Europe and the direction of future Communist party action. The second document would consist of slogans applicable to the communists' tactic of cooperation with other leftist forces. At the insistence of the Yugoslavs and other independent parties, the Soviets agreed that the final documents would reflect the "consensus" of all participants, although Ponomarev noted for the record that any delegate would be able to present differing views in his conference address. The Soviets' satisfaction with the conference preparations at this embryonic stage is evident in *Pravda*'s description of the Warsaw meeting as a reflection of the "tendency toward unity and cohesion . . . now dominant in the Communist movement."[45] That the Soviets perceived their basic objectives as still on track is indicated by *Pravda*'s editorial assessment that the subsequent preparatory session in Budapest in December 1974 marked further progress toward elaborating a "common stand of the European Communist movement. . . ."[46]

Nevertheless, as conference preparations proceeded through a lengthy series of meetings, it became evident that the severity of the interparty disagreements and the consensus rule would prevent the conference from meeting its mid-1975 target date. In May 1975 it was reported that a "balanced" subgroup of eight parties (Soviet, East German, Danish, and French; and Yugoslav, Romanian, Italian, and Spanish) had been established to try to arrive at an acceptable compromise after the independent parties had rejected an East German draft calling for unified action and common ideological positions by all parties. The interpretation that the disagreements reflected division between the "centralists" and the "autonomists" was, however, heatedly rejected by the PCF, which protested that it "is not less attached to its independence" than the Yugoslav or Italian Communists.[47] Rather, the PCF declared, the crux of the conflict was the issue of whether the conference should stress the necessity of combining detente with the antiimperialist strug-

---

*Including Yugoslavia, but excluding Albania, Iceland, and The Netherlands; the Dutch Communists eventually participated in the Berlin conference.

gle, as the PCF insisted; or, as favored by "several European parties already building socialism," it should modulate support for the anti-imperialist struggle in the interest of detente.

The deliberations of the subgroup were further complicated by the events in Portugal in the spring and summer of 1975. The Italian and Spanish parties opposed the revolutionary tactics of the Moscow-oriented PCP and openly supported Mario Soares and the Socialists; the Romanians and Yugoslavs, although more subtly, did likewise. The PCF, conversely, joined most of the other Communist parties in defending the PCP. The subgroup was unable to reach agreement, and the drafting task once again fell to the East Germans as hosts. According to a well-informed Yugoslav source, the draft submitted to the October meeting in East Berlin by the East German Socialist Unity Party (SED) was close to a possible compromise acceptable to the majority of parties.[48] The PCF, however, objected to the vacuousness of the draft, particularly the absence of a class analysis of the crisis of capitalism and the modalities for exploiting it.

At this point, the Soviets apparently reassessed how much they were willing to compromise in order to convene the conference as planned, prior to the 25th CPSU congress. What was reported as a "great sharpening of the Soviet positions" produced a scrapping of the October East German draft at the November 17 editorial commission meeting, in favor of a new SED draft embodying Soviet formulas on "insistence on the leading role of the USSR and the Socialist camp, on [proletarian] internationalism," and on the fact that the final document would be an "obligatory general line for all European Communists."[49] While the Soviet and all the Eastern European delegations except the Romanians and Yugoslavs enthusiastically supported this change, according to the Yugoslav source, the Yugoslav, Italian, Spanish, British, Swedish, "and to some extent the French" delegates strenuously objected. In the light of the emerging PCF positions, it is evident that what the PCF resisted was not the Soviet call for a denunciation of U.S. "hegemonic pretensions" in Western Europe or condemnation of the NATO threat to the Socialist community, but the restrictive definition of the type of leftist alliances in which communists could participate.[50]

According to the Yugoslav analyst, this instance of Soviet hardening was not an isolated case, but corresponded to a harder line on detente, relations within the Socialist community, and on the assertion of independence by the leading Western European Communist parties.

> ... the Soviet party views with great doubt and mistrust the direction of the Italian, French, and Spanish Communists toward unconventional new forms of struggle for socialism in their countries and also toward the new, unconventional, pluralist image of socialism which these parties are building. The Soviet criticism at the expense of the largest West European Communist

> parties is increasingly more frequent and sharp and sometimes one has a strong feeling that the Soviet dissatisfaction with West European Communists has gone so far that only another step is needed and Moscow will accuse the largest West European Communist parties of revisionism and a social democratic attitude.[51]

At the January 1976 preparatory meeting the East Germans presented a new draft, reflecting a more conciliatory Soviet line and therefore more acceptable to the independent parties on some of the key issues. A major impediment to further progress intruded at the March meeting of the editorial commission, however, when the PCF decided to vent its dissatisfaction with the emerging document's analysis of the aggravation of the crisis of capitalism and how the Communist parties should exploit it. Objecting to the draft's lack of militancy on the class struggle, as well as to the Soviets' continued benignancy toward French foreign policy (see Chapter 6), the PCF declared its intention to reserve judgment on its participation in the conference. At the follow-up editorial commission session in May, the PCF announced that it would await the outcomes of the final draft before making its decision on whether to attend. Not until June 22 did the PCF Central Committee decide, on the basis of Kanapa's report which emphasized the limited nature of the conference, the absence of an imposed single strategy, and the recognition of party autonomy, to accept the draft and send a delegation to Berlin.[52]

What this episode of PCF intransigence reveals about the PCF's evolution is well illustrated by contrasting its position as a leading proponent of party autonomy and potential absentee at the 1976 conference with its expressed great satisfaction with both the manner of preparation and the content of the documents issued by the 1969 International Conference of Communist and Workers' Parties, all of which documents the PCF (in contrast to the PCI and 13 other parties) signed without reservation. It also testifies to the complexity of the contentious issues within the international Communist movement. For crosscutting the "autonomist" versus "centralist" cleavage are other issues, such as anticapitalist and anti-NATO militancy, on which the alignments differ. What was probably a Soviet concession on the latter issue in order to secure participation of the Yugoslavs almost precipitated—if one can believe the PCF threat—a boycott by the French. Finally, Soviet vacillations during the conference preparations also dramatize the lack of consensus within the Soviet hierarchy itself on how to deal with the upsurge of independent sentiment within the international Communist movement, and how to reconcile promotion of detente with support for the class struggle.

The conference itself, which finally convened a year behind schedule on June 29, 1976, was a victory not for the unity so ardently sought by the Soviets but for the diversity advocated and practiced by the "independent" parties. The final document, a lowest-common-denominator statement necessitated by the consensus rule, contained nothing of the binding detailed political action platform the Soviets had sought.[53] It was also reticent on the subject of the Soviet example, limiting its praise to recognition of the USSR's economic and foreign policy achievements. It explicitly rejected the notion of universal models of socialism, asserting that the future Socialist society "will be built up in accordance with the desires of each people." Most notable was the absence of the sacrosanct phrase "proletarian internationalism," which had figured prominently in the 1969 document. In its place was a remarkable affirmation of party autonomy, the impact of which was not diminished by its insertion in a complex formulation endorsing "mutual solidarity." The Communist and workers' parties of Europe, the document declared:

> will develop their internationalist, comradely, and *voluntary cooperation and solidarity* on the basis of the great ideas of Marx, Engels, and Lenin, strictly adhering to the principles of *equality and sovereign independence of each party, noninterference in internal affairs, and respect for their free choice of different roads in the struggle for social change of a progressive nature and for socialism.* The struggle of each party for socialism and its responsibility towards the working class and the people of that country are bound up with mutual solidarity among working people of all countries and all progressive movements and peoples in their struggle for freedom and the strengthening of their independence, for democracy, socialism, and world peace.[54]

The persistence of diversity was most sharply reflected in the individual delegates' speeches. Brezhnev's speech demonstrated how the CPSU hoped to recoup its losses in the final document's omissions by purposefully stamping its imprint on the public interpretation of the conference results.[55] The Soviet leader made certain the USSR received its due in a highly flattering recitation of Soviet achievements. He also characterized the final document as "binding" on the CPSU, contrary to the nonbinding character agreed to in the preparatory sessions. And he made sure to compensate for the regrettable absence of the phrase "proletarian internationalism" by launching a campaign in its defense that was pursued vigorously in the Soviet press in the postconference period. While dismissing as "strange" the apprehensions of those who interpret the calls to strengthen proletarian internationalism as signifying a Soviet desire to recreate an organizational center, Brezhnev strongly defended the validity of the concept itself. Proletarian internationalism, he declared, "preserves all its significance . . . in our time. It was and remains the powerful and tested tool of the Communist parties and the working-class movement in general."

Brezhnev also renewed the CPSU's call for collective appraisal of the strategy and tactics pursued by the individual parties. Only practical experience can determine the correctness or erroneousness of a given approach, he averred; but "even before practice pronounces its final verdict" the Communist and workers' parties should engage in "comradely debate" involving a broad comparison of the views and experiences of the different parties. To this end, he endorsed the convening of future multilateral meetings to facilitate the exchange of views. The tortuous record of preparations for the 1976 conference strongly suggests, however, that any attempt at closer coordination of the activities of the Western European "autonomist" parties by the CPSU are certain to be vehemently resisted. As Marchais bluntly declared in Berlin, such conferences no longer meet the requirements of a period in which communist diversity precludes the elaboration of a joint strategy.[56]

The fact that the individual delegation leaders' speeches provided a platform for airing views not included in the final document did not guarantee that such views would receive equal coverage. Aside from the East German *Neues Deutschland,* which, as the official organ of the host party, was obliged to print the delegates' speeches in their entirety, the state-controlled Soviet and Eastern European media heavily censored offensive or sensitive passages. A Soviet reader perusing the July 3 issue of *Pravda* would have had no way of knowing, for example, that Marchais had made a blistering attack on French President Giscard d'Estaing's foreign policy, since the Soviets, assiduously trying to rekindle enthusiasm for detente in Paris, chose to ignore that portion of Marchais' speech. Marchais' brazen assertion that, as far as the PCF was concerned, such conferences as the Berlin assemblage are no longer appropriate because the elaboration of a common strategy "is completely out of the question" was likewise considered unprintable.

Perhaps most revealing of Soviet sensitivities was *Pravda's* treatment of Marchais' explanation of the PCF interpretation of democratic socialism. A *Pravda* reader would have assumed complete PCF-CPSU agreement on this subject, since, according to the newspaper's account, Marchais had stated that the future French socialism would be profoundly democratic since it would be founded on "social ownership of the basic means of production and exchange and on political power of the working people with the working class having the dominating role." The crucial following sentence, however, was obviously deemed too tendentious by the Soviet censor: "It will be most profoundly democratic, but not only because by eliminating exploitation it will guarantee to the working people the essential conditions for their freedom, but also because it will guarantee, develop, and expand all liberties which our people have attained by struggle."[57] And the fact that Marchais concluded this passage by reminding his comrades of the PCF's decision to drop the dictatorship of the proletariat because the concept "does not coincide with the reality of political power in a Socialist France for which we are fighting" was also considered inappropriate material for *Pravda's* columns.

Like *Pravda,* the Polish paper *Trybuna Ludu* omitted from its summary of Marchais' speech references to civil liberties, including the touchy issue in Poland of the right to strike. It also deleted the passage on the possibility of democratic alternation in power, as did its Soviet counterpart. Marchais' comments on democratic liberties were likewise censored in the Romanian press, as was his statement on the PCF's decision to abandon the concept of the dictatorship of the proletariat. The Bulgarians went a step further, paraphrasing Marchais' appeal for pluralism and democracy in such a way as to distort its true meaning; while, conversely, the Czechoslovak newspaper *Rude Pravo* used boldface type to emphasize Marchais' statements about how the changed correlation of forces curbs "imperialism's" freedom of action, and the capitalist states' official acceptance of peaceful coexistence.[58]

Soviet satisfaction that the conference outcome provided at least a minimum springboard for the further dissemination of CPSU views was apparent in the postconference Politburo assessment. The Politburo referred to the "immensely important" provisions concerning the need to defeat anticommunism and anti-Sovietism, the injunction against Communist parties' submerging themselves in leftist alliances, and the pledge to develop international cooperation and solidarity "on the basis of the great ideas of Marx, Engels, and Lenin."[59]

Not surprisingly, the PCF Politburo communiqué gave the conference quite a different slant. It hailed the conference results in the major area of PCF concern, recognition of party autonomy and the importance of the search for original paths to socialism. It also leveled a broadside attack on the Giscard government for impeding further steps toward detente in Europe by its refusal to participate in disarmament negotiations. Finally, it declared that, based on the "two inseparable principles of its independence and the mutual internationalist solidarity to which it is profoundly committed," the PCF would strive to develop its relations with other Communist parties and other forces prepared to undertake "united or convergent action."[60] Kanapa subsequently specified the joint initiatives undertaken by the Western European Communist parties as "particularly fruitful" examples of the new forms of cooperation the PCF has in mind.[61]

Following the conference, a host of articles appeared in the Soviet press designed to give the conference an ex-post-facto Soviet imprimatur. Any impression of conciliation on party autonomy that may have been conveyed by Brezhnev's speech and the conference document was dispelled by articles such as that by Ponomarev in the CPSU journal *Kommunist,* in which solidarity with "real" socialism was defined as the sine qua non of an effective revolutionary policy.[62] A blatant Soviet claim to leadership of the international Communist movement was even more forcefully asserted in a postconference article in the Soviet military paper *Krasnaya Zvezda,* which stressed that although all Communist parties are "politically equal . . . *the leading detachment of the international working class is the Soviet working class and its vanguard—the CPSU.*" In an obvious criticism of the tactics of the "autonomist" Western European parties, the author condemned deviating "even one iota" from Marxist-Leninist teaching or proletarian internationalism "for the sake of acquiring a respectable image in the eyes of the bourgeoisie. . . ."[63] The post-conference period also witnessed an intensification of the Soviets' insistence on opposition to anti-Sovietism as a prerequisite for successful accomplishment of the fraternal parties' domestic and international goals. The elaboration of a *"positive action program"* directed at peace and progress in Europe is inextricably linked with a *"profound, well-argued critique of anticommunism and anti-Sovietism,"* an article in *Kommunist* declared.[64]

Despite this renewed evidence of Soviet hardening, the effort to find common ground between the views of the orthodox and the independent Communist parties continues. One prominent Soviet official whose writings suggest understanding of the autonomists' position is Zagladin, who, as deputy head of the International Department of the CPSU Central Committee, is responsible for relations with the Western European parties. The Berlin Conference produced a new formulation of the relationship between party autonomy and interdependence, he wrote, and offered the following accommodative formulation as an expression of the common viewpoint on the question: the independence and autonomy of the fraternal parties are a *precondition* for the development of equal cooperation among them.[65] Even so, the principal thrust of Zagladin's article is the need for increased unity and solidarity within the Communist movement, and the rejection of any attempts by the "enemies of socialism" to drive a wedge between ruling and nonruling parties.

Some of the most accommodative and flexible language expressed in a major Soviet journal in the latter half of 1976 was contained in an article that otherwise took quite conventional positions on the validity of proletarian internationalism and the necessity of solidarity with "real socialism." Each ruling and nonruling party, operating under differing conditions, is "fully independent *[polnost'yu samostoyatel'na]* in its appraisals and opinions, in defining political goals and tasks, and in elaborating the tactics most appropriate" to its country's situation and historical period, the author declared. Not only does Marxism-Leninism not limit, it actively promotes, the search for new methods of revolutionary struggle. International tasks can be accomplished only if they become "interwoven in the tightest possible way" with the resolution of national tasks—a reversal of the customary emphasis. "Loyalty to the principles of proletarian solidarity consists not in ignoring or artifically removing" differences which exist among Communist parties, but in understanding their causes and strengthening the movement's unity and cohesion "even while maintaining a certain noncoincidence in views. . . ." "All Communist parties are equal and are *responsible only to the working class and working masses of their own countries [otvetstvennyy tol'ko pered rabochim klassom i trudyashchimisya massami svoikh stran].*"[66]

Zagladin returned to print in the first issue of the journal of the Institute of the International Workers' Movement of the Soviet Academy of Sciences for 1977 with an article that leaves little doubt, however, that the CPSU is firmly opposed to opening the Pandora's box of heterodoxy. In language strongly suggesting that the targets of his rebuke included the author of the above article and the autonomist European parties, he wrote: "In some articles the question has been posed in such a way as to imply that the principles of the autonomy, independence, and equality of fraternal parties must take precedence over internationalist solidarity and cooperation. . . ." This is an erroneous interpretation. Independence means being "independent of any influences from the class enemy," while autonomy is understood in the sense that "only a party which is a really autonomous working class party is capable of achieving" its objectives. Harking back to his own August article, Zagladin seemed intent on clarifying its meaning: "In other words, autonomy, independence, and equality are not an end in themselves. They are a most important condition and precondition—but only a condition, precisely a condition, precisely a precondition—for what? They are a precondition and condition for success in resolute class struggle within the country and in the international arena."[67]

Zagladin moreover rejected the claim, which, he stated, "it is extremely common to encounter," that the successful activity of a given Communist party within its own country constitutes the fundamental criterion of proletarian internationalism. Moreover, at times the "absolutely specific international obligations" must take precedence over the interests of the particular Communist party, he declared, as was the case, he pointedly reminded the PCF, during the French colonial wars in Indochina and Algeria. Finally, taking note of the "considerable talk in the Communist movement at present about updating internationalism," Zagladin disavowed any notion about the creation of a "new internationalism" based on greater regard for the national characteristics of each Communist party, and underscored this intransigence by likewise rejecting elimination of the word "proletarian" from this basic Marxist-Leninist concept.

These articles, taken together with the relative down-playing of the more orthodox views at the conference itself and other instances of the muting of the most hard-line views, suggest that while the CPSU is still threading its way gingerly in its relations with the increasingly successful autonomist Western European parties, it is not prepared to yield on matters of substance. The growing stature of the PCI, as witness the June 1976 elections, in which it received 33.7 percent of the popular vote, and the electoral success of the Communist-Socialist alliance in France, are realities the Soviet authorities cannot ignore. Although, as the following chapter will discuss, the Soviets may have ambivalent feelings about these parties' advent to power from the perspective of Soviet national interest, the arguments for reaching an accommodation with them are compelling. On the other hand, the Soviets' first priority must always be preservation of the integrity of the Socialist bloc, to which the independence of the Western European Communist parties poses an increasing challenge. The major Western European parties for their part also have no desire to push their disagreement with the USSR to the breaking point. What is likely to emerge, therefore, is a continued pattern of selective dissent, tolerated with continued irritation by the CPSU.

NOTES

1. Moscow broadcast in French to Europe, February 28, 1976.

2. "PCF Can Insure Best Real Change," *L'Humanité,* April 1, 1976.

3. François Billoux interview in *La Nouvelle Critique,* February 1969, no. 2.

4. *L'Humanité,* February 6, 1976.

5. A. I. Sobolev, "Communists and the Modern World," *New Times,* November 1975, no. 47.

6. Vitaliy Korionov, "Communists' Banner," *Pravda,* January 24, 1976.

7. *Pravda,* February 25, 1976.

8. As a historical footnote, Khrushchev's reflections on his experience with Tito are instructive. As he wrote in his memoirs: "My experience with Comrade Tito showed me that there are different ways of going about the building of socialism. There's no single model or model which fits all the countries of the world. . . . More patience should be shown to parties that are experimenting with slightly different approaches . . . on the one vital condition, of course, that the means of production and the banks belong to the people, and that the state is run by the dictatorship of the proletariat." *Khrushchev Remembers* (New York: Bantam Books, 1971), p. 428.

9. See the monthly publication of the Center for Advanced International Studies, University of Miami, *Soviet World Outlook* 1, No. 7 (July 15, 1976).

10. "On an Article by Manuel Azcarate, a Leader of the Spanish Communist Party," *Partinaya Zhizn,* February 1974. As evidence of the importance the Soviets attached to this article, translations or summaries were broadcast to 20 countries or regions of Europe, Asia, and Latin America, February 14–19, 1974.

11. This passage was apparently considered too inflammatory vis-à-vis the autonomists and therefore counterproductive to the Soviets' efforts to convene the Berlin Conference of Communist and Workers' Parties, and it was deleted from the March 19 *Pravda* version of the original TASS text; see *Le Monde,* March 28–29, 1976.

12. See Timur Timofeyev, "The New and the Old in Anticommunism," *Kommunist,* November 1976, no. 16. *Le Point* (Paris), July 5, 1976, reported that the CPSU is closely monitoring Marchais' popularity within the PCF. Marchais' rejoinder to Suslov's reported remarks was to defend the PCF's record on internationalism, but also to remind the Soviets of the necessity of reciprocity in its practice. *L'Humanité,* March 19, 1976.

13. *Pravda,* November 6, 1976.

14. Paul Courtieu, "France's Future: Socialism," *World Marxist Review* 19, no. 6 (June 1976):35.

15. René Andrieu, "The Righters of Wrongs," *L'Humanité,* December 16, 1970.

16. "Rebuffing Anti-Sovietism is a Matter for All Who Want Democratic Change and Socialism," *L'Humanité,* February 9, 1974. *Pravda* took note of the PCF campaign against anti-Sovietism on February 18, 1974.

17. Georges Marchais, speech to the 22nd PCF congress, *L'Humanité,* February 5, 1976.

18. *L'Humanité,* September 18, 1973.

19. *L'Humanité,* January 28, 1974.

20. *L'Humanité,* September 10, 1976.

21. Ibid.

22. See Kevin Devlin, "Mao's Death Widens Gap Between Loyalist Regimes and Eurocommunists," RAD Background Report/196, September 16, 1976.

23. L'Humanité, May 29, 1973.

24. L'Humanité, January 28, 1974.

25. France nouvelle, February 5, 1974.

26. L'Humanité, February 5, 1976.

27. On the genesis of the PCF-PCI rapprochement, from the signing of a joint declaration in December 1958 through 1966, see François Fejtö, The French Communist Party and the Crisis of International Communism (Cambridge, Mass.: M.I.T. Press, 1967).

28. The PCI has also supported de facto the Christian Democratic government's austerity program, while the PCF has vigorously opposed the solutions to France's economic problems proposed by the Giscard government. On the PCI's strategy and tactics, see Donald L. M. Blackmer, "Continuity and Change in Postwar Italian Communism," in Blackmer and Sidney Tarrow, eds., Communism in Italy and France (Princeton, N.J.: Princeton University Press, 1975); and Giacomo Sani, "The PCI on the Threshold," Problems of Communism, November-December 1976.

29. L'Humanité, November 20, 1975; and L'Unità, November 18, 1975.

30. For the text of the leaders' speeches at the June 3 rally, see Georges Marchais, "Change: The Big Question on the Agenda," and Enrico Berlinguer, "For a Democratic Alternative to the Crisis," L'Humanité, June 4, 1976.

31. Le Monde, January 31, 1976. The PCE has been the most outspoken proponent of party autonomy and of a model of socialism tailored to European conditions. Like the PCF and the PCI, it is an advocate of coalition politics and political pluralism. See Eusebio M. Mujal-Leon, "Spanish Communism in the 1970's," Problems of Communism, March-April 1975.

32. L'Humanité, March 4, 1977. Pravda, after a delay in which the CPSU was undoubtedly weighing how to treat the Madrid communiqué, on March 7 finally published a heavily censored version in which this section, with its enumeration of over a dozen specifically guaranteed freedoms, was omitted. See also the report of the three leaders' joint press conference, which L'Humanité (March 5) called "An Event of the Highest Importance."

33. Moscow Radio, February 5, 1970.

34. Yu. Bochkarev, "Loyalty to Leninism," Sovetskaya Rossiya, February 7, 1970; and TASS, February 8, 1970.

35. TASS, March 31, 1971.

36. L'Humanité, July 6, 1971.

37. Pravda, December 15, 1972.

38. C. Ratiani and V. Sedykh, "With the French Communists," Pravda, June 23, 1974; TASS, June 24, 1974; and Pravda, June 26, 1974.

39. L'Humanité, July 29, 1974.

40. Pravda, October 24, 1974, and February 7, 1976.

41. "A Demonstration of Solidarity," Pravda, February 7, 1976.

42. Le Monde, June 23, 1976, report on an article by Francis Cohen in the May issue of La Nouvelle Critique.

43. Kevin Devlin, "The Interparty Drama," Problems of Communism, July-August 1975, p. 22; and "The Challenge of Eurocommunism," Problems of Communism, January-February 1977.

44. Pravda, October 18, 1974.

45. Pravda editorial, October 30, 1974, which stressed that several speakers at the meeting had emphasized that European Communists reject "Eurocentrism" as an alien concept, and asserted that attempts by "bourgeois propaganda" to divide the European parties should be firmly rebuffed.

46. *Pravda,* December 31, 1974.

47. *L'Humanité,* May 14, 1976.

48. Janez Stanic, "Moscow is Sharply Changing Directions," *Delo* (Ljubljana), December 27, 1975.

49. Ibid.

50. Based on report by Jacques Amalric, *Le Monde,* December 30, 1975, cited by Devlin, "The Challenge of Eurocommunism," p. 9.

51. Stanic, op. cit.

52. *Le Monde,* March 28–29, 1976; *L'Humanité,* May 12, 1976; *L'Humanité,* June 23, 1976; see also *Le Monde,* June 30, 1976.

53. "For Peace, Security, Cooperation, and Social Progress in Europe," final document adopted at the Conference of European Communist and Workers' Parties in Berlin, TASS, June 30, 1976, and *New Times,* 1976, no. 28.

54. Ibid.; italics added. PCF spokesman Kanapa asserted that the omission of proletarian internationalism "is not our doing" (*Le Monde,* June 30, 1976).

55. *Pravda,* June 30, 1976.

56. According to PCF Central Committee Secretary Paul Laurent, the PCF is not opposed to future regional or global Communist meetings; it is only "the type of conference, like the one at Berlin, that aggravates us and seems a little outdated to us." Gatherings requiring lengthy preparation should be replaced by "more lively, more topical, and more efficient relations. . . ." Michele Cotto interview with Paul Laurent, Paris Radio, July 20, 1976.

57. *L'Humanité,* July 1, 1976.

58. See Radio Free Europe Research Situation Reports SR/23, July 13, 1976, p. 5; July 14, 1976, p. 11; and SR/27, July 7, 1976; and J. L. Kerr, "The Media and the European Communist Conference: a Study in Selective Reporting," RAD Background Report/173, August 11, 1976, p. 5.

59. *Pravda,* July 3, 1976.

60. *L'Humanité,* July 8, 1976.

61. Jean Kanapa, "Berlin Conference: Under the Conditions of Our Era," *L'Humanité,* July 10, 1976.

62. Boris Ponomarev, "The International Significance of the Berlin Conference," *Kommunist,* July 1976, no. 11.

63. V. Yegorov, "The Party of Proletarian Internationalism," *Krasnaya Zvezda,* August 5, 1976; emphasis added.

64. Timofeyev, op. cit.; emphasis in the original. Timofeyev also warned against regarding the USSR's revolutionary experience as inapplicable to contemporary Western Europe.

65. V. Zagladin, "An Outstanding Contribution to the Cause of Peace and Progress," *Mirovaya Ekonomika i Mezhdunarodnyye Otnosheniya,* August 1976, no 8.

66. Yu. Stepanov, "Proletarian Internationalism—The Most Important Principle of Marxism-Leninism," *Mirovaya Ekonomika i Mezhdunarodnyye Otnosheniya,* 1976, no. 11, p. 28; emphasis added.

67. V. Zagladin, "The Development of Proletarian Internationalism under Contemporary Conditions," *Rabochiy Klass i Sovremennyy Mir,* 1977, no. 1 (January–February); see also the 50-page report on a conference on the subject of "Proletarian Internationalism in World Development," organized by the leading international political affairs journals of Eastern Europe (minus Romania and Yugoslavia) in *Mezhdunarodnaya Zhizn,* March 1977, no. 3, in which a Soviet delegate declared that "the support of all workers' and Communist parties to the first country of socialism . . . represents a criterion of real internationalist solidarity, a yardstick of the real revolutionary character of any Socialist movement."

6

SOVIET-FRENCH
RELATIONS AND THE
FRENCH COMMUNIST PARTY

The Soviet Union's outreach to France as the Western European anchor of its detente policy has been a significant limiting factor in the PCF's domestic posture and, to some extent, in its relationship with the CPSU. The Soviets value their relations with France highly, as Brezhnev conspicuously asserted in his report to the 25th party congress, and continuously endeavor to expand their scope. The PCF, with its opposition role thus circumscribed in the foreign policy field, has followed a course of encouraging the "positive aspects" of French foreign policy, while constantly goading successive French governments to pursue the independent foreign policy launched by de Gaulle and move further and faster along the path of detente. This approach complemented the PCF's domestic strategy of appealing to French patriotism and particularly to the Gaullist electorate. It succeeded as long as the basic compatibility between Franco-Soviet detente and the PCF's pursuit of its domestic goals endured. This convergence of interests eroded, however, as the Soviets pressed their courtship of an increasingly reluctant and "Atlanticist" post-Gaullist French government, advancing their own state interests in their quest for Western trade and technology (so the PCF charged) at the expense of the revolutionary cause in France. Thus, in an ironic twist of interparty relations, the PCF accused the CPSU of pursuing an "opportunistic" foreign policy incompatible with proletarian internationalism.[1]

FRANCO-SOVIET DETENTE

The political rapprochement between the USSR and Fifth Republic France was inaugurated by de Gaulle's historic visit to the USSR in June 1966, which launched an era of *détente-entente-coopération* between the two nations.

A commercial agreement in October 1964 had already proposed doubling trade between them over the ensuing five-year period; a subsequent agreement signed in May 1969 again provided for the doubling of trade in 1970–74. By 1973, France was the USSR's third largest Western trading partner. In the decade following de Gaulle's visit, trade between the USSR and France grew eightfold, reaching a level of 1,697,000 rubles in 1976, a 20 percent increase over the previous year.[2] Of even greater significance was the pattern of regular political consultations at the summit and foreign ministerial level established under the terms of an October 1970 protocol. Five Brezhnev-Pompidou summit meetings took place from 1970 to 1974, the second of which, in October 1971, produced a declaration of Principles of Cooperation setting forth the fundamentals of Franco-Soviet relations. Three summit meetings have been held between Brezhnev and Pompidou's successor, Giscard d'Estaing, in December 1974, October 1975, and June 1977.

Franco-Soviet accord was made possible by the existence of complementary national interests: the French desire to play an independent major role in international relations, which required maintaining aloofness from the United States and NATO, dovetailed with the Soviet drive to undermine the Atlantic Alliance, weaken United States influence in Western Europe, and increase Soviet influence and prestige in that part of the continent. By early 1969 the Soviets regarded their relations with Gaullist France as "the most brilliant example" of the peaceful coexistence of states with different social systems, based on the successful development of political, economic, and scientific-technological relations.[3] France's withdrawal from the NATO military organization was hailed as liberating it from a position of subordination to the United States, and its opposition to British Common Market membership as helping thwart Washington's interventionist intentions in "little Europe." Moreover, de Gaulle's ideas of an independent "European Europe" were seen as complementary to the Soviets' ambition to establish a European collective security system transcending East-West borders.

The Soviets were clearly stunned by de Gaulle's precipitous disappearance from the French political scene.[4] Soviet apprehensions about the future direction of French foreign policy were evident in the report of *Izvestiva*'s correspondent of rumors that "rightwing forces" were trying to portray the results of the referendum as indicating dissatisfaction with "France's independent foreign policy with regard to NATO and Atlanticism," and intended to use the outcome and de Gaulle's departure "to revise French foreign policy in the direction of putting the country back on the rails of Atlanticism."[5] The Soviet press and French-language broadcasts to Europe weighed in with endorsements of continued Franco-Soviet cooperation. Declared *Pravda*'s Paris correspondent: "To repudiate the policy of international detente and to align itself with the aggressive NATO bloc ... would conflict with the interests of France."[6] Soviet apprehensions were by no means assuaged by the "new notes" enunciated in the foreign policy sphere by de Gaulle's heir and UDR candidate for the presidency, Pompidou, particularly his pronouncement that "Europe needs Britain" and his indication of an intention to pursue closer ties with the United States.[7] However, although the Soviets effusively praised the personal qualities of the PCF candidate, Duclos, they clearly favored Pompidou as the most likely of the electable candidates to perpetuate the Gaullist foreign policy which he had served for six years as prime minister.[8]

Franco-Soviet relations continued to expand in the early 1970s, but the changed international context inevitably curtailed their initial élan. Robert Legvold points out that, in retrospect, the Soviets comprehended that the first signs of falling off of the tempo of Franco-Soviet relations had occurred as early as 1968. Despite de Gaulle's reaffirmation of the basic premises of Franco-Soviet cooperation in his September 9, 1968, press conference, it was after Czechoslovakia that the French articulated their reservations concerning the Soviet ambition to convene an all-European security conference, increased their cooperation with NATO surveillance in the Mediterranean, and registered their apprehensions over the expansion of Soviet power in the region.[9] A temporary stagnation in trade relations also occurred at this time. The inauguration of Brandt's Ostpolitik deprived the Franco-Soviet relationship of its uniqueness in Europe (particularly after the Soviet-West German treaty in August 1970), while after the Nixon-Brezhnev summit in 1972 the United States superseded France as the Soviets' principal interlocutor under detente. Moreover, Soviet attainment of nuclear parity had caused de Gaulle to revise his post-Cuban missile crisis perception of United States strategic might as posing the sole threat to French independenence.[10] As evidence of the changed French position, Pompidou reversed the traditional French opposition to British entry into the Common Market at the Hague Conference in December 1969, which signaled an important French accommodation to Western European economic and monetary union.

If the utility of France as an instrument for undermining Western unity in NATO and the EEC had somewhat depreciated, however, the Soviets still valued the role of Franco-Soviet relations as a model of peaceful coexistence. As an *Izvestiva* correspondent affirmed:

> Of the West European states, France objectively has the best chance of undertaking the difficult but lofty and noble mission of pioneer along the path of relaxing tension, since it is divided from the Socialist countries, primarily the USSR, by the least number of disputed problems and is drawn close to them by the maximum number of common interests. Therefore, it is France, rather than any other country, which is capable of graphically demonstrating the fruitfulness of peaceful cooperation between states with differing socioeconomic systems and, moreover, of creating an example, a working model, of such coexistence.[11]

Brezhnev flattered Gaullist egos by traveling to France in October 1971 on his first state visit to the West, and by his deliberate emphasis on the special quality of the Franco-Soviet relationship. "To the Soviet people France is not only a major state," he declared; "to the Soviet people France is a friendly power. This is most important."[12]

The highlight of the Brezhnev-Pompidou Paris summit was the signing of an accord providing for a new impetus in Franco-Soviet political consultations and pledging the two countries to work for detente in Europe based on the inviolability of existing borders, noninterference in internal affairs, equality, independence, and renunciation of the threat or use of force.[13] In concrete terms, with the September four-power agreement on the status of Berlin agreement having removed the final obstacles, the Soviets won Pompidou's commitment to work for the convening of a conference on security and cooperation in Europe.[14]

Soviet officialdom portrayed the October 1971 Brezhnev-Pompidou summit as having raised Soviet-French cooperation to a qualitatively new level and as marking a historic turning point for Europe.[15] The PCF, too, expressed great satisfaction with the results of the Brezhnev visit. As PCF Politburo member and Central Committee secretary Plissonnier declared: "L. I. Brezhnev's official visit to France is a political event of prime importance. . . . The Soviet Union's foreign policy and Franco-Soviet cooperation fully accord with the interests of my country and the strivings of the French people."[16]

The Franco-Soviet rapprochement confronted the PCF with two contradictory priorities: weakening the existing regime in an effort to eventually supplant it in power, while at the same time supporting the "positive aspects" of its foreign policy—its detente with the USSR and Eastern Europe and its divergence from U.S. policies on NATO, the EEC, the Middle East, and Vietnam—with the inevitable result of helping shore up its popular support. PCF Secretary General Rochet's speech to the 1969 Moscow International Conference of Communist and Workers' Parties well illustrated this dichotomy. "We have waged a just and uncompromising class struggle against the Gaullist power of the monopolies and we shall continue to wage it against any attempts at a reactionary continuation of Gaullist power," he declared. "At the same time," he added, "we . . . will continue to act in favor of an independent French policy. . . ."[17]

For the Soviets, the resolution of the dichotomy in favor of the promotion of Soviet national interest at the expense of the PCF's interest in advancing the cause of revolution in France was less complex. As Brezhnev was reported to have asserted:

> . . . take de Gaulle. Have we not succeeded, at no risk to ourselves, in driving a breach through the imperialist camp? De Gaulle is our enemy and we are well aware of it. The French Communist party was narrow-minded enough

to try to stir us up against de Gaulle for their own particular interests. But look at our achievements! We have weakened the American position in the heart of Europe and this weakening will continue . . . look at the balance-sheet from our point of view. . . . To the Devil (*k'chortu*) with those parties that set themselves up as our mentors![18]

PCF support of Soviet foreign policy was the area of its most steadfast allegiance. It staunchly defended the CPSU against charges by the PRC and others that the Soviet Union was participating in establishing a "superpower condominium" with the United States for the promotion of its state interests at the expense of proletarian internationalism. Thus, the PCF was left very little latitude in the foreign policy field, except to snipe from the sidelines at French divergence from the independent Gaullist line. *L'Humanité* attacked the Pompidou regime for deviating from the Gaullist policy of opposition to British entry into the EEC, complained of a considerable increase in the regime's "pro-Atlantic tendencies," and accused it of "working to reinforce its political and military alliance with the United States."[19] The PCF Politburo also took the Pompidou government to task for predicating the convening of a European security conference on prior resolution of the Berlin issue.[20] In January 1972, following the Nixon-Pompidou meeting in the Azores, Marchais accused the Pompidou government of "an accelerated slide toward Atlanticism, closer links with Washington, and a closer integration of French foreign policy with the general strategy of U.S. imperialism."[21] Such PCF criticism posed no threat to Soviet-French relations, and probably performed the useful function of serving as a more militant surrogate spokesman for the Soviets, allowing them to take the diplomatic highroad. It also furthered the PCF goal of dividing the Gaullists over the issue of fidelity to de Gaulle's legacy, and salvaged a modicum of maneuvering room for the party in the electoral arena.

THE FOREIGN POLICY NEXUS

The March 1973 French parliamentary elections brought the complexities of the foreign policy nexus to the fore. The Gaullists, shown to be behind in the polls, launched a strident anticommunist campaign, while the conservative French press attacked the Soviet Union for interfering in French domestic affairs. The Soviets, while continuing to praise Soviet-French cooperation as an instrument for achieving peace in Europe, countered with attacks on the "extreme rightists and the pro-Atlantic press in France" for their "fabrications" concerning Soviet interference in French domestic affairs.[22] The announcement that French President Pompidou would pay a visit to the Soviet Union in January caused raised eyebrows over the coincidence in timing, coming in such close proximity to the French elections. Marchais' assertion that "it is ridiculous to claim, as certain commentators are doing, that this meeting could embarrass French Communists because it is a few weeks before the parliamentary elections" did not dispel the impression that the Soviets indeed preferred the continuation in power of the Gaullists to the unpredictability and risks inherent in a leftist victory.[23]

In any event, following the announcement of Pompidou's impending visit, Marchais journeyed to Moscow to confer with his Soviet counterpart. Whether Marchais complained to Brezhnev in private about the damage to the PCF's domestic position caused by the announcement of the Pompidou visit is not known; the ensuing communiqué merely noted that unanimity had been reached on all subjects discussed. The two party leaders confirmed the significance of comprehensive Soviet-French cooperation, but also stressed that peaceful coexistence does not mean the weakening of the working-class and anti-imperialist struggle. Besides according with the Soviets' own views on detente,[24] reiteration of this caveat was an important legitimization of the domestic electoral efforts of the PCF. This dialectical interweaving of the positive impact of Soviet-French relations with a reassertion of the continuation of the class struggle under detente was also a key theme of CPSU Politburo member Suslov's address to the PCF 20th congress in mid-December.[25]

The January 1973 Brezhnev-Pompidou summit in Zaslavl, near Minsk, focused on developments in Europe. Pompidou acceded to the Soviet position that the convening of the all-European security conference (CSCE) should not be made dependent on progress in talks on troop reductions in Central Europe (MBFR), as the United States had proposed. The two sides pledged to work for a convening of the conference "in the nearest months to come," thus putting pressure on the United States, Britain, and West Germany to agree. On other topics, Brezhnev and Pompidou confirmed the harmony of Soviet and French positions on a settlement of the conflicts in Indochina and the Middle East and also agreed to maintain a regular exchange of views on developments in Europe. The joint communiqué described the conversations as having taken place "in an atmosphere of trust and mutual understanding, in keeping with the special character of the relations of friendship and respect between the peoples of the Soviet Union and France."

The official Soviet press greeted the Zaslavl summit as an "event of great importance in international life," and hailed its results as a refutation of allegations of a "cooling down" in Soviet-French relations.[26] At the same time, however, the Soviets expressed increased annoyance at the anticommunist and anti-Soviet attacks in the French press, which, for the first time, they specifically linked to Gaullist circles. The PCF meanwhile renewed its criticism of the French government for restraining the development of Franco-Soviet relations because of its ever closer identification with the United States.[27]

French apprehensions about the impact of bilateral U.S.-Soviet cooperation on Western Europe became increasingly apparent in 1973. The signing of the U.S.-Soviet treaty on the prevention of nuclear war at the June Nixon-Brezhnev summit, in particular, aroused French doubts over the credibility of the American nuclear guarantee to Europe, while the agreement to hold a European security conference at the summit level now gave rise to an impression of Soviet-U.S. collusion in determining the fate of Europe. Brezhnev's stopover in France on his return from the United States did little to quell French fears. The PCF dutifully praised the results of the Soviet-U.S. summit, just as it had done following the Nixon-Brezhnev Moscow summit the previous year, and as it would do after the Vladivostok agreement the following year. The Soviets prominently reported the PCF's position that Brezhnsv's visit to France demonstrated irrefutably the fallaciousness of the charge of superpower collusion.[28] Nonetheless, the concerns of the French government surfaced dramatically in the speech of Foreign Minister Michel Jobert to the Helsinki Conference on Security and Cooperation in Europe in July. Warning against the illusory acceptance of a deceptive "moral disarmament" which would dull the vigilance of the West, he insisted that genuine security required each nation to defend its own peace and security, and affirmed France's resolve to strengthen its own defenses.[29] The Soviets did not criticize Jobert directly but, in attacking the British foreign secretary for warning against excessive euphoria or optimism concerning the prospects of the CSCE, indirectly expressed their dismay at France's hardening position.[30]

During this period the momentum in Soviet-French relations was sustained largely due to progress on the commercial and scientific-technological front. In July the two countries signed a ten-year agreement for cooperation in trade and industry and in December a ten-year protocol on scientific-technological cooperation. Large-scale compensatory deals involving French construction of a pulp and paper mill and a styrene plant were also sealed. In March 1970 France had agreed to extend a 4.5-billion-franc long-term credit to the USSR to finance shipments of French capital goods, and additional credits were granted in 1973, raising the level to 9 billion francs for 1975–80. Work was proceeding on the basis of a September 1970 agreement reached with the state-owned Renault company for cooperation at the Kama River truck factory. Trade turnover between France and the Soviet Union increased by 40 percent in 1973 over the 1972 level, although the Soviets were not happy with the persistent unfavorable balance of trade and made continuous representations to their French counterparts to obtain an increment in French imports of Soviet goods. The Soviets continued to give favorable marks to the overall status of Soviet-French relations, while the PCF contented itself with harping on the government's failure to take full advantage of the existing opportunities.[31]

In the fall of 1973, however, following the outbreak of war in the Middle

East, anti-Soviet feelings in France and unmitigated frustration over the mounting evidence of French impotence in asserting its voice in world affairs combined in an outpouring of French pique. Speaking in the National Assembly on November 12, Foreign Minister Jobert expressed exasperation over Soviet and U.S. efforts to arrange a Middle East cease-fire in total disregard of the views of Western Europe. On December 8 the Soviet journal *Novoye Vremya* attacked Jobert for referring to a Soviet-United States condominium. Nonetheless, despite acknowledged differences on certain issues, the Soviets continued to press for the further development of mutually beneficial Soviet-French cooperation. In February Jobert conferred in Paris with his Soviet counterpart, Andrei Gromyko, and arranged for the fifth Brezhnev-Pompidou summit the following month in the Soviet Union. Gromyko especially noted the two sides' convergent positions on energy questions, particularly France's rejection of the U.S. proposal for a common front of energy consumers at the Washington conference, which had been partly responsible for the reinvigoration of Franco-Soviet relations.[32]

Despite the impression of a successful meeting conveyed by the Soviet press, little of substance was accomplished at the Brezhnev-Pompidou summit in Pitsunda in March 1974. Perhaps the meeting's greatest significance was the mere fact of its being held, maintaining the regularity of Soviet-French consultations at the summit. Evoking the issue that overshadowed the conference, in a presummit press conference with French journalists Brezhnev denounced the bourgeois French media for using the term "superpower" to refer to the Soviet Union.[33] The two sides did agree to coordinate their efforts toward consolidating detente in Europe and bringing the CSCE to a successful conclusion, and—perhaps in response to French dissatisfaction at being disregarded in the past—agreed to "activate consultations" aimed at bringing peace to the Middle East. Brezhnev, speaking at Alma-Alta on March 15, called the meeting "fresh evidence of the stability of traditional Soviet-French friendship. . . ."[34]

The French presidential elections following the death of Pompidou three weeks after the Pitsunda meeting confronted the USSR with another of its periodic choices between raison d'état and promotion of the revolution of its once again the choice in favor of the former was made with little apparent difficulty. The Soviets by no means found the Gaullist candidate, Chaban-Delmas, entirely to their liking with respect to perpetuation of the close Franco-Soviet relationship, but he offered more hope for continuity than did either the Independent Republican Giscard d'Estaing, who was too profiled as a European integrationist, or Mitterand, who, though running as a joint Socialist-Communist candidate, led a party containing a strong pro-Atlantic and pro-European integration faction and whose election might upset the French domestic stability essential for detente. After the defeat of Chaban-Delmas in the first round, the Soviet press seemed to go out of its way to accord the two remaining candidates equal treatment. A *Pravda* dispatch from Paris made a point of noting that *both* candidates had expressed favorable views concerning the continuation of close Franco-Soviet relations.[35] However, one well-publicized incident was interpreted by many observers as a blatant attempt by the Soviets to influence the outcome of the election in Giscard's favor. (As the French official responsible for drafting the 1964 commercial agreement and the 1973 trade and industrial cooperation agreement, Giscard had laid the basis for future good relations.) On May 7, prior to the second round of voting, Soviet Ambassador Stepan Chervonenko, a member of the CPSU Central Committee, paid a call on Giscard, ostensibly in his capacity as Minister of Economy and Industry and copresident of the Franco-Soviet bilateral commission. Although the PCF's statement the following day noted that "relations between states . . . neither can nor should be affected by or even suspended during an election period," its displeasure was evident in the reproach which followed: "Nonetheless, the fact remains that, considering that Giscard d'Estaing is one of the two candidates in the presidential elections, the *démarche* of the USSR ambassador to France was inopportune. It is the more regrettable because it has been used as a pretext for political speculations which have represented it as an adoption of an attitude favorable to the candidate of the Right."[36]

Soviet indulgence toward Giscard was all the more remarkable in the light of the fierce anticommunist and anti-Soviet campaign waged by the Right during the electoral contest. After his victory the Soviets concentrated on Giscard's record as an "energetic promoter" of detente. Commentators again emphasized that "all the leading claimants to the presidential office" had stressed the importance of continuing the Pompidou independent foreign policy line.

The persistent Soviet courtship of the new French leadership finally overtaxed PCF tolerance. The immediate target of its ire was an article in *Le Monde* by the director of the Soviet Institute of World Economics and International Relations. The PCF took strong exception to two "errors" committed by the author, Yuriy Rubinskiy: first, that he had claimed that no French presidential candidate had "deemed it profitable" to openly employ anti-Sovietism; and second, that he had stated that peaceful coexistence would solve France's economic and social problems.[37] In fact, the PCF declared, one candidate—Giscard d'Estaing—had blatantly indulged in a massive propaganda campaign slandering the Soviet Union and accusing the PCF of being "Moscow's agent." In the second place, the PCF huffed, it is a "grave error" to suggest that coexistence alone will suffice to solve France's great economic and social problems, which only the elimination of the "domination of the monopolies" can accomplish. Therefore, the PCF concluded, venting its accumulated spleen over the Soviet behavior during the just-concluded election campaign, "it was not a matter of indifference—whatever Professor Rubin-skiy's personal views may suggest in this respect—whether the candidate of the Right, whose only objective is to maintain the authoritarian rule of big capital, or the candidate of a united Left, was elected."

Whatever strain this electoral contretemps produced in PCF-CPSU relations was not apparent, however, at the meeting between Brezhnev and PCF Secretary General Georges Marchais in Moscow in July, which *L'Humanité* described as "very cordial." The two Communist leaders affirmed that greater utilization of the opportunities available to expand Soviet-French cooperation constituted a "clear national imperative" for both countries.[38] The same month the new French foreign minister Jean Sauvagnargues met with Brezhnev in Moscow, prompting an optimistic Soviet assessment of the future prospects of Soviet-French relations. The PCF, however, intensified its criticism of the desultory French performance, accusing the government of failing to honor its commitment under the 1971 agreement to "cooperate closely" in promoting detente in Europe. It specifically criticized the French refusal to participate in the disarmament talks and alignment with the "Atlantic bloc" on issues of European security and cooperation.[39]

PCF MILITANCY ON DETENTE AND THE SUPERPOWER CONDOMINIUM

In December the first Brezhnev-Giscard summit took place in Rambouillet. While asserting that it was "unreservedly pleased" about the meeting between the two leaders, the PCF again expressed strong dissatisfaction with the current status of Franco-Soviet relations and with the French government's policies regarding NATO military integration, transformation of the Common Market into a political bloc, and creation of a Western European defense alliance within which West Germany would have the right to "control" nuclear arms. It also very deliberately noted that the prospects for further development of Franco-Soviet cooperation, which it encouraged, "in no way mortgage the struggle we are waging against the present government because it represents big capital. . . ."[40] The Soviets, for their part, underscored the importance of this meeting in marking the continued pursuit of detente over three French presidencies. Two significant outcomes were French acquiescence in the conclusion of the Helsinki talks at the summit level and the signing of a major new five-year trade agreement for 1975–79.

While in France, Brezhnev also met again with Marchais and other PCF officials, whose warm endorsement of Soviet-French relations elicited the appreciative Soviet comment that "France is one of the capitalist countries where the force of the working class and its battle vanguard, the Communist party, plays an exceptionally important role in the rapprochement and cooperation with the Soviet Union."[41]

Following the meeting, however, Marchais issued a separate statement in which he made four points. First, the Soviet Union's peace policy and efforts to insure security in Europe and end the arms race accord with long-standing positions of the PCF. Second, while it welcomes any moves that strengthen Franco-Soviet relations, the PCF believes that much remains that the French government could do to strengthen detente and cooperation in Europe. Third, the PCF will continue its pressure on the French government in this direction, by "combating the cold war concepts and anti-Sovietism" prevalent among French "leading circles." Fourth, the PCF remains adamant in its determination to continue its drive to supplant the current government with a government of the Left, irrespective of any possible Soviet preferences to the contrary —as Marchais reminded Brezhnev in no uncertain terms.

> I related to him the current aspects of our struggle to defend the working people's interests, for a democratic change and for socialism. This was a natural thing, since for Communists—and we reaffirmed in this connection what we indicated in our previous meetings—the peaceful coexistence for which we strive in no way ends the struggle of the working class and the peoples for social progress, democracy, and socialism. Thus, it in no way signifies the maintenance of the social and political status quo.[42]

The mounting PCF impatience and irritation with the CPSU's promotion of Soviet state interests over the prospects of socialism in France again surfaced on the occasion of Prime Minister Jacques Chirac's March 1975 visit to the USSR. In contrast to Soviet reports, which portrayed the visit in positive terms, the PCF assessed its results as "slender" and its chief benefit the resultant "political capital" accruing to the Giscard regime.[43]

With no improvement, from the Soviet point of view, in the French position on key issues, tensions flared. In his April 1975 talks with French Socialist leader Mitterand, CPSU Politburo member Suslov deplored the "unconstructive positions" of the French government on disarmament and French relations with NATO. On July 2, the eve of the departure for Moscow of the French ministers of economy and finance and foreign trade, TASS attacked Interior Minister Michel Poniatowski for calling the *Quotidien de Paris* publication of the so-called Ponomarev document from the banned Portuguese *República* (see Chapter 2) a Communist blueprint for seizure of power.[44]

The conflict between state interests and revolution again surfaced publicly on the occasion of Giscard's October 1975 visit to the Soviet Union. The official Soviet press censored a PCF statement issued prior to the trip which emphasized the French Communists' hard line on detente and the party's determination to continue its struggle to replace the incumbent government with a government of the Left. Under no conditions, the PCF declared, would it "abandon or abate its struggle to substitute as soon as possible a democratic unity government for the present 'grand bourgeoisie' power structure and implement the new policies defined by the Common Program of the Left."[45] The PCF's articulation of this position in connection with Giscard's visit coincided with its expression of the same view at the October preparatory session of the Conference of European Communist and Workers' Parties, where PCF delegate Kanapa stressed the party's axiom that purusit of detente does not signify perpetuation of the sociopolitical status quo in Europe.[46] *Pravda* confined itself to the anodyne statement that the PCF "will never abandon or abate its struggle for the realization of the objective defined in the Common Program."[47] The CPSU daily also deleted the PCF's views on the crisis in France resulting from the "policy of austerity, authoritarianism, and national recklessness" being pursued by the chief of state. It obliterated the meaning of the PCF's expression of annoyance that the USSR had never publicly protested Prime Minister Chirac's direct intervention with Brezhnev during his visit to Moscow in March 1975, when he had reportedly asked the Soviet leader to intercede with the PCF to cease its agitation within the French armed forces.[48] Finally, *Pravda* blue-penciled the PCF's assertion that its policy would not be changed by "any interference, pressure, or foreign reprisals whatsoever."

The censorship of the PCF's statement appeared even more striking when compared with the verbatim reportage in the same issue of *Pravda* of a speech by Giscard, which included a call for "detente with respect to ideological competition," an anathema to Marxists. The PCF, however, did not remain silent on the "ideological detente" issue, wondering in print whether Giscard, by invoking a concept whose implication was preservation of the sociopolitical status quo, was trying to make an end run around the Helsinki agreement commitments to self-determination.[49]

A CHANGING SOVIET ASSESSMENT

Giscard's reference to a cessation of ideological competition highlighted the differences in the French and Soviet interpretation of the Helsinki accords, and was one of several areas of disagreement that contributed to the chilly tone of this encounter. The perception of discord was such that Brezhnev's cancellation of one session was interpreted by observers as due more to a diplomatic than to a physical indisposition. The French did not alter their position on MBFR, which they continued to fear would lead to the creation of a neutralized or demilitarized zone in Central Europe. They did, however, subscribe to the convening of a world disarmament conference to which all nuclear powers would be invited, and, although remaining adamant against signing the nonproliferation treaty, agreed to take steps to insure that transfer of French technology would not aid other countries to acquire nuclear arms. Despite the signing of a "Declaration on the Further Development of Friendship and Cooperation between the Soviet Union and France," the results of the talks were disappointing to the Soviets.

At this point, however, the Soviets apparently still regarded their stake in preserving the close working relationship with France as sufficiently high to justify special pains to nurture it, as Brezhnev's 25th party congress remarks indicated. This relentless Soviet effort to woo the French government, which had by now reached the point of diminishing returns for the Soviets' detente policy, produced the apex in PCF-CPSU friction over foreign policy: Marchais' decision to boycott the CPSU party congress. When Marchais' stand-in Plissonnier declared in his congress address that "the French government has, in fact, put our country back into NATO, which is led by American imperialism," *Pravda* eliminated the final clause.[50] Plissonnier's diatribe against French foreign policy, like Marchais' comments at the PCF's own congress earlier that month, was in stark contrast to Brezhnev's own remarks. Subsequently, at an unprecedented Moscow press conference, Plissonnier bluntly declared: "The PCF does not share Leonid Brezhnev's assessment of French foreign policy."[51] Mindful, perhaps, of not pushing matters too far, *L'Humanité* did not print Plissonnier's critical press conference remarks.

Soviet Foreign Minister Gromyko's visit to Paris the following April, timed to highlight the tenth anniversary of de Gaulle's visit to Moscow, clearly was aimed at restoring some of the original warmth to the Soviet-French relationship. However, while the joint communique spoke of the "special importance" that both countries attach to political consultations and to their "close or similar views" on a number of international issues, it was nonetheless clear that important differences remained on MBFR, the reduction of military budgets, and underground nuclear testing.[52]

PCF public criticism of Soviet policy toward France and the West in general continued to attract attention in the months preceding the convening of the Berlin conference. At the March preparatory session the PCF delivered its sharp critique of the Soviet failure to exploit the crisis of capitalism, took exception to the draft document's lack of militancy and threatened to boycott the conference.[53] Later the same month the PCF youth movement angrily rebuked the Soviet and Romanian youth organizations for extending invitations to delegations from Gaullist and Independent Republican youth groups, which it viewed as lending support to the incumbent regime. In May the PCF monthly *La Nouvelle Critique* published an article containing a forthright explanation of the reasons for the PCF-CPSU differences over detente. These differences, wrote Francis Cohen, an expert on and longtime supporter of the Soviet Union, "are aggravated by the confusion between party and state" in the Soviet Union.

Everything still happens there as if any change were regarded as threatening to upset a precarious balance. Hence reliance must be placed on whatever is safe ... meaning principally the European Socialist community (plus Cuba). The victory of the worker movements in the capitalist countries (in particular, Western Europe) is uncertain and hence cannot be envisaged as a starting point.

The PCF's strategy is based on the global nature of the imperialist system and monopoly state capitalism and regards anything which could consolidate all or part of the imperialist system as contrary to the revolutionary Socialist outlook.[54]

At the Berlin conference Marchais launched a vehement attack on Giscard's foreign policy, terming it "one of the most flagrant manifestations that imperialism has no intention of abiding voluntarily by commitments it has been forced to accept." While endorsing the principles of peaceful coexistence, Marchais emphasized PCF opposition to the practice of superpower condominium.

But peaceful coexistence in no way signifies preservation of the social and political status quo in our country, nor the partition of the world into spheres of influence among the most powerful states. On the contrary, we are urging French working people to seek in the new correlation of forces in the world and the detente which characterizes the situation in Europe new grounds for confidence in the outcome of their struggle for democratic changes and socialism. That, in our view, is the main thing.[55]

The Soviets initially ignored the domestic aspect of the discord between Gaullist Prime Minister Chirac and Independent Republican President Giscard—notably, the former's desire to wage a more aggressive campaign against the Left—and portrayed Chirac's resignation in August 1976 as due to unhappiness over the Atlanticist and pro-European integration drift of French foreign policy. They also linked it to the enunciation of a new defense policy by French Chief of Staff General Guy Méry, which opened the possibility of redeployment of French troops to a forward position along the eastern border of West Germany. "Chirac and his colleagues in the Gaullist party obviously did not want to continue linking themselves with those aspects of French policy which they see as a departure from the course charted by General de Gaulle," the Soviets declared. "The overwhelming majority of Frenchmen, whatever else divides them, stand for a fully independent and self-reliant French foreign policy," they added, in obvious reference to the convergence of views on this issue between the Gaullists and the PCF.[56] Continuing their pattern of nurturing Soviet-French relations through this difficult period, however, the Soviets emphasized the favorable outlook of the incoming prime minister, Raymond Barre, on the prospects for expanded trade between the two countries, expressed in his address to the July meeting of the Soviet-French joint commission in Paris.

The Soviets were clearly engaged in a holding action designed at least to safeguard the progress in Soviet-French relations made over the past decade. As a Soviet international affairs commentator observed in an article devoted to the July 16, 1976, signing of the Soviet-French accord on the prevention of accidental or unsanctioned use of nuclear weapons, the task is to insure that the differences in views between the two countries "do not lead to zigzags in and departures from the general line of cooperation" established between them.[57] For Franco-Soviet cooperation to continue, the Soviets peevishly admonished, the French side must show its willingness to "make full use of the available opportunities" and "not allow anyone to erode" the understanding and trust that had been established.[58]

By year-end 1976 a marked change in attitude was evident in Soviet treatment of relations with the Giscard government. While still going out of their way to encourage a renewal, the Soviets stepped up their criticism of the Giscard regime and simultaneously gave more favorable coverage to the positions of the Left and to the similarities of the foreign policy views of the leftwing Gaullists and the Communist-Socialist alliance. The fact that for the first time in the history of the Fifth Republic neither the president nor the prime minister was a Gaullist was undoubtedly a factor in the Soviets' calculations. The emphasis now was on the need to exploit the "many untapped possibilities" for strengthening Soviet-French cooperation, as Brezhnev stated in a special interview over French television.[59] Acknowledging differences with the Giscard government, Brezhnev announced that he would visit France in the near future, and expressed the hope that his visit would "generate an impulse for new initiatives. . . ."[60]

The strains and paradoxes in Franco-Soviet relations were clearly evident beneath the overlay of diplomatic protocol during Brezhnev's June 20–22 visit to France. The summit meeting, Brezhnev's first trip abroad in his added capacity as Soviet chief of state, also inevitably entailed ramifications for French domestic politics and PCF-CPSU relations. As was not the case on previous Brezhnev visits to France, the Soviet and French Communist leaders did not meet; by contrast, Brezhnev's schedule did include a visit with Jacques Chirac, the Gaullist mayor of Paris and chief rival of Brezhnev's host, Valéry Giscard d'Estaing. Reflecting the Soviets' obviously keen interest in improving Franco-Soviet relations as a response to the faltering of detente with the United States, the meeting nonetheless highlighted the persistence of disagreement between the two sides over human rights, the tempering of ideological conflict, and French defense policy. The chief tangible accomplishments were agreements on scientific and cultural exchanges, the expansion of French credits, and the tripling of Soviet-French trade over the 1974 level.

Clearly, however, the Soviets are not content to let their relations with France ride on the crest of the continued expansion of economic, scientific, and cultural ties. What matters most for them is the shoring up of the political side of detente and progress in the military sphere. As Brezhnev rather sardonically commented in a March 1977 address:

> In their time the USSR and France were, so to say, the trail blazers of detente and their mutual relations were described as "preferential" ones. To a certain extent this is true to this day: We are maintaining lively ties in the economic and cultural fields. We cooperate also in some foreign policy matters as well.[61]

When French officials speak positively about Soviet-French relations the Soviets take note, such as when Foreign Minister Luis de Guiringaud reaffirmed the Gaullist formula of *détente-entente-coopération* with the Soviet Union, or Giscard pledged France's continued adherence to de Gaulle's policy vis-a-vis NATO.[62] On the other hand, the Soviets were quick to attribute the losses sustained by Giscard's Independent Republicans in the November 1976 parliamentary by-elections to the government's increased cooperation with NATO and agreement to direct elections to the European Parliament. In contrast, the Soviets noted, the Gaullists, who increased their votes slightly, had "recently made several attempts for the defense of France's national independence."[63]

Soviet criticism of French foreign policy was carried directly to the National Assembly chamber by Ponomarev, candidate member of the CPSU Politburo and Chairman of the Supreme Soviet of Nationalities' Foreign Affairs Commission, who led a Soviet delegation to Paris for a meeting with the Foreign Affairs Commission of the French National Assembly. Ponomarev scored France for its "passivity" with regard to efforts to curb the arms race and ban nuclear weapons, for its opposition to the Warsaw Pact's proposal for a treaty renouncing first use of nuclear weapons, for its renewed cooperation with NATO, and for its increased military expenditures.[64] According to the French press, only Billoux, the PCF's representative on the commission did not seem surprised by Ponomarev's indictment.[65] Two months later Marchais declared over French television that "as far as the problems of peaceful coexistence and international detente are concerned, we have no reproach to make about the USSR's foreign policy."[66]

The Soviets have also stepped up both their self-defense and militancy on the issue of proletarian internationalism versus detente and state interests. As one of the Central Committee's leading experts on relations with the nonruling Communist parties, Zagladin, wrote, "In the history of the revolutionary movement in the last six decades there has not been a single instance when the

CPSU has not displayed solidarity with any given struggling people or any given fraternal party needing support . . . irrespective . . . of the state of our party's relations with the party or country needing support."[67]

The Soviets' behavior inevitably suggests that in weighing the likely outcome of the 1978 French parliamentary election they have substantially upgraded their estimate of the chances either of a leftist victory, or, alternatively, of a resurgence of genuine Gaullism around the dynamic figure of former Prime Minister Chirac. A tougher Soviet stance on current French foreign policy is the logical consequence of such an evaluation.

NOTES

1. *L'Humanité*, February 28, 1976. The Soviets maintain that in strengthening their economy they are in fact fulfilling their internationalist duty; see T. T. Timofeyev, "Implementation of the Peace Program and Certain Questions of the Ideological Struggle," *Voprosy Filosofii KPSS*, January 1976, no. 1; greetings of the CPSU Central Committee to the PCF 22nd party congress, *Pravda*, February 7, 1976; Brezhnev's address to the Berlin conference, *Pravda*, June 30, 1976; and V. V. Zagladin, "The Development of Proletarian Internationalism under Contemporary Conditions," *Rabochiy Klass i Sovremennyy Mir*, 1977, no. 1 (January–February).

2. TASS, December 31, 1976; *Foreign Trade* (USSR), supplement to No. 3, 1977; and TASS, February 28, 1977.

3. S. Zykov and M. Mikheylov, "Little Europe and Big Europe," *Izvestiya*, March 27, 1969.

4. See, e.g., Anatoliy Krasikov report, TASS, April 18, 1969; and Yuriy Bochkarov, "The President Resigns," *Literaturnaya Gazeta*, April 30, 1969. The Soviets had not previously reported de Gaulle's threat to resign in the event of an unfavorable outcome on his referendum on administrative and territorial reorganization and Senate reform.

5. S. Zykov, "The Results of the Referendum," *Izvestiya*, April 29, 1969.

6. V. Sedykh, "Tense Days," *Pravda*, May 1, 1969. Sedykh asserted that the negative referendum vote was a condemnation of the "ruling circles' domestic social and economic policies" and quoted the *Le Monde* editorial position that "in spite of difficulties, French-Soviet cooperation is now on a big enough scale to become an 'institution' which could not be seriously affected" by the referendum outcome.

7. M. Molchanov, "France Between Past and Future," *Literaturnaya Gazeta*, May 28, 1969.

8. Anatoliy Krasikov commentary, TASS, June 3, 1969.

9. Robert Legvold, "The Franco-Soviet Rapprochement after de Gaulle," *Survey*, 20, no. 4 (Autumn 1974):73–74; see also Yuriy Bochkarov, "France: Foreign Policy after de Gaulle," *New Times*, January 20, 1970, no. 3, p. 27.

10. Legvold, op. cit., p. 75.

11. Yu. Rubinskiy, "The USSR and France—a Dialogue for the Sake of Peace," *Izvestiya*, October 24, 1971; see also former Soviet President Podgorny's remarks on the occasion of Pompidou's visit to the USSR, *Pravda*, October 7 and 14, 1970.

12. L. I. Brezhnev, speech at the Elysée Palace, Moscow Radio, October 25, 1971. Speaking on French television on October 29, Brezhnev applauded the "independent foreign policy of France. . . ."

13. "The Principles of Cooperation between the Union of Soviet Socialist Republics and France," TASS, October 30, 1971.

14. Soviet-French communique, TASS, October 30, 1971. The French also endorsed the Soviet proposal to convene a world disarmament conference and the two sides expressed their

support for the U.N. Security Council resolution of November 22, 1967 on withdrawal of Israeli troops from all occupied territories and for an end to foreign intervention in Indochina.

15. Editorial, "In the Interest of World Peace," *Pravda,* November 1, 1971; and Vadim Zagladin, "Turning Point," *New Times,* November 1971, no. 46.

16. TASS, October 24, 1971. Indicative of the delicate state-party balancing act the Soviets pursue, official contact between Brezhnev and the PCF was limited to a visit to Lenin's Paris apartment.

17. *L'Humanité,* June 7, 1969.

18. Erwin Weit, *At the Red Summit: Interpreter Behind the Iron Curtain,* trans. Mary Schofield (New York: McMillan, 1973), p. 140; the author, Gomulka's former interpreter, was reporting remarks by Brezhnev to Gomulka and Ulbricht at the Seventh SED Congress in April 1967.

19. *L'Humanité,* November 24 and December 11, 1969.

20. *L'Humanité,* December 11, 1970.

21. *L'Humanité,* January 6, 1972. The PCF also opposed Pompidou's foreign policy by urging a "no" vote on the April 23, 1972, referendum on enlarging the Common Market.

22. Nokolai Kononov, "Soviet-French Cooperation is in the National Interest," Moscow broadcast in French to Europe, January 8, 1973; Prof. M. Krutogolov, "The USSR and France: Traditions of Friendship," *Izvestiya,* February 9, 1973; and Vsevolov Grigoriyev, "Will Anticommunism Help Them?" Moscow broadcast in French to Europe, March 10, 1973.

23. *L'Humanité,* December 7, 1972, published in *Pravda,* December 9, 1972; cf. Yu. Zhukov and V. Sedykh, "A Permanent Policy," *Pravda,* February 9, 1973.

24. The Soviet position is that detente creates the optimum external conditions for successfully waging class struggle by nonmilitary means. One of the most unequivocal Soviet statements on the inclusions and exclusions of detente (razryadka mezhdunarodnoy napryazhënnosti, literally "relaxation of international tension") appeared in Zinovy Mirsky, "The Dialectics of Détente," *New Times,* 1975, no. 36. For a detailed analysis of the Soviet views on detente see Foy D. Kohler, Mose L. Harvey, Leon Gouré, and Richard Soll, *Soviet Strategy for the Seventies: From Cold War to Peaceful Coexistence* (Coral Gables, Fla.: Monograph in International Affairs, Center for Advanced International Studies, University of Miami, 1973).

25. *Pravda,* December 15, 1972.

26. Soviet-French communique, TASS, January 12, 1973; editorial, "In the Interests of the Peace and Security of Peoples," *Pravda,* January 15, 1973; and V. Matveyev, "Europe: The Path to Security," *Izvestiya,* January 18, 1973.

27. V. Sedykh, "Security for Europe," *Pravda,* January 25, 1973; *L'Humanité,* January 11, 1973.

28. Yu. Zhukov and V. Sedykh, "A Permanent Factor of International Life," *Pravda,* June 26, 1973, quoting a statement to *Pravda* by PCF Politburo member Jean Kanapa.

29. *Le Monde,* July 5, 1973.

30. See L. Vidyasova, "The Conference on Security and Cooperation in Europe," *International Affairs* (Moscow), no. 10, October 1973, pp. 15–16; Legvold, op. cit., p. 89.

31. See, for example, A. Ilyin, "Soviet-French Cooperation Gains Strength," *International Affairs* (Moscow), no. 9, September 1973; interview with PCF Central Committee secretary Roland Leroy, "Our Cooperation Will Develop," *Sovstskaya Kultura,* October 19, 1973.

32. TASS, February 16, 1974. The Soviets had also hailed the French decision to float the franc in January 1974 as evidence of dissention within the Common Market, and had commended the French decision to continue selling arms to the Arabs.

33. Reported by G. Lebanidze and G. Ratiani, "A Fresh Impetus to Cooperation," *Pravda,* March 14, 1974.

34. *Pravda,* March 16, 1974.

35. V. Sedykh, "The Struggle Grows More Acute," *Pravda,* May 16, 1974.

36. *L'Humanité,* May 9, 1974. Two years later in a radio interview Marchais condemned this event as representing "an opportunistic position, not in conformity with proletarian internationalism," reported in "A Day on Europe—1 with the PCF Secretary General," *L'Humanité,* February 28, 1976.

37. Yuriy Rubinskiy, "A Constant," *Le Monde,* June 8, 1974; *L'Humanité,* "Two Errors," June 9, 1974; and *"L'Humanité* Points Out 'Two Errors' Made by Soviet Prof. Rubinskiy," *Le Monde,* June 9–10, 1974.

38. *L'Humanité,* July 29, 1974.

39. Statement by the PCF Central Committee Secretariat, "The Fiftieth Anniversary of the Establishment of Diplomatic Relations between France and the Soviet Union," *L'Humanité,* October 29, 1974.

40. Jean Kanapa, "Bringing French-Soviet Cooperation up to Date," *L'Humanité,* December 2, 1974.

41. V. Sedykh, "A Meeting of Major Significance: On the Results of the Soviet-French Summit Talks," *Kommunist,* 1974, no. 18.

42. "Last Night Georges Marchais Met the CPSU General Secretary," *L'Humanité,* December 7, 1974. The Soviets reacted angrily to the public allegation by PCF author Jean Ellenstein in his book *Le P.C.—La Parti communiste* that the USSR equates detente with preservation of the social status quo; see Yu. Sedov, "Falsification instead of Objective Study," *New Times,* 1977, no. 5.

43. PCF Politburo Communique, "The Results of Chirac's Trip to the USSR," *L'Humanité,* March 26, 1975. When the communique charged the members of the Giscard government with "duplicity" and asserted that "The workers and the French people certainly have every reason for not trusting them," it is difficult to avoid making an inferential extension to the Soviet leadership. Marchais is reported to have blurted over the air "to hell with them" as a commentary on the alleged tranquility of the Brezhnev-Chirac encounter; reported by Pol Mathil in *Le Soir* (Brussels), June 8–9, 1975.

44. *Le Monde,* May 4–5, 1975; "French-Soviet Misunderstandings," *Le Monde,* July 4, 1975.

45. *L'Humanité,* October 13, 1975.

46. Ibid.

47. *Pravda,* October 15, 1975.

48. See editorial, "Unusual Remarks in Moscow," *Le Monde,* March 23–24, 1975. At that time Chirac also revealed the same canny understanding of the separation of issues the Soviets employ. Asked about the polemics between himself and Marchais, Chirac declared: "This has absolutely nothing to do with relations between two great countries such as France and the Soviet Union, and particularly nothing to do with the talks I may now be having . . . with the Soviet leaders"; telephone interview from Irkutsk, USSR, on "Douze-Quatorze" program, Paris, March 22, 1975.

49. Yves Moreau, "Ideological Détente?" *L'Humanité,* October 17, 1975. The PCF termed Giscard's visit "far less fruitful than it should have been . . . ." Yves Moreau, "Declarations and Facts," *L'Humanité,* October 18, 1975. Moreover, Marchais asserted that the PCF found it "very interesting" that the USSR signed trade agreements with France "despite the fact that the trade balance with France is against it" (*L'Humanité,* October 22, 1975).

50. *Pravda,* February 29, 1976.

51. *Le Monde,* March 2, 1976.

52. See, e.g., report of Gromyko's press conference, "M. Gromyko Wants Paris to Do More for Disarmament," *Le Monde,* May 2–3, 1976; V. Kuznetsov, "Détente: A Process to Carry Forward," *New Times,* May 1976, no. 19.

53. See Flora Lewis, "French Communists Say Moscow is Soft on Capitalism," New York *Times*, March 28, 1976.

54. Reported in *Le Monde,* June 23, 1976.

55. *L'Humanité,* July 1, 1976; significantly, *Pravda* (July 3) reprinted this paragraph from Marchais' speech, but deleted the above attack on French foreign policy. (It should be pointed out that PCF and CPSU declaratory positons on detente do not differ; it is with Soviet practice that the PCF has quarrelled.)

56. International Observers' Roundtable, Moscow Radio, August 29, 1976; popular discontent over the government's inability to resolve France's economic difficulties was the explanation given for the dispute in "After the Change of Cabinet in France," *Pravda,* September 2, 1976, and S. Petrov, "Change of Cabinet in France," *New Times,* June 1976, no. 36.

57. G. Dadyants, "A Principled Course," *Sotsialisticheskaya Industriya,* July 20, 1976.

58. Alexei Ilyin, "USSR-France: The Past Ten Years," *New Times,* June 1976, no. 26.

59. L. I. Brezhnev interview with Yves Mourousi in the Kremlin, TASS, October 5, 1975. The Soviet media censored Giscard's reciprocal interview on Soviet television, omitting passages concerning the standard of living of French workers (*Le Figaro,* October 15, 1976).

60. L. I. Brezhnev, speech to the CPSU Central Committee plenum, TASS, October 25, 1976.

61. L. I. Brezhnev, speech to the 16th congress of trade unions, TASS, March 21, 1977.

62. TASS, December 2, 1976; "A Constant Factor," *Pravda,* November 11, 1976; and TASS, January 28, 1977.

63. Vsevolod Grigoryev commentary in French to Europe, November 22, 1976. The same commentary asserted that the Left was becoming an "increasingly important factor in France's political life."

64. TASS, December 10, 1976.

65. J.M.K. commentary, *Le Figaro,* December 15, 1976.

66. *Le Monde,* February 24, 1977.

67. V. V. Zagladin, "The Development of Proletarian Internationalism."

CHAPTER 7

It is appropriate to recall our initial premise: 1968 was a watershed year in relations between the PCF and the CPSU. Punctuated by the May-June student and worker strikes in France and the Soviet-led invasion of Czechoslovakia in August, the year marked the launching of the PCF on a path of autonomy from the CPSU in which national considerations would henceforth be the foremost determinant of party conduct. Perhaps Annie Kriegel's concept of the "consciousness lag" can be appropriated here. When one examines the events at work on the PCF since 1968, the independent line drawn at the 22nd party congress in 1976 does not appear so extraordinary. As Kriegel noted with respect to a different context, "certain signs of upheaval, working deep under the surface, have been picked up only much later and at a great distance from their point of origin."[1]

Our analysis was confirmed by PCF Politburo member Kanapa. "As far as we are concerned," he wrote in his January 1977 article in *Foreign Affairs*, "the year 1968 played a decisive role . . . in what our policy line has become."[2] For the PCF, the lessons of 1968 were that renewed efforts to solidify its alliance and broaden its base of support in the French electorate in domestic affairs, and autonomy and independence of decision making in international and interparty affairs, were imperative if it were ever to attain power in France. Ideally, this would be accomplished in harmony with the policies of the CPSU. But, in the event of a major conflict between the PCF's domestic strategy and the interests of the CPSU, the former would prevail.

The Soviet's distress over the centrifugal tendencies in the international Communist movement, of which the PCF assertion of autonomy is one of the most striking recent phenomena, is evident in the vigor of their reassertion of their leadership role in the post-Berlin conference period. The strategy and tactics of the Western European parties and their challenge to Soviet authority expose a vulnerability of the Socialist system. Just as detente and increased trade and cultural exchange with the West compound the problems of internal control and expose the Soviet leadership to criticism for squandering revolutionary opportunities in the name of detente, so the Western European Communists' endorsements of political pluralism, individual liberty, and national roads to socialism raise the possibility that pluralistic contagion could ultimately threaten the stability of the Socialist community itself. By their defense of human rights under socialism, the Eurocommunists inevitably make common cause with dissidents in the Socialist bloc; their advent to power would further enhance their image as a pole of attraction for Eastern European liberalizing elements, providing a "viable within-system alternative to the Soviet model."[3]

The continued strengthening of the position of the PCF-PS alliance, as evidenced by the results of the March 1977 municipal elections, increases the possibility of a leftist victory in the 1978 parliamentary elections. Soviet statements indicate a revised assessment of the Left's chances, which is partly responsible for a perceptible cooling toward the Giscard regime. At the same time, both the PCF and the CPSU are trying to achieve a modus vivendi in order to prevent their disagreements from escalating to a breach that would be disastrous to both.

The CPSU believes it must avoid a schism along Eurocommunist lines, which would immeasureably diminish its position as a leader of a powerful revolutionary force linking the Socialist countries, the nonruling Communist parties, and the national-liberation movement. Moreover, despite the serious inconveniences posed by the growing power and prestige of the Western European prodigals, their advent to power and the resultant disruption of the Atlantic Alliance hold obvious benefits for the Socialist bloc. For the PCF, at stake is the preservation of its ties to an international movement it believes in the historical ascendancy and to an ideology it has espoused throughout its existence, not to mention the certain divisiveness within its ranks an outright break with the CPSU would provoke. Marchais' conduct at the March 1977 "Eurocommunist summit" in Madrid—at which he refused to join in a concerted condemnation of Soviet human rights violations and continued to eschew the antagonizing term "Eurocommunism"—reflects these exegencies.

This is not to imply, however, that the accommodation will be smooth. Even if the PCF discreetly refrains from attaching a "Eurocommunist" label to its activities, the CPSU is just as surely to continue interpreting such regionalization of communism as a threat to Communist unity. The swelling of PCF ranks with newcomers attracted by the party's pluralist and autonomist stance makes a reversion to traditional orthodoxy unlikely. Moreover, in the changed domestic and international context, when the Western European Communist parties' legitimacy depends more on the votes of domestic electorates than the approval of an international mentor, it is also unlikely that direct Soviet pressure could undermine these parties' strength; such is not the case with some of the smaller parties, however, as witness the Swedish Communist split in March 1977 over the issue of Eurocommunism versus Soviet or-

thodoxy.[4] Rather, for the PCF, the challenge is to find the right balance
between electoral appeal and symbolic loyalty to international communism to
keep its credentials with both constitutencies in satisfactory standing.

It also bears repeating that the PCF is continuing to evolve, that its 1976
congress was merely a benchmark along a path of uncertain destination. What
Marchais told the 20th party congress remains valid today: "The PCF," he
said, "pays constant attention . . . to the evolution of the situation in the
country and throughout the world. . . . the PCF is changing and will continue
to change."[5] But it would be erroneous to anticipate the PCF's becoming "a
party like the others" within the French political system, losing its distinctiveness in an amalgam of social democracy. Not even the advent to power in a
multiparty coalition will efface either the democratic centralism of its internal
organization, which requires strict loyalty to the party line once enunciated,
or its almost messianic vanguard zeal. And it is these two aspects of the PCF
—democratic centralism in its internal organization and vanguard pretensions
with respect to its allies—that raise the most serious questions about its commitment to play by the democratic rules of the political game.

Sufficient divergencies exist between the Communists and their Socialist
allies over economic and foreign policy issues unresolved by the Common
Program to portend a rough relationship within a future Left governmental
coalition. An unfavorable economic situation, competition for leadership
within the alliance, and disagreement over policy issues could well give rise to
a period of instability following the Left's advent to power.[6] Conceivably, a
rupture in the Communist-Socialist alliance could ensue, leading to the creation of a new center-left governmental coalition. On the other hand, if the Left
is defeated in 1978, it is by no means certain that the Union de la gauche could
survive another prolonged period in the opposition.

These are turbulent times in both French politics and Communist interparty relations. For France the 1978 election is a major crossroads. The choice
is not just between alternative political parties and programs but between
competing conceptions of society. For the PCF and the CPSU, the question
is whether a new accommodation can be achieved to encompass the PCF's
insistent challenge to Soviet authority. If so, it could represent a new stage in
the evolution of Communist interparty relations, in which the transformation
of the PCF-CPSU relationship is playing a central part.

NOTES

1. Annie Kriegel, "The International Role of the French Communist Party since World War
II," in Donald L. M. Blackmer and Kriegel, *The International Role of the Communist Parties of
Italy and France* (Cambridge, Mass.: Center for International Affairs, Harvard University, 1975),
p. 38.

2. Jean Kanapa, "A 'New Policy' of the French Communists?" *Foreign Affairs,* January 1977, p. 280.

3. Charles Gati, "The 'Europeanization' of Communism?" *Foreign Affairs,* April 1977, p. 547.

4. A Soviet broadside against Spanish Communist leader Santiago Carrillo following the PCE's weak electoral showing in the June 1977 elections indicated a revived Soviet effort to divide Spanish Communists and buttress the challenge to Carrillo's leadership by pro-Soviet elements within the party. The attack on Carrillo's views, which came in the form of a widely disseminated *New Times* editorial, also marked a new level of intensity in the Soviets' confrontation with Eurocommunism, as well as an attempt to exploit existing differences among the Western European parties. See "Contrary to the Interests of Peace and Socialism in Europe," *New Times,* June 1977, no. 26.

5. *L'Humanité,* December 18, 1972.

6. These problems were dramatically previewed by the PS's angry reaction to the PCF's untimely release in May 1977 of its economic plan for a future leftist government. The PS immediately repudiated the PCF proposals that called for vastly increased wages and social security benefits, job-creating, and social welfare programs, to be financed by a near doubling of corporate taxes and an unrealistic projected increase in GNP.

ANNETTE EISENBERG STIEFBOLD is a member of the research faculty of the Center for Advanced International Studies at the University of Miami. Prior to that she was on the research and editorial staffs of the Carnegie Endowment for International Peace, the Institute of African Studies of Columbia University, the Institute for Research on Poverty, and the International Confederation of Free Trade Unions (ICFTU).

Ms. Stiefbold has published several books and articles in the field of international relations, including *Convergence of Communism and Capitalism: The Soviet View; The Uncertain Alliance: The Catholic Church and Labor in Latin America;* and "Syria, Lebanon, and the Crisis of Soviet Policy in the Middle East ."

Ms. Stiefbold holds a B.A. from Cornell University, an M.A. from Columbia University, and the Certificat d'Etudes Politiques from the University of Paris.

FOREIGN POLICIES OF WEST EUROPEAN
SOCIALIST PARTIES
edited by Werner J. Feld

YUGOSLAVIA AFTER TITO
Andrew Borowiec

THE PORTUGUESE REVOLUTION AND THE
ARMED FORCES MOVEMENT
Rona M. Fields

THE FATE OF THE ATLANTIC COMMUNITY
Elliot R. Goodman

ALLENDE'S CHILE
edited by Philip O'Brien